A HISTORY
OF SOCIALISM
AND COMMUNISM
IN MODERN TIMES

# A HISTORY OF SOCIALISM AND COMMUNISM IN MODERN TIMES:

## Theorists, Activists, and Humanists

WARREN LERNER
Duke University

Prentice-Hall, Inc., Englewood Cliffs, N.J. 07632

*Library of Congress Cataloging in Publication Data*

LERNER, WARREN.

A history of socialism and communism in modern times.

Bibliography
Includes index.
1.–Socialism—History.  2.–Communism—History.
I.–Title.
HX36.L434      335'.009      81-10541
ISBN  0-13-392183-2      AACR2

© 1982 by Prentice-Hall, Inc., Englewood Cliffs, N.J. 07632

Printed in the United States of America

10   9   8   7   6   5   4   3

Editorial/production supervision
  and interior design by Joyce Turner
Cover design by Wanda Lubelska
Manufacturing buyer: Edmund W. Leone

Prentice-Hall International, Inc., *London*
Prentice-Hall of Austrailia Pty. Limited, *Sydney*
Prentice-Hall of Canada, Ltd., *Toronto*
Prentice-Hall of India Private Limited, *New Delhi*
Prentice-Hall of Japan, Inc., *Tokyo*
Prentice-Hall of Southeast Asia Pte. Ltd., *Singapore*
Whitehall Books Limited, *Wellington, New Zealand*

For FRAN,

whose book this always was

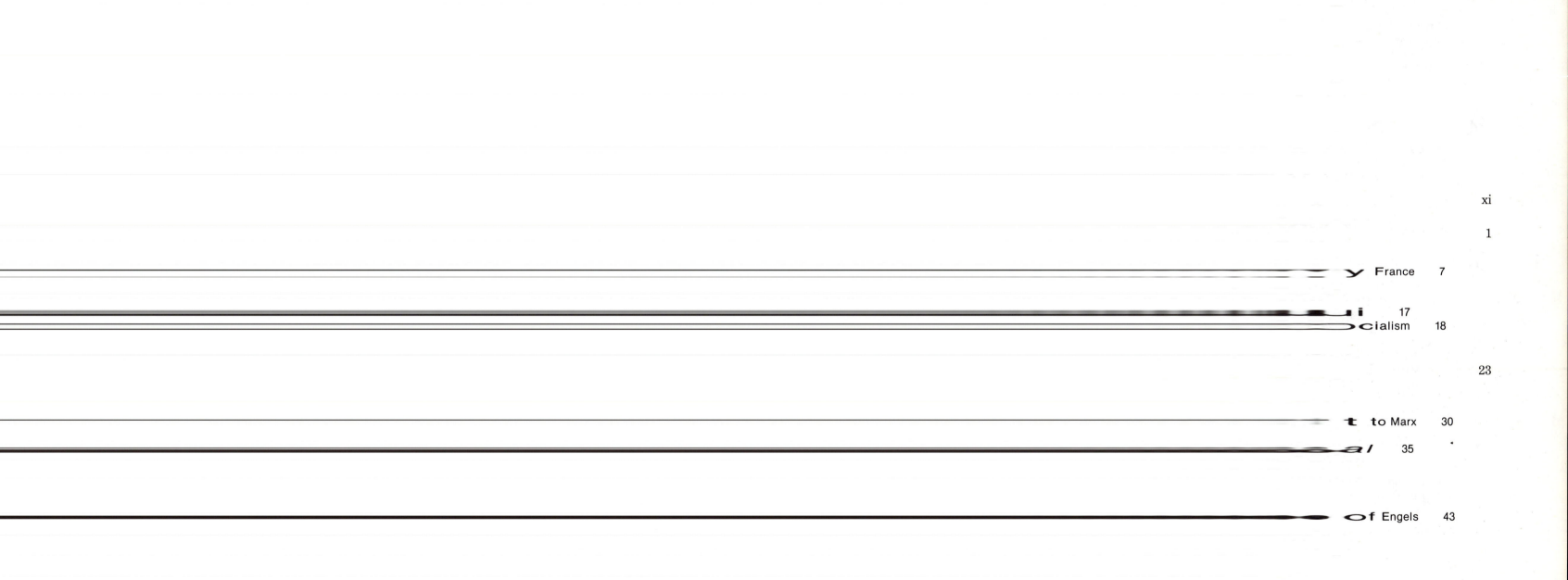

# Contents

# Preface

The history of socialism is the history of the quest for social and economic justice in the modern world. It derives from a loss of faith in western institutions, especially capitalism, as a provider of this justice. In this century, the hegemony of capitalism has been substantially eroded by two world wars that have inflicted great hardship on millions of people and have shattered the myth of western omnipotence over nonwestern countries. In recent times, a variety of socialist, political, and economic arrangements have taken the place of traditional capitalist systems, or in some cases substantially modified them. In western Europe there has been a strong commitment to democratic socialism; in the communist societies of the Soviet Union, China, Southeast Asia, and East Europe, highly monolithic governments have become well entrenched. One way or another, much of the contemporary world is ruled by regimes that subscribe to some form of socialism or to one of its mutations.

In the years since the Second World War, interest in socialism as a political and economic phenomenon has soared. In the more than two decades that I have been teaching courses in the history of socialism, the literature on the subject has multiplied severalfold. There has been a deluge of new works as well as a rediscovery of old works that had been out-of-print, untranslated, or even forgotten. The contemporary student of socialism will find a veritable cornucopia of readers, analytical studies, biographies of major figures, and various other works. What has been lacking is a reasonably concise historical

presentation of the development of socialism from the putative beginnings of socialist thought in the era of the Enlightenment
and the French Revolution, to the highly diversified forms of
socialism and communism that exist in the contemporary world.

In attempting to remedy this need, the present volume makes
no pretense at being comprehensive. Such a work, if indeed possible,
would require a number of volumes. Instead, this book is intended as
a historical overview that will enable the reader to investigate further the sources of socialist development and the literature of the
history of socialism. Toward this end, each chapter has been provided
with an annotated selection of readings relevant to the material discussed in the chapter. Insofar as practical, these readings have been
chosen to provide a blend of primary materials on the history of socialism, studies of special problems, and an assortment of biographies
of the people whose lives were involved in the movement. It is hoped
that this brief volume will spark the reader's interest into exploring
further into the history of socialism.

Where does one begin the history of socialism? The case can be,
and has been made, that socialism is old as recorded civilization. The
intellectual origins of socialism can easily be ascribed to the philosophers of ancient Athens and to various ideologies and movements of
the past two thousand years of recorded history. An investigation of
the history of socialism might begin with the works of Plato, or with
the medieval guilds, or with the communal religious groups that pro-
liferated in the sixteenth century, or with the British Leveller movement of the seventeenth century, or with other historical movements.
However, as a *continuous* political ideology, socialism emanates
from the values of the eighteenth century movement known as the
Enlightenment, and was a response to the socioeconomic problems
that emerged with the modern industrial age. For this reason, the
late eighteenth century has been chosen as the beginning point of
this volume. Many of the earlier phenomena, such as those noted
above, are worthy of extended coverage as precursors to socialist
history, but there is no direct linkage between them and the modern
socialist movements.

Socialism is a term that defies a standard definition. That idea
or institution which is "socialist" is often that which is so perceived
by the beholder; the designation can be either complimentary or de-

rogatory depending on the source. However, all professed socialists share the belief that within the capitalist system, the ownership of private property, particularly revenue producing property, has led to the economic and social exploitation of human beings. How to replace this system with one that will provide a just society is the issue with which socialists have been, and still are, concerned. The history of socialism reveals a broad potpourri of ideas, values, tactics, and priorities for solving this dilemma of modern times.

Defining communism is even more nebulous than defining socialism. All communists consider themselves socialists; a great many socialists do not consider themselves communists. From this simple observation one may deduce that communism can be viewed as a form of socialism; this is the view adopted here. After the Russian Revolutions of 1917, those revolutionary socialists who refused to be involved in the affairs of capitalist societies and maintained a loyalty to the Bolshevik Revolution came to be known as communists. The term communism took on particular meaning in the context of Lenin's Russia and its challenge to the outside world. In recent years, communism has undergone considerable redefinition, particularly in western societies, but one can say that to be *communist* is to identify with a more radical and more revolutionary approach to society than is suggested by the more generic term *socialist*. Throughout the text, this is the usage generally observed.

In any work, regardless of subject, the author's views and opinions may well differ from those of other writers in the field; this is all the more likely in the case of a polemical field such as the history of socialism. Obviously, I accept full responsibility for such views as well as for any errors of fact or interpretation that may emerge.

W. L.
Durham, North Carolina
March 1, 1981

A HISTORY
OF SOCIALISM
AND COMMUNISM
IN MODERN TIMES

# 1

# Socialism Before Marx

Modern socialism owes its origins to the eighteenth-century philosophical and political movement sometimes called the Enlightenment, the Age of Reason, or the Age of Newton. The selection of the English scientist-philosopher Isaac Newton as the intellectual godfather of the age was singularly appropriate. Toward the end of the seventeenth century, Newton's laws of motion led to the generalization that the universe was governed by discernible laws which were ascertainable. The impact of Newton's work was enormous: in science, in political thought, and even in religion (where he became the unwilling touchstone for the Deist movement). It gave impetus to the eighteenth century's preoccupation with the development of scientific laws to explain political arrangements. Toward this end, political philosophers attempted to separate all political laws into two categories: man-made laws and natural laws. Man-made laws were obviously those proclaimed by kings and parliaments. Although they might very well be good laws, they were neither scientific nor eternal; rather they were subject to error and revision. On the other hand, natural laws, such as Newton's laws of motion, were by definition immutable. And if one could ascertain the "natural laws" of political behavior, it followed that one could prescribe a just society which would be viable and permanent. The natural laws of political behavior, however, required scientific proof of a different nature than that for the laws of motion. The quest for this proof became the obsession of the political philosophers of the Enlightenment.

## THE SEEDS OF SOCIALISM

For the purpose of tracing the development of socialist theory, the most important of the Enlightenment philosophers was the Frenchman, Jean Jacques Rousseau (1712–1778). Rousseau led a bizarre, inconsistent, and even irresponsible personal life, a life which might belie his intellectual and personal commitment against the injustices of his society. He seduced servant girls and noble ladies alike, sired illegitimate children whom he placed in orphanages, and generally, behaved like a cad. In an age that prized brilliance of thought, he was perhaps one of the most brilliant and was certainly one of the most eloquent in his writings, which ranged a full gamut of subjects from education to the origins of political authority.

One of his early works, *The Discourse on the Origins of Inequality* (1755) established his "credentials" as the intellectual father of the modern socialist movement. In that work, Rousseau described the virtues of humanity in a natural state, uncorrupted by the materialism of modern society and, consequently, untroubled by hostility, destruction, and oppression. Laws or legal codes were no more than rules invented by the propertied elements of society to maintain their tyranny over the unpropertied. They were violations of natural law because they led to the aggrandizement of private property and the victimization of one person by another. Property, and the rights and privileges entailed by its possession, were seen as the source of the modern person's alienation from true humanity. In effect, Rousseau seemed to be summoning the "have nots" of the world to class warfare against the "haves."

Rousseau's *Discourse on Inequality* found echoes among later political philosophers but gathered little response from contemporaries. The work even failed to win the philosophical competition in which it was entered, and some observers wondered whether Rousseau was not playing devil's advocate rather than offering a serious critique of contemporary society. Retrospectively it appears that he was quite serious indeed, and his denunciations of idle luxury, economic exploitation, and social indifference opened one of the rawest nerves of his time.

In a later, better-known work, *The Social Contract* (1762),

Rousseau advanced the then revolutionary idea of popular sovereignty, a notion which led him to declare that the good of society was advanced by a force which he called "the general will." The "general will" was seen as an expression of humanity's better instincts, which evoked a society of a community of individuals. To Rousseau, the "general will" was the basis of authority and the only legal basis for government, a force that transcended all other societal organizations and groupings: towns, classes, guilds, and so forth. Rousseau has been much criticized for having formulated a "general-will" idea that suggested that people would be *forced* to be free and to promote egalitarian and natural forms of association. Yet Rousseau—who, it must be remembered, lived before the emergence of modern democracies—was suspicious of unknowing minorities, who might fail to appreciate the importance of a society that sought social justice for all, and who would seek to fulfill their own self-serving aims.

One could read Rousseau in various ways. Several dictators of later generations were to cite Rousseau's conception of the "general will" as a rationalization for their own exercise of unfettered authority that they would claim was vital to impose a better society on humanity. On the other hand, latter-day socialists also were impressed by Rousseau and his devastating critique of the economic, moral, and social injustices of existing society. Yet he left no immediate followers and his diverse writings were interpreted in equally diverse ways.

A generation later, France, and then all of Europe, was thrown into turmoil by the outbreak of the great French Revolution (1789). The Revolution itself was not initiated by the unpropertied poor but, on the contrary, by the people of property who believed, with justification, that they were being excluded from the day-to-day decision-making process of their society. At that time the clergy composed what was known as the First Estate, and the nobility, the Second Estate. The so-called "Third Estate"—in theory the bulk of the French population, but in practice the propertied middle class—was the driving force of the Revolution. In the early stages of the French Revolution the Third Estate tore down the privileged position of the first two estates but held back from redistributing property amongst the entire population. In fact, the great manifesto of the Revolution, "The Declaration of the Rights of Man and the Citizen" (1789), sanctified the right of private property.

In proclaiming the idea of citizenship, however, the Declaration lent itself to an egalitarian interpretation far beyond the intentions of its middle-class promulgators. In the French countryside, the response of the peasantry was often to burn the deeds that conveyed landownership rights and to declare that the land belonged equally to all. The slogan which soon emerged as the credo of the Revolution— "Liberty, Equality, and Fraternity!"—was considered by many of the French to imply economic and social, as well as political, equality.

The Revolution became further radicalized in the early 1790s with the emergence of the Jacobins as the dominant force of the new revolutionary regime, particularly after the execution of Louis XVI in 1793. Though the Jacobins themselves originally had been rooted in the middle class, many of them yielded to the excitement engendered by the *sans-culottes* (so-called because they wore the long trousers favored by workers and not the knee-length garments of the middle class). The *sans-culottes* might themselves be described as lower middle class, since many of them were small shopkeepers or artisans, but they consistently exerted pressure on the Jacobins for more radical changes.

These pressures upon the regime for direct intervention in the economic life of the country and for actions against foreign threats to the Revolution brought to the forefront the enigmatic but dynamic Maximilien de Robespierre. History, perhaps unfairly, has associated Robespierre's name with the mass terror that prevailed between 1793 and 1794, but he was far more than a blood-thirsty tyrant. Although he never articulated a clearly defined program, he did attempt a balance of social and economic reform. In any case, a coalition of various forces, alarmed by the escalation of terror and economic regimentation, arrested and executed Robespierre in the summer of 1794, thereby ending the radical phase of the Revolution.

Whatever Robespierre's intentions, his connection with terror had damned his program. Rightly or wrongly, the episode of terror had been associated with an overextension of the Revolution from its original mandate. Power in France passed to an oligarchy known as the Directory, and attempts at social and economic change came to a halt. Although neither the monarchy nor feudal privileges were restored, many of the erstwhile aristocrats returned to France, and forms of social and economic privilege began to reappear. In short, although France remained a republic in name, a revolutionary society by its own self-estimation, and was still at war with most of Europe as a result of the Revolution, it had in effect become once again a status-quo society.

## EARLY "SOCIALISM" IN POSTREVOLUTIONARY FRANCE

It was in this France of the Directory, a period when the revolutionary fervor of earlier years had apparently been spent, that the first, active "socialist" movement emerged. In 1795 François Noel Babeuf, a journalist from the provinces, began to disseminate in Parisian circles a new doctrine of economic and social revolution. Babeuf was, by all accounts, an imperfectly educated person according to the standards of his time, but he had read Rousseau, from whom he seemed to have developed the idea that a "natural society" was an egalitarian one, and that economic and social disparity was an offense to nature. Carrying the doctrine of equality to what he considered its logical extension, he urged the forging of a society in which there would be a single standard of living. In line with his growing commitment to revolution, he changed his first name to Gracchus in memory of the two brothers of that name who had vainly attempted, in the Roman Republic of ancient times, to stem the eroding economic status of the lower and middle classes.

Exploiting the rising urban discontent, Babeuf and his followers began to rally Parisian workers to voice demands for a fair share of society. At any other time Babeuf might well have been ignored, but in the later 1790s the suffering and casualties that had been inflicted upon the workers in the name of revolution—with no real revolution having taken place for the urban poor—now met with some interest. Babeuf grandiosely titled his movement "The Conspiracy of Equals." Though his own sense of political philosophy was rudimentary at best, he attracted to his cause several more-gifted supporters, notably Phillipe Michel Buonarotti, A. A. Darthe, and Sylvain Maréchal. The theme of the "Conspiracy" was quite simple:

so much had been promised and so little had been delivered.

Maréchal, who had been a writer of some note before the Revolution, apparently contributed the group's major theoretical pronouncement, "The Manifesto of Equals," although Babeuf is usually cited as the author. The Manifesto was one of the first avowedly revolutionary socialist documents in modern history, although the word "socialism" did not yet exist. Addressing itself to the problems of Parisian workers, the Manifesto proposed the expropriation of all property and the elimination of inheritance. Government was to pass to the control of a proposed dictatorship of the Parisian workers.

The Conspiracy of Equals failed to develop the discipline characteristic of successful conspiratorial groups. Instead, it tried to broaden its base by recruiting supporters from diverse social groups, with the result that it inevitably compromised its secrecy and was betrayed to the authorities. The conspirators were arrested and charged with treason. Babeuf and Darthé were sentenced to death and summarily executed. Other conspirators, including Buonarotti— who years later was to tell the story of Babeuf—were deported.

Babeuf has been called the first socialist activist; he could, because of his fate, be called the first socialist martyr as well. Despite his sketchy knowledge of the political and economic theories of his time, he had created a movement which had attacked economic exploitation through the use of property and identified it as the major evil of humankind. Furthermore, he had attempted, albeit unsuccessfully, to translate his political views into political action.

Within France itself, the memory of the Conspiracy of Equals was quickly suppressed. The triumph of the Directory over the Conspiracy, however, was short-lived. The Directory collapsed of its own dead weight in 1799, yielding to a new oligarchy in which the young general, Napoleon Bonaparte, quickly emerged as leader. Within a short time, Napoleon brought the Revolution full cycle: in 1804 he crowned himself Emperor of the French. From that lofty post Napoleon dominated not only France but most of the European continent for a decade.

There has been continuing historical controversy concerning Napoleon's achievements, failures, and aspirations. In no way could Napoleon be considered a socialist; indeed, he was a firm believer in economic privilege and dispensed it freely to his friends, relatives, and supporters. Nevertheless, a mystique about Napoleon developed amongst the downtrodden of Europe, for whom Napoleon represented a challenge to the status quo and, by logical extension, to national oppression and economic exploitation. Although in reality Napoleon's efforts in this regard were minimal, one should note the zeal with which Poles flocked to his standards, anticipating that he would be the liberator of Poland. The weavers of Silesia, and other economically oppressed groups, declared their support of Napoleon as the man who would end their poverty and suffering. Even the middle classes of Central Europe looked to him as one who would break the power of the nobility.

He failed all of these people badly, and yet they did not blame him. When he was defeated and banished in 1815, it was widely noted that the victors—the Tsar of Russia, the King of Prussia, and the Emperor of Austria—were all champions of the old order. Passwords like "legitimacy" and "restoration," which were used by the new powers of the post-Napoleonic world, implied the continuation of the privileges of property and inheritance as well as the continued exploitation of the rural and urban poor. From his exile, even Babeuf's coconspirator, Phillipe Buonarotti, mourned the defeat of Napoleon as a defeat for revolution.

## THE INDUSTRIAL REVOLUTION

Hitherto, the discussion of socialism's early beginnings has been peculiarly centered on France, notably because of the Revolution that dominated that country's history. Yet the history of socialism owes at least as much to activities taking place concurrently in England, whose economic development had moved in a direction considerably more likely to produce a denouement between classes. For quite some time there had been a systematic policy of excluding the small farmers from the land by fencing off once commonly held areas such as pasture lands. These "enclosure acts," as they were called, had the effect of concentrating more and more land in the hands of the already wealthy landowning class and creating a new class of dispossessed rural poor, who now were not only landless but unemployed and living on the margin of survival.

In fact, the plight of the new landless rural poor aided considerably the development of industry in England. The new larger farms were actually more efficient and did not require as much labor as the older individual small farms. Thus, merely to survive, the rural poor were forced to find employment in various forms of manufacturing. The availability of a mobile labor supply was perhaps one reason why eighteenth-century England became the first country to undergo what commonly has been called the "Industrial Revolution." In barely the space of a generation, England developed a machine economy, particularly in the area of textiles. The economic ramifications of the Industrial Revolution were mind-boggling. And as the gross national product of England multiplied geometrically, so did economic disparity.

The landless exiles from the countryside were quickly recruited into the labor force of the new factories. Even though the demand for labor was strong, they had virtually no bargaining power since the only alternative to employment in the factories was starvation. They accepted employment on whatever terms were offered, which, more often than not, were the barest survival wages. Thus the dichotomy arose that England as a nation and its new class of factory owners became fabulously wealthy, whereas much of its population became mired in inextricable poverty. As a British conservative of a later generation was to aptly sum up the situation, England had become two nations: one of the very rich, and one of the very poor.

The eighteenth-century English were neither unaware of, nor indifferent to, the growth of poverty in the midst of wealth. Industrialization had increased the complexity of English society and brought with it challenges to the economic and political, as well as the social, order. The beginnings of an attempt to analyze the economic system came with the publication of Adam Smith's *An Inquiry into the Nature and Causes of the Wealth of Nations* (1776), which postulated a theory that came to be known as *laissez-faire* economics; this theory held that an economic system functions best when it is free from government interference. Free competition would result in the maximizing of individual welfare, Smith believed, to the benefit of all. Smith was not an apologist for economic exploitation or an uncaring individual indifferent to suffering; he sincerely believed that the free economy would produce so much wealth that everyone, owners and workers alike, would fare better. Regardless of his intentions, his work became—after his death, at least—an apologia for the unbridled power of the industrialists.

The chaos and chronic warfare engendered by the French Revolution did little to advance the cause of social change in England. In fact, the French Revolution had the opposite effect: many English observers of the turn of events in France believed that the moderate reforms proposed in 1789 had led to the terror of 1793. Yet there were still English people who could not ignore the social challenge and proposed schemes to end or alleviate the economic exploitation of the many by the few. Most radical of these economic theorists was Thomas Spence (1750–1814) who considered as the basic evil of his time the expulsion of the small farmers from their farms earlier in the century. To rectify this situation he devised a program for the collectivization of land and spent his life unsuccessfully agitating for his plan. Spence was, if anything, too late, and in any case radical schemes such as his were badly received at a time when England was perennially at war with revolutionary France.

More important was the work of William Godwin (1756–1836) who in 1793 published *An Enquiry Concerning Political Justice*, in which he argued that the root of the problem lay in the coercive effect of government upon the individual. Godwin had an overriding belief in the inherent goodness of people: strip away the corrupting structure of government, he believed, and people will behave decently toward each other. Some of Godwin's arguments seem ridiculous or oversimplified by present-day standards—for instance, his blanket condemnation of all contracts and associations, or his absolute belief in the perfectability of humanity. In its time, however, his *Enquiry* was almost alone in its aspiration to a better society, and despite its high price the work enjoyed tremendous sales.

Godwin may appear to be no more than a precursor of anarchism, and an unstable precursor at that, but in fact his contribution to the development of socialism was far more substantial.[1] His wife,

---

[1] For a fuller discussion of anarchism, including Godwin's influence on it, see chapter 3.

Mary Wollstonecraft, introduced another dimension of the social problem with the publication of *The Rights of Women* (1792), and Godwin had considerable influence on a number of British intellectuals, most notably the poet Percy Bysshe Shelley. Shelley's prestige in literature enhanced retrospectively Godwin's circle, as did Shelley's later marriage to Godwin's daughter Mary (who was to achieve fame in another field as the author of *Frankenstein*). Although Godwin himself left behind no lasting movement—and, considering the inchoate state of his ideas, perhaps it is just as well—he did contribute to the discussion of the problem of social and political justice in an industrial society. If one thinks of the edifice of socialism as a wall, Godwin must be credited with placing several of the bricks into its base.

No intelligent analyst of eighteenth-century England could disregard the plight of the industrial worker. Some sought to blame the poor themselves for a lack of self-discipline, or for having too many children and thereby exacerbating their poverty. There was a tendency to consider poverty a sociological problem rather than an economic problem, even though economic analysts of this persuasion curiously overlooked the fact that the more workers in a family—and one became a worker at a very very young age—the greater the family income.

Thomas Malthus (1766–1834) offered the gloomy prediction that in the foreseeable future food supplies would fail to expand enough to feed the ever-burgeoning population. More profoundly, David Ricardo formulated the persuasive "Iron Law of Wages," which asserted that wage increases would not substantially improve workers' conditions because their consumption requirements and ever-growing families would tend to keep them at the subsistence level. Ricardo was not unsympathetic to the lot of the worker, but he maintained that, in an economic system where labor is the basic measure of value, the workers, who ultimately would be more numerous than the demand for them, simply would receive a smaller portion than the value of their productivity. Later theorists, including Karl Marx, were to make much of Ricardo's labor theory of value, but for the first part of the nineteenth century his views dominated economic analyses and were interpreted as a judgment that the workers were doomed to the lower echelons of the economy.

Ricardo's idea that labor was the major measurement of economic value (Adam Smith and other earlier writers had subscribed to similar ideas) could be put to use in various ways, both to the benefit and detriment of the workers. One of the more enterprising of Ricardo's contemporaries to develop the theme was the British industrialist Robert Owen, considered by some to have been the founder of British socialism.

As a prosperous Manchester factory owner, Robert Owen would seem to be a singularly unlikely candidate for founding a socialist movement. Yet, as a man possessing a peculiar combination of social conscience, creative initiative, and personal ego, he came to perceive that his wealth derived from the poverty and exploitation of others, and he sought to demonstrate that this economic parasitism was not inexorable. After acquiring in 1800 the New Lanark mills in Scotland, he proceeded to make them models for their time in employer-employee relations, providing workers with good housing and sanitation, schools, and nonprofit stores.

When England was faced with growing unemployment after the Napoleonic Wars, Owen began to develop ideas for small cooperative communes, at first meant only to provide a place for the unemployed . But as time went by, Owen began to wonder out loud if some form of cooperative society might not have greater dimensions and indeed offer an alternative to the factory towns that so exploited workers. His proposals, never really well presented, had few supporters in England or on the European continent. In 1824, feeling politically repressed in England, Owen emigrated to the United States and, after buying land from a religious sect in New Harmony, Indiana, sought to build there the cooperative society which most of his European colleagues had spurned.

New Harmony was marked by everything save harmony. The community had been launched on idealistic goals as an assemblage of equals, but many of the settlers had their own ideas on who should do what and bickering amongst individuals and groups of settlers was common from the beginning. Owen was a major part of the problem himself, for he was not willing to be simply one more member of a cooperative community. By 1828 the experiment at New Harmony had broken down and Owen returned to England. There he turned away from cooperative communities and devoted his energies to the nascent trade-union movement, which he now believed was the vehicle for relieving the exploitation of the workers. Owen lived to a ripe old age, dying in 1859 at eighty-eight. For all practical purposes, however, his work was completed by the 1830s when, save for one last brief try at developing a new cooperative unit, he ceased to work with trade unions. His last years were marked by forays into religious debates, sociological exegeses, and various other endeavors which testified to the enormous breadth of his interests but unfortunately also revealed the shallowness of his thought. Yet Owen was by no means a failure. He had given voice to the needs of the English working class, and though his cooperatives failed they continued to be emulated in the West even to the present day, albeit not in as all-encompassing a form as Owen had projected. Whatever his shortcomings, Owen had introduced humanism into the nascent socialist movement, an achievement quite sufficient in itself to guarantee his place in history.

## THE UTOPIAN SOCIALISTS

Although the industrial revolution was not well established in France until the nineteenth century, old social and economic inequities persisted throughout the Napoleonic period and the Restoration which followed. Enlightenment philosophers such as Rousseau had addressed themselves to universal problems rather than to the specific problems of French society. Though they had damned tyranny and exploitation, they had failed to prescribe any specific reforms. Rousseau was a theorist, not an activist. Even Babeuf, who certainly was committed to activism and who spoke in terms of building an egalitarian society, never really presented a serious economic program in any detail.

Proponents of social change in France in the early nineteenth century tended to carry further the ideas of Rousseau and Babeuf; they now began to advocate the rebuilding of society according to principles of economic justice. Even so, rather than offering immediate solutions to contemporary problems, they merely presented ideas that they believed were capable of being translated into future action. For these reasons, they became collectively known as "Utopian socialists," a term emanating from Thomas More's sixteenth-century classic *Utopia*, a description of an ideal state in which social evils such as poverty and despair have been eliminated.

Although such figures as Robert Owen in England are usually counted among the "Utopian socialists," the majority of this group's more prominent theorists came from the Parisian postrevolutionary generation. One of the first and most influential was the volatile Count Henri de Saint-Simon (1760–1825). As his noble title indicates, he was descended from the old aristocracy—he claimed direct descent from Charlemagne—but he renounced his title during the Revolution. Spurned by Napoleon, he turned his thoughts toward the reorganization of society, pouring out a torrent of writings interspersed with periods of depression and withdrawal.

Saint-Simon's works were not systematic or even consistent; by modern-day standards they would not even be considered socialist. Eventually he preached a doctrine calling for the redistribution of rewards so that the productive classes, whom he called *les industriels*, would benefit in place of the old privileged and nonproductive classes, whom he dubbed *les oisifs*. Though he was inconsistent as to which groups were to be included in *les industriels*, he emphasized the solidarity of the productive elements of society and advocated the restructuring of society on the basis of labor divisions. Saint-Simon particularly emphasized the importance of technology and productivity for building a more prosperous and harmonious social order. For this reason he attracted supporters among scientists and industrialists as well as humanitarians.

After his death, Saint-Simon's disciples extrapolated from his ideas a program which, among other things, called for the abolition of private property ownership and for public control of the means of production. This system became known as Saint-Simonianism. Prominent among its leaders was Barthelemy Enfantin (1796–1864), who in the late 1820s did much to popularize Saint-Simonianism. However, within a few years Enfantin moved to deemphasize the social ideology of the movement and concentrated instead on the establishment of a quasi-religious commune. The commune was rumored to be indulging in all sorts of immoral activity, and, when the authorities cracked down on it, the entire Saint-Simonian movement suffered, causing its disintegration by 1833. Saint-Simonian ideas were to

have influence on future socialist ideology not as a cohesive movement but because they stressed the rational use of economic factors
and working-class solidarity.

A contemporary group of the Saint-Simonians, the followers of
Etienne Cabet (1788–1865), more directly foreshadowed later socialist programs. In 1840 Cabet published *The Voyage to Icaria*, a "Utopian" prospectus for the model egalitarian community. Icaria was to
encompass a population of one million and provide a simple but equi-
table subsistence for all. Cabet actually did establish an "Icaria" in
1849 at Nauvoo, Illinois (and later in Corning, Iowa), but few people
were attracted by its spartan and authoritarian, even if egalitarian,
regimen.

A better blend of socialism and humanism was to be found in the
work of Charles Fourier (1772–1837). Like most of the early socialists, Fourier came from comfortable circumstances, and, like some
others, he tended to be a bit eccentric both in his writings and his activities. He, too, was substantially influenced by the writings of
Rousseau and by the experience of the French Revolution. He scorned
Saint-Simon's admiration for technology and wistfully projected the
idea of a simpler, basically agrarian society in which the community
would see to all needs. In his "Utopian" society, people were to be organized into "phalansteries"—a term derived from the *phalanx* of
ancient-Greek military formations—of 1620 people each. In these
relatively small communities—certainly small by comparison to
Cabet's projected community of a million—people would be able to
follow their own life-styles and vocational inclinations.

One of Fourier's objectives was to avoid, in his ideal community,
the deadly monotony which had been a by-product of the introduction
of the factory system. To accomplish this he proposed the rotation of
tasks so that, where possible, every person would be engaged in an
activity of interest and challenge, leaving no one to bear the unre-
lieved burden of a disagreeable assignment. He has often been derided for his proposal that children be assigned the task of garbage
disposal, but his reasons for this emanated from the simple observation that children did not mind handling garbage and adults did.

Fourier was not an egalitarian; he was quite willing to allow for
differentiated rewards for differentiated contributions to society,
provided gross discrepancies were mitigated by a progressive in-

come tax. Exploitation would not exist in the harmonious society he envisioned.

Fourier never succeeded in establishing a single phalanstery in France, although some experiments in the United States, notably at Brook Farm in Massachusetts, were influenced by Fourier. Here a cooperative community, long popular with Boston literary figures (Nathaniel Hawthorne, Margaret Fuller, Charles Dana, and others), was converted into a phalanstery in 1844 and for a few years seemed to embody the practice of Fourier's ideas. The experiment was short-lived, however, and never revived after a fire devastated much of the farm. The idyllic features of his plan, combined with his eccentric personality, inhibited potential support. Among Utopians, Fourier must be rated with the most impractical. By his emphasis on a humane economy, he had, however, made a major contribution to the growing body of socialist and quasi-socialist thought.

## THE REVOLUTIONARY ACTIVISM OF BLANQUI

One of the consistent attributes of the early Utopians was their unwillingness to confront the established order with an activist revolutionary strategy. Although an important reason for this was undoubtedly the fate of Babeuf, in general Utopian socialists were not admirers of violence or of any form of confrontation for that matter. They were basically gentle people who simply sought to change society by creating a better method of organization. Besides the Utopians, however, there were many socialist-oriented revolutionaries who fervently believed that only the overthrow of existing governments could make possible the conditions that would create a just society. The most famous advocate, and practitioner, of confrontation tactics was the French revolutionary Louis-Auguste Blanqui (1805–1881), who was prominent in every revolutionary upheaval in France from 1824 to his death.

Blanqui's first serious revolutionary activity appears to have been in the Parisian Revolution of 1830, in which Charles X was re-

placed by a new monarch, Louis Philippe, who, although more responsive to the French middle class than his predecessor, was not so
to the French workers. The experience committed Blanqui to a lifetime as an insurrectionist in the service of the French workers. He
joined and later organized numerous conspiracies and spent most of
his adult life in jail. At one of his trials, when asked his profession, he
proudly proclaimed "proletarian," by which he meant to describe his
allegiance to all the productive classes of France, agrarian as well as
industrial. The targets of his conspiracies were the "exploiters"—the
alliance between the government and the industrialists. Blanqui, in
his own way, combined the heritage of the Jacobins, Babeuf, and
Saint-Simon. As a theorist of the future "socialist" society he was de-
ficient, but his conception of class struggle and his commitment to
direct revolutionary action had a lasting influence on the socialist
movement.

    Nineteenth-century socialists were at best ambivalent toward
Blanqui and even coined the term "Blanquism" to designate any
movement committed to violent tactics in the name of socialism. On
the one hand, they admired any person so willing to undergo
repeated incarceration for the cause of socialism; on the other, they
tended to be wary of his obsession with insurrection and his espousal
of revolutionary dictatorship should the insurrection succeed.

## 1848: THE CLOSING CHAPTER
## OF EARLY SOCIALISM

Certainly there had to be a middle ground between the passive idealism of the Utopians and the uncompromising activism of the Blan-
quists. The French labor leader Louis Blanc (1811–1882) seemed to be
the first person of any prominence to attempt to find this middle
ground, utilizing a meld of republican and socialist aspirations. In the
tradition of the modern Social Democrat, Blanc hoped that democratic
procedures could be used to end the kind of society that exploited its
workers and that, through the concept of a "right to employment"
(under fair conditions, of course), a just society could be built. In his

famous work *The Organization of Labor* (1840), he advanced the economic argument for socialism and its compatibility with a democratic society. In contrast to the more radical ideas of Saint-Simon and Fourier, or the extremism of Blanqui, Blanc appeared to be advocating a feasible program, based on a system of state, or national, workshops whose policies would be determined by the workers rather than by capitalist owners. In February 1848, when a "republican" revolution overthrew the monarchy of Louis Philippe, Louis Blanc was suddenly catapulted into national prominence as a member of the Provisional Government. Quite naturally he used his position to promote some of the labor reforms he had advocated, but although his fellow republicans wanted to change France into a constitutional republic, he found that they drew the line on basic socioeconomic reform.

The French workers, in the stormy revolutionary spring of 1848, were unwilling to wait while Louis Blanc persuaded the others in the Provisional Government to make social changes. The much-ballyhooed National Workshops—which were only a shadow of Blanc's original ideas—frustrated both the workers by their impotence and the Constitutional Assembly by their implied threat of a future socialist society. When the government tried to close down the Workshops in June 1848, riots ensued, and the army was called in with chilling results. Several thousand people were killed, eleven thousand others were deported to French colonies overseas, and the National Workshops were dissolved. Blanc himself managed to flee to England, from where he could morosely survey the ruins of the "democratic" revolution. The June Days of 1848, as they became known to history, closed a chapter in the development of socialism. In essence, the Utopian theories of Saint-Simon and Fourier, the activism of Blanqui, and the republicanism of Blanc were all casualties of that year. It now appeared that no socialist program could be built by any of these routes. Only by a total separation of socialist goals from the ideas of existing society, and with proper timing, did there appear to be any hope for those who espoused socialist solutions to the problems of society.

# SELECTED READINGS

MARTIN BUBER, *Paths in Utopia* (Boston: Beacon Press, 1960).
Buber was one of the most-prominent theologians of the twentieth century; in this work he offers an overview of the Utopian experience with considerable sympathy for its leaders.

G.D.H.COLE, *A History of Socialist Thought*, vol. 1: *The Forerunners, 1789–1848* (New York: St. Martins, 1953).
The first of a multivolume study of the history of socialist thought, may well be the best in the set, offering a broad panorama of the varieties of pre-Marxian socialism.

PAUL KAGAN, *New World Utopias* (New York: Penguin, 1975).
An illustrated essay on the transfer of Utopian ideas to communities in the western United States, this book offers some evidence of the lasting hopes of the Utopians.

GEORGE LICHTHEIM, *The Origins of Socialism* (New York: Praeger, 1969).
This is an erudite and thoughtful discussion of the development of socialist ideology in the first half of the nineteenth century and a little beyond.

FRANK E. MANUEL, *The New World of Henri Saint-Simon* (Cambridge: Harvard University Press, 1956).
Manuel develops a scholarly insight into the thought and vision of one of the best-known Utopian socialists.

JEAN-JACQUES ROUSSEAU, *The Social Contract* (New York: Penguin, 1978).
This is the classic statement of Rousseau's view of the dynamics of society.

HENRI DE SAINT-SIMON, *Social Organization, the Science of Man and Other Writings* (New York: Harper & Row, Pub. Inc., 1964).
This sampling of the writings of one of the more-important Utopians offers insight into both Saint-Simon's original ideas and his erratic presentation of them.

JACOB L.TALMON, *The Origins of Totalitarian Democracy* (New York: W. W. Norton & Co., Inc., 1976).
Talmon covers a broad panorama but is particularly concerned with Rousseau's ideas and their interpretation in nineteenth-century Europe.

E. P. THOMPSON, *The Making of the English Working Class* (New York: Penguin, 1967).
   Thompson's work is very broad in its coverage, offering a full description of the life of the industrial workers of England and their development into a social force.

# 2

# Marx and Engels

None of the early socialists had the impact upon the history of socialism that one attributes to Karl Marx. Not only is he indisputably the primary theorist of modern socialism, but he is one of the most influential political philosophers of modern history. His impact on socialism of the past century has been so extensive that it can be compared to that of a prophet upon his flock. His ideas have been so pervasive that the terms *Marxism* and *socialism* are often used interchangeably, even though in today's world there are socialist movements that do not trace their origins to Marx.

## EARLY INFLUENCES ON KARL MARX

Karl Marx was born on May 5, 1818, in the small Rhineland city of Trier. Although Trier had a continuous history dating back to Roman times and had been the seat of an elector of the Holy Roman Empire, in Marx's time it was a small town of little note. It had no university, and most commercial activity in the town emanated from its modestly prosperous wine and river-commerce businesses. On the whole, however, there was little to distinguish it from a dozen other nineteenth-century Rhineland towns.

On both sides of his family Karl Marx was descended from a long line of rabbis. Little is known of Marx's mother save that she was the daughter of a Dutch rabbi and apparently a woman of limited education and intellect. She was evidently proud of her rabbinical heritage, and one may surmise that she often reminded Karl of the tradition and responsibilities inherent in that heritage. Beyond this, her influence on Karl's values and education appears to have been minimal, and he never held her in high regard.

A great deal more is known of Karl's father, a descendant of the rabbis of Trier. A child of the Enlightenment and its secular outlook, Heinrich Marx had broken with his family tradition, scorned the rabbinate, and trained instead as a lawyer. Following the territorial adjustments of the Napoleonic Wars in which Trier became part of the Prussian kingdom, he became a loyal subject of the King of Prussia. If nothing else, Heinrich Marx was an ambitious man, anxious to become a financially successful Prussian citizen. Even though Prussian Jews enjoyed considerable emancipation when compared to Jews elsewhere, Jewish lawyers were nevertheless subject to very real professional constraints, especially after the passage of new anti-Jewish laws in 1816. Since Heinrich Marx's true religious proclivities were of the Deist variety, it is understandable that he saw no point in enduring these constraints when he had the option of conversion. In 1817, the year before Karl's birth, he formally converted to the local Protestant church, an act based on professional considerations and not on religious conviction.[1]

Karl Marx himself formally scorned both his Jewish ancestry — later in life he was to give vent to feelings that could only be described as anti-Semitic — and also the Protestant church into which he was baptized as a child. Yet he was not unaware of his distinguished rabbinical heritage. His forbears included some of the greatest rabbis of their time, notably the famous Rabbi Meier Katzenellenbogen, a sixteenth-century sage. It is interesting to note that in the European tradition rabbis are not clergymen; they are arbitrators and teachers of immutable law (Jewish Scripture), and their interpretations of truth and natural law (or God's Law) are binding on the community. The role of discovering and interpreting natural law — in this case the laws of history — was to become Marx's obsession in his adult life.

An obviously talented student, Marx's academic success pleased his father, who was a well-read man and delighted in having at least one offspring who shared his intellectual aspirations. It was neither at home nor at school, however, where Marx received his most impor-

---

[1]Karl's mother declined for years to go along with the family's conversion, delaying her own baptism until 1825, presumably out of respect for her father who was Rabbi of Nijmegen until his death that year.

tant intellectual stimulation. Rather, it was at the home of Ludwig von Westphalen, a local official of aristocratic background who ran an informal literary salon for the more-gifted youth of Trier. At the Westphalen's Karl not only dabbled in poetry but received a thorough introduction to the humanities as well. In 1835 he passed the college entrance examinations and prepared to enter the University of Bonn.

It is curious that the unconventional young Marx should have chosen to attend the very conventional University of Bonn. His behavior once he arrived at Bonn was puzzling; he apparently spent little time with his studies, drank constantly, may have been involved in a duel, and at the end of the year, having literally wasted his time at the university, he returned to Trier.

Whatever his problems at the time, Marx apparently resolved them during the summer of 1836. He secretly became engaged to Jenny Westphalen, daughter of his former mentor, and publicly announced his intention to resume his education at the relatively new and unconventional Friedrich Wilhelm University of Berlin.

## HEGEL, HESS, AND FEUERBACH

In the 1830s Berlin was a heady destination for a youth who had hitherto never been away from the small towns of the Rhineland. The city was both the seat of a repressive, anti-intellectual monarchy and a dynamic university. The latter had only been founded during the Napoleonic period but had quickly developed into an innovative and exciting institution, attracting some of the best minds in Germany.

When Karl arrived at the university he was immediately swept into the constant exchanges of ideas, challenges, and ideological debates that seemed to pervade the student body. Still influenced by the humanism that marked his Trier education, he turned to the composition of poetry in the tenor of the romantic movement then prevalent. Though his class attendance was casual and erratic, as was the case with most Berlin students, he avoided the totally dissolute experience of his year at Bonn.

Marx's poetry—such of it as survives—was neither poor nor distinguished by contemporary standards. As time passed, however, he became progressively less interested in poetry and more interested in the theories of political philosophy then abundant at the university. A faculty roster during that period would have provided a truly distinguished compendium of scholars. By far the most influential among them was the philosopher Georg Hegel (1770–1831), who had died several years prior to Marx's arrival but who had left his permanent imprint on the students. Hegel's idealism and provocative analysis of historical development had caught the imagination of the more radical students. It was ironic that Hegel should have become their hero, even if posthumously, since his own career had been anything but radical. Quite to the contrary, in his later years he had become a champion of the Prussian state and of German culture and had, all too obviously, aspired to a position in the Prussian Court. Even his most ardent disciples were embarrassed by his identification with the established state, to say nothing of his obsession with Christianity.

It was not Hegel's life but his teachings and their implications that attracted a following. His philosophy was a highly complex attempt to solve what he considered the open questions left by his predecessors, notably Immanuel Kant. No brief comment on his works can be satisfactory; they were so diverse and so complex that they became rallying points for both conservatives and radicals, who professed to see in them the philosophical justification of their own positions. What chiefly interested the young Karl Marx and his radical friends was Hegel's theory of the instruments of change in historical development.

Hegel taught a scheme of historical progression by which mankind painfully ascended to higher and higher stages of civilization. There were, of course, setbacks to this pattern of progression—and as a good conservative, Hegel viewed the French Revolution with its seeming lack of logic and direction as one such setback—but nevertheless, propelled by a force which Hegel dubbed "the Absolute," progress did occur. Borrowing on a system of argumentation developed by the ancient Greeks and known as the dialectical method, Hegel argued that progress in history was achieved by the reconciliation of opposites or "alienations." He made the case that one concept, the *thesis*, inevitably produced its opposite or contradiction, the *antithesis*. The interaction of thesis and antithesis refined the thesis, rejecting what had become invalid or anachronistic in the thesis, to produce a more-advanced concept known as the *synthesis*. The synthesis became the symbol of the progress achieved. Inevitably the synthesis became the thesis of a new and higher stage, and the system of reconciling opposites began again.

For the radicals at Berlin, or as they became known, the Young Hegelians, this analysis of history implied that revolutionary change was the force that moved history, for how else did the antithesis transform the thesis into synthesis? The romantic poet Karl Marx had difficulty in accepting Hegel, but once his poetic zeal had yielded to his interest in problems of philosophy, the ideology of Hegel seemed more worth the intensive study it required. He was attracted by the idea of a total scheme of history even though he found many aspects of Hegel's philosophy unsatisfactory.

Marx's ideological development was far from complete at Berlin. He finished his formal education in 1841 with a mail-order doctorate from the University of Jena—such things were rather common—and began to contemplate what he should do with his life. After a brief flirtation with the idea of an academic career, in the 1840s Marx became involved in journalism, first in Prussia and then after 1843 in France and Belgium. During this time, he came in contact with a dynamic writer from Cologne, Moses Hess (1812–1875), a man who was responsible for introducing Marx to socialism.

Hitherto, there had been little in Marx's experience or background to make him sensitive to social and economic problems. His radical affiliations as a student of Hegelian philosophy were essentially romantic and idealistic. Hess, himself an idealistic humanitarian, introduced Marx to the idea that injustice had basically economic origins. He convinced Marx that the quest for a just society had to be directed at the elimination of private property and of national frontiers, both of which contributed to poverty and degradation. Apparently impressed with Marx's response to these ideas, as well as his general intellect, Hess became Marx's patron as well as tutor.

In later years Marx deprecated Hess and minimized Hess's influence on him. Probably Hess's strong commitment to Jewishness offended Marx and led him to make these disclaimers, although Marx was generally not gracious in acknowledging his debts to others. Nevertheless, Hess was clearly responsible for bringing Marx from a nebulous Hegelian radicalism to a total commitment to socialism.

During these crucial years another philosopher, Ludwig Feuer-bach (1804–1872), had an influence on Marx. Feuerbach's outlook, personality, and values were the opposite of those of the gentle Hess. Whereas Hess had been reluctant to give economics exclusive impor-tance in historical events and had remained idealistic in the Hegelian tradition, Feuerbach challenged Hegel's idealism, particularly his commitment to Christianity, and stressed material conditions in-stead. Feuerbach advanced the idea that God was man's creation and hence philosophies of history should stress man and not God. Though Marx was highly critical of much of Feuerbach's work, particularly the latter's lack of interest in political activity, he was overwhelmed by Feuerbach's convincing substitution of materialism for Hegel's vague idea of an "Absolute." The theory later known as Marxism was still many years from creation, but Marx had in effect moved into the socialist camp, although he denied any common sympathies with the Saint-Simonians, Fourierists, Owenites, or any other of the exist-ing socialist groups.


## FRIEDRICH ENGELS
## AND HIS COMMITMENT TO MARX


In the summer of 1843, frustrated by the Prussian censorship and generally unhappy with the German situation, Marx decided that the time had come to leave Prussia and start an entirely new life. As men-tioned before, he was already engaged to his childhood sweetheart Jenny von Westphalen; now they married, and together they emi-grated to Paris. There he began to work on his new ideas, to involve himself in socialist groups, and to develop openly the bellicosity that was to mark his personal relationships for the rest of his life. Yet it was also in Paris that he formed the lifelong association with the scion of a textile fortune, Friedrich Engels. Marx had known Engels slightly in Prussia but had not been particularly close to him then. Like Marx, Engels had been a young Hegelian at the University of Berlin and had come under the influence of Moses Hess. In other respects, their backgrounds and experiences were quite different: Engels had learned about the operations of industrial society in a more direct fashion than Marx, through his involvement in his family's factories in Barmen, Germany, and Manchester, England. His studies at the University of Berlin had already predisposed the young Engels toward the cause of social change. His visit to the family holdings in Manchester in 1843–1844 completed the conversion.

The Manchester that Engels visited in the 1840s was a classic example of the social cost of unfettered industrialization. In hardly more than a century Manchester had grown from a mill town to one of England's larger cities. The growth, however, had been devoid of social conscience and Engels was profoundly shocked by the endless rows of squalid slums, the lack of basic municipal services or sanitation, and, most shocking of all, the anger and helplessness of the workers who saw their lives being wasted by an apparently uncaring group of factory owners, of whom Engels himself was involuntarily a member.

It was in Manchester that he became thoroughly committed to the cause of the worker; there he became convinced that the moment was at hand for the exploited workers of Europe to turn on the upper and middle classes who oppressed them. He kept careful notes of his observations, eventually publishing them as, *The Condition of the Working Class in England in 1844.*

Returning to Paris in September, 1844, Engels met Marx, whom he had once before briefly encountered, and he now intuitively recognized Marx's potential as the genius who would develop and articulate the revolutionary changes in society that Engels considered inevitable. In forming one of the most-unusual intellectual partnerships in history, one which was to last almost four decades, Engels deliberately cast himself in a subservient role. He was a gifted writer and theorist in his own right—more able than Marx at turning out lucid prose—but he never dared equate his talents with those of Marx. Instead he became Marx's editor as well as collaborator, preferring to be Marx's helpmate rather than rival. In doing so, Engels provided Marx with an essential service, without which it is doubtful that Marx could have produced the theoretical framework of socialism and historical view that became his monument.

Prior to his collaboration with Engels, Marx's work was in a state of flux. His journalism, not yet couched in socialist terms, was nonetheless sufficiently radical to earn him an *ex post facto* banishment from Prussia in 1844 and expulsion from France the following year. Yet he remained dissatisfied with what he considered his own incomplete mastery of economics and its role in history. It was now that he imposed upon himself a regimen of serious study and reflection, during which he began to write in notebooks and produce articles, all the while trying to formulate a theoretical justification for the political objectives which were taking shape in his mind. He also attended the meetings of a group of German emigres known as the Communist League, an organization committed to spreading the doctrine of socialism and given to revolutionary language that sometimes exceeded its own aspirations.

During these years Marx also met various other socialists, many of whom were to become later adversaries: most notable were the Frenchman Pierre Joseph Proudhon, the Russian Mikhail Bakunin, and the Prussian Wilhelm Weitling. When Marx was exiled to Belgium in 1845—ironically not because he presented a threat due to any specific action, but because of the complaints of the Prussian government over the tone of emigré publications—he had already learned enough from his socialist colleagues to benefit from their experience, and also to judge almost all of them to be completely wrong in their analysis of society and history. He became obsessed with developing a scientific system that demonstrated how socialism was the only logical outcome of human experience, and he displayed a total intolerance to the views of his fellow emigrant socialists when they dared to dissent or criticize his views. In the emigrant circles of the 1840s, Karl Marx was known as a fiery genius with whom one disputed at considerable peril.

The late 1840s were a time of peculiar stagnation for Europe. The social problems of industrialization were as vexing as ever, and workers chafed under the continued hardships they endured. In East and Central Europe monarchies sought to act in the old manner of heavy-handed authoritarianism, while in West Europe the regimes fought off with alternate tactics of repression and indecision the republican aspirations that had flourished since the French Revolution. In such an atmosphere political intrigues were commonplace, and secret and not-so-secret societies harboring all sorts of political schemes flourished. The Communist League was but one of these secret societies, and hardly one of the better known.


## THE *COMMUNIST MANIFESTO*


More than a few members of the Communist League had had difficulties dealing with Marx, but, impressed with Marx's genius and willing to overlook his irascibility, they nonetheless commissioned him to write their manifesto. After considerable maneuvering by Engels, who had made an early attempt at writing one himself, the League was persuaded to accept Marx's document, which had been produced with substantial assistance from Engels. The resulting product was the work known to history as the *Communist Manifesto* (1848), by far the most widely read of any of Marx's writings.

The *Communist Manifesto* is not the most profound of Marx's works, but it may well be the best written, and it certainly is one of the least obscure. In terms of its rhetoric, at least, it is the most overtly revolutionary of his works. Using the language of revolutionary confrontation, the *Manifesto* proclaimed the historical inevitability of a denouement between the workers, now referred to as the *proletariat*, and the propertied classes, or *bourgeoisie*.

The *Communist Manifesto* starts with an accolade to the dynamics of historical change: "The history of all hitherto existing society is the history of the class struggle." The *Manifesto* then divides society into two hostile camps: the proletariat and the bourgeoisie, recounts the exploitation of the former by the latter, and literally proclaims class warfare by summoning the proletariat to the fulfillment of its historic mission. The Utopian socialists are dismissed as visionaries, and workers are urged to follow the true revolutionaries, the communists (defined here as simply "the vanguard of the proletariat"). At the end, in an appeal to the solidarity of class over nation, the *Manifesto* concludes with the heady slogan: "Proletariat of the world, unite! You have nothing to lose but your chains!"

By coincidence the *Communist Manifesto* appeared in January 1848, one month before the previously mentioned Parisian revolution triggered a series of revolutions across the European continent. The *Communist Manifesto* played no role whatsoever in the revolutions of 1848, but its first appearance has always been linked with that date—the year of revolution.

From the point of view of inflammatory rhetoric, Marx never again matched the *Communist Manifesto*, nor did he attempt to do so. In these years Marx was more disposed toward an active approach to socialism and more willing to speak in terms of imminent confrontation than he would be in later years, but still he shrank from any direct involvement in revolutionary action. Terminology was one thing, personal activity was another. In the *Communist Manifesto* as well as in several other statements of the late 1840s, Marx often used revolutionary hyperbole that suggested a more directly active approach than he was personally ready to launch. In the specific case of the *Communist Manifesto*, however, there were other considerations. The radical, angry tone of the *Manifesto* may well reflect the fact that it was commissioned by the Communist League, which indulged, as did most secret groups of the time, in exaggerated statements of its own intentions and used overly dramatic language when stating its position vis-à-vis established society. In any case, the *Manifesto's* language, its call to arms, and its suggestion of an *immediate* confrontation are not typical of most of Marx's writings and belie the developmental approach to socialism which Marx had been pursuing in the years prior to 1848.

While in Paris in the 1840s, Marx had kept a series of notebooks which he had prepared for his own self-education and reflection rather than for publication. In them he had given his major attention to unraveling the causes and subsequent effects of the exploitation of the worker in industrial society. In a superb analysis of how the system alienated the worker not only from the fruits of his or her labor but from humankind as well, Marx explored the role of private property and its manipulation, concluding that this was the source of alienation. He used the term *communism* to differentiate his views on the role of private property from those of other socialists, whom he felt had not adequately perceived nor sufficiently stressed its fundamental importance.

Marx never finished, nor published, these notebooks.[2] Yet they provide evidence of the serious thinking he was doing at the time, and they reflect his perception of socialism as deriving fundamentally from a concern with the betterment of the human condition. In the notebooks Marx was trying to explore, in a substantial way, the historical processes that determine human progress; the *Communist Manifesto*, despite its effectiveness as an incendiary document, was out of keeping with the general tone of his work, both prior and subsequent to its publication.

It was, however, quite in keeping with the furor in Europe in 1848. Yet for all their importance in European history, the revolutions of 1848 were essentially revolutions that failed; except for France, the established regimes survived for the time being. Throughout Europe, the scene was repeated in which the revolution first seemed to succeed and then, being unable to coordinate its goals, failed to defend its initial gains. In Vienna, Rome, Berlin, Budapest, and in other capitals, short-lived revolutionary regimes were again replaced by the regimes they had challenged. Marx remained a passive bystander through this period. Never again was he in such proximity to revolutionary activity, yet he took no part. After a brief visit to the Rhineland, Marx proceeded to England, where he remained in permanent exile from his native land.

## MARX'S EXILE AND THE WRITING OF *CAPITAL*

England in the second half of the nineteenth century was a highly complex and troubled society, but it was not one on the verge of revolution. Marx at this time seems not to have been involved with English workers nor particularly interested in the problems that were excit-

---

[2]The very existence of these notebooks was unknown until the end of the 1920s when they were published by the Institute of Marxism-Leninism in Moscow. Essentially two generations of Marxists formulated their views of Marx without recourse to these notebooks, which are important to anyone studying the development of Marx's ideas on society and its problems.

ing English politicians. Essentially, his English exile was marked by years of poverty—at least until the later years when Engels was able to provide him with a regular income—and intensive study of economics, philosophy, and history. In London, he strove to synthesize the ferment and ideas of the previous years. It took him a full decade to produce his first work, *The Critique of the Political Economy*, and, when the slender volume finally appeared in June 1859, it was somewhat of a letdown to his admirers. The stress on class warfare of the *Communist Manifesto* was conspicuously absent; the book's only innovation was a new emphasis on the labor theory of value, with particular attention to the importance of manual labor. He was, however, at work on his greatest work, *Capital*. (Although the first, and most important, volume was ready in a few years, various problems with publishers delayed the appearance of *Capital* until 1867.)[3] A massive publication, both in part and in entirety, it was the closest he ever came to a systematic exposition of "scientific socialism." As he had been doing for many years, his exposition was couched in the Hegelian terminology of thesis, antithesis, and synthesis to explain the dynamics of change in history, but it was clearly evident how far Marx had traveled from the dialectical idealism of Hegel to the dialectical materialism with which he supplanted it. The transition, which had already been evident in the *Communist Manifesto*, was refined and more fully developed in *Capital*.

## DIALECTICAL MATERIALISM

According to Marx, *dialectical materialism* organizes society into economic classes which serve as the transition forces for moving society to progressively higher stages of historical development.

---

[3]Marx never published the second and third volumes of *Capital*; they appeared only after his death, as edited by Engels and others.

Marx's application of dialectical materialism to explaining history is known as *historical materialism*, or the view of history as being changed by economic forces.

Marx summarized human history as being encapsuled in five basic "stages": primitive communism, slavery, feudalism, capitalism, and the as-yet-unfulfilled stage of socialism. According to historical materialism, each of these stages constitutes a thesis, and each will eventually develop an antithesis—a socioeconomic class which becomes aware that it has been denied its full economic reward for its productivity. The alteration of socioeconomic relationships which inevitably occurs as a result of the challenge to the established order produces a synthesis of antagonistic classes—or a new, higher historical stage—which, like its predecessor, will eventually produce an antithesis and give way to a new synthesis. To illustrate, feudalism can be viewed as the thesis of the Middle Ages; when feudalism was challenged by the rise of the middle class (or bourgeoisie)—which lacked the power commensurate with its economic importance—the middle class was functioning as the antithesis; the middle class successfully broke down feudalism and replaced it with capitalism, which was the resulting synthesis. As capitalism developed, however, it in turn generated its own antithesis in the form of the working class, which became the most productive element in society but was denied the full rewards of its productivity. It is the detailed exposition of the rise of capitalism and the attendant exploitation of the working class that constitutes the major share of *Capital*.

Expanding upon ideas introduced in his earlier *Critique of Political Economy*, Marx stressed the labor theory of value as the cornerstone of society. He explained that labor was both the source of the workers' livelihood and of their exploitation. Since capitalist society denied a worker a fair return for his or her labor, a substantial proportion of the worker's productivity was returned to the capitalist as profit or, in Marx's terminology, as "surplus value" stolen from the worker. Greater productivity fails to benefit workers because capitalists always seek to increase the "surplus value," thereby worsening the workers' economic status and driving them into increasing impoverishment and misery. The result of this class exploitation is inevitably the rise of the workers against their capitalist exploiters in order to create a just society, that is, the socialist society.

All of this represented a substantial refinement and development of Marx's earlier thought. In his unpublished writings of the 1840s he had concerned himself primarily with alienated labor. Although a generation later his mature theoretical work went beyond the issue of alienation, his concern remained fundamentally humanist. The idea voiced in the *Communist Manifesto* that "the history of all hitherto existing society is the history of the class struggle" now culminated with *Capital*'s emphasis on the polarization of the impoverished working class vis-a-vis the gluttonous bourgeoisie and the presumption that the next step for the working class was to settle its accounts by overthrowing capitalism. The *Communist Manifesto* summoned the workers to revolution; *Capital* offered the rationale for such a revolution.

With *Capital* Marx reached the apex of his career as a political and economic theoretician. His later writings tended to be topical; he never produced another, so comprehensive work on "scientific socialism, " or what has become known in the modern world simply as Marxism. The erudition and thought that went into Marx's theory is evident even to the most hostile observer. Essentially, it was more than a theory; it was a world view—and a faith—for understanding humanity and the dynamics of historical change. It drew on almost all known bodies of knowledge: philosophical, historical, economic, sociological, and even scientific.

As thorough and exhaustive as the system seemed, there were still unanswered questions, at least as far as future events were concerned. That the workers would confront capitalism and achieve the destruction of the latter was implicit in the doctrine; how they were to do this was more uncertain. Marx was not one for defining tactics in detail. The forces of history made inevitable the conflict between proletariat and bourgeoisie; the mechanics of pursuing this conflict were quite another matter. Similarly, Marx offered no detailed analysis of the future socialist society that was to arise once the capitalist stage had been ended. He contented himself with the observation that in a society that had ended class differences, class exploitation would also be ended. Such a society was by definition a just society.

## THE FIRST INTERNATIONAL

After he completed the writing of *Capital* in the early 1860s, Marx became interested in practical matters as he had been previously in theoretical endeavors. In 1861, with the political climate of Europe more sedate, he was able to make a trip to Berlin, where he was truly impressed with the growth of social consciousness among the Prussian workers. What distressed him, however, was that much of this growth was due to the energetic proselytizing and organizing of Ferdinand Lassalle (1825–1864), who had more or less filled the void left by Marx's long residence in England.

In many ways Lassalle was a more youthful and charismatic version of Marx himself, although his bizarre personal life scandalized Marx. Lassalle, who had always paid homage to Marx as a thinker, had his own very different ideas on socialist tactics. He had invested prodigious energies in what today would be called "consciousness-raising" activities amongst the workers, an activity which Marx had somehow found unappealing. Perhaps Marx saw in Lassalle a rival for primacy amongst socialists; certainly the fact that he perennially owed Lassalle money did not endear the latter to Marx. He bitterly dismissed Lassalle—in the most caustic of references—as a "Jewish nigger" and returned to England wishing Lassalle considerably less than good fortune in his efforts to organize the Prussian workers. The rivalry resolved itself in 1864 when Lassalle, in a fit of anger, provoked a duel over an affair that had nothing to do with Marx or politics and was fatally wounded. The ironic result was that Lassalle, in his brief but meteoric career, had created the organizational base for a Marxist party in Prussia. His sudden death left the embryonic party leaderless and susceptible to the "Marxist" influence of Marx himself, who never appreciated the importance of Lassalle's contributions.

Marx never had much direct influence on the British working class, nor had he ever tried particularly hard to win any. In the 1860s, however, he began to attend various worker meetings and to take careful note of those who had connections or aspirations beyond England. A series of meetings between British and French worker groups commencing in 1862 had led to the formation of a so-called "international federation of working men," which then turned to Marx to write its credo, remembering perhaps the dramatic manifesto he had written for the Communist League in 1848.

The new group, however, was nowhere near as confrontation-oriented or as activist as the Communist League had been in 1848, and Marx was quick to perceive the difference in sponsorship. The Inaugural Address he prepared for this group was hardly in the same vein as the *Communist Manifesto*, although some of the old rhetoric came through; it was certainly less bellicose and tended to avoid very specific commitments to socialism. Yet it was sufficient to give Marx a position of leadership in the new organization—known retrospectively as the First International—and he quickly became its most prominent and outspoken member.

The organization grew steadily, too steadily for Marx who was unhappy over some of the dissident and uncertain groups who were joining its ranks. Marx had emerged as the undoubted ideological leader of the organization, and it was probably the one time in his life when he enjoyed high visibility in socialist circles and when his reputation was such that the other socialists would refer to him in terms usually reserved for the leader of a movement.

In 1868, despite Marx's misgivings, the First International absorbed an organization known as "The International Alliance of Socialist Democracy." What Marx found disquieting about the new organization was not so much the group itself as its charismatic leader, Mikhail Bakunin. The latter, an activist of long standing—he had been deeply involved in the Italian revolution of 1848—was an admirer of Marx, but the admiration was hardly reciprocated. In part, Marx may well have feared losing his leadership to a dynamic personality such as Bakunin, but more importantly, he could hardly overlook the nondeterminist and non-"scientific" approach to socialism espoused by Bakunin, who was later to be one of the founders of modern anarchism. The two highly egocentric men never really did function as collaborators, and the International became an arena in which each vied for primacy amongst the European socialists.

The issue came to a head with the startling victory of Prussia in the Franco-Prussian War of 1870 and the emergence of a united German Empire dominated by the victorious Prussian regime. Marx, and even more so Engels, applauded this turn of events as the triumph of an advanced industrialized society. Germany was to be hailed in the name of economic and historical progress. Bakunin, on the other hand, had open misgivings about the impact of a victorious Germany on proletarian activism. Feelings became more exacerbated in March 1871 when a mixed group of radicals and liberals seized control of a large portion of the city of Paris, proclaiming themselves an independent entity known as the Commune of Paris. For two months they withstood the forces of the French central government, until, in a wave of terror and counterterror, the Commune was overthrown, the conflict causing frightening casualties numbering into the thousands.

The Commune of Paris was not a socialist enterprise and certainly owed little to Marx or the International. Yet Marx identified with it as a manifestation of working-class solidarity, choosing to overlook the fact that embroiled in it were far more followers of Bakunin (and Blanqui) than of Marx.

Oddly enough Marx's exuberant support of the Commune vitiated his position in the International, where many of the labor leaders recoiled from the idea of "claiming credit" for an episode they considered ill-timed and illfated. Recognizing the erosion of his position, Marx responded in the most vindictive manner possible by utilizing his remaining influence to have the International's headquarters transferred to the United States, where it floundered in the disputes of small factions and eventually disappeared as he expected it would. By use of innuendo and slander he also succeeded in having Bakunin expelled from the organization on a spurious charge of embezzlement.

It was, however, a Pyrrhic victory in every sense. Marx never again rose to a position of leadership among socialists. Indeed the remaining decade of his life was marked by very little productivity, a situation caused at least partially by his wife's terminal illness, and by the vexing fact that he was being increasingly ignored even by those who were committed to his version of socialist ideology.

His last years were a physical as well as an emotional trial. The death of Jenny in 1881 was compounded by the news of the death of his eldest daugher. On March 14, 1883, he himself died, bitter at his personal tragedies and unaware of the enormous impact his work was to have in the near future. His funeral was sparsely attended and, despite Engels's moving eulogy, little noted by the general public or the press.

## LIEBKNECHT, BEBEL, AND THE SOCIAL DEMOCRATIC WORKERS' PARTY

All of his disappointments notwithstanding, even during his lifetime Marx's doctrines of socialism and historical determinism had had a substantial impact on others. Amongst Marx's disciples—excepting, of course, Engels, who was more of a collaborator—by far the most influential were two German socialists who worked closely together, Wilhelm Liebknecht (1826–1900) and August Bebel (1840–1913). Bebel was one of the very few major socialist leaders with a genuine proletarian background. Liebknecht, on the other hand, was a trained philologist. The two men seemed to appreciate each other's different yet complementary attributes, and both of them were convinced, for various reasons, that Marx had a great deal to offer the European working class, even if he was a theorist rather than an activist.

Capitalizing on the vacuum left by the death of Lassalle, in the late 1860s Liebknecht and Bebel had succeeded in organizing a socialist movement in Germany based on Marxist principles. Called the Social Democratic Workers' Party, it was the first recognizably Marxist organization in the world, and in 1869 it met as a political party in the German city of Eisenach.

Bebel and Liebknecht were not content with having formed only a splinter group of German socialists. Lassalle had left behind a formidable organization of his own, and it seemed wasteful and self-defeating for socialists to compete with each other when they shared a common philosophical outlook. Without fully apprising Marx, who detested even a dead Lassalle, Bebel and Liebknecht began to inquire as to what premises might be acceptable to both groups. The situation was a delicate one, but in 1875, after several years of negotiation, a so-called "unity congress" was convened at the city of Gotha. The result was a single German Social Democratic Party.

Marx and Engels, who had not been party to the negotiations, were infuriated when informed of the basis of the "compromise." Marx was irritated at the theoretical placebos given to make palatable some of Lassalle's ideas on the wage system and labor, but he took particular exception to the provisions which suggested working for democratic reforms within the context of the newly created German Empire. In his *Critique of the Gotha Program*, Marx complained that the program was too accepting of the "police-guarded military despotism" that was the German state, and that it ignored the revolutionary goal Marx had defined as "the dictatorship of the proletariat." Marx defined the latter as a transition stage between capitalism and communism; this goal, essential to any revolutionary program, was conspicuously absent in the Gotha program.

In point of fact, Liebknecht and Bebel had deliberately modified Marxian goals so they might form a more viable option to offer the German workers, who were not about to seek the overthrow of their recently unified country. Rather than engage in a theoretical dispute with Marx, Liebknecht deliberately suppressed Marx's *Critique*—it was not published until 1891—and proceeded with the business of organizing German socialism. Privately, Bebel complained to friends that "the two old men in London" were simply out of touch with the realities of the German situation. In his memoirs, Bebel noted that virtually up to the time of Marx's death it had been necessary for one socialist or another to journey to London and soothe Marx's bruised feelings over the Gotha compromise. Marx's objections notwithstanding, the Gotha compromise in effect made European Marxism a political fact of life.

## MARXISM REINTERPRETED: THE WRITINGS OF ENGELS

Beginning in 1878, and to some extent even earlier, the German Chancellor Otto von Bismarck promoted a massive antisocialist campaign in Germany. Considering the problems involved in combatting these attacks, the internecine warfare over the Gotha program seemed irrelevant, and Liebknecht and his colleagues simply ignored objections from London. In any case, Marx's will to keep up the argument was dissipated by his own declining health as well as the various problems besetting members of his immediate family. Engels, though he too had opposed the Gotha program, was not ready to launch a crusade to undo it. Instead he turned his efforts to other challenges to the doctrinal purity of "scientific socialism."

In the 1870s a certain Dr. Eugen Dühring had celebrated his conversion to socialism with a massive publication in which he criticized some of the philosophical bases of scientific socialism as espoused by Marx. Dühring's work was actually quite shallow and could have been fruitfully ignored with few consequences. Engels, however, decided to rebut it in order to offer a new clarification of the bases of scientific socialism. It was at this point that Engels emerged from Marx's shadow as a theorist in his own right. In 1877, he wrote a massive polemic known popularly as *Anti-Dühring*, a work which became a milestone in the history of socialist thought.[4]

What Engels did, with Marx's overt approval, was to restate the tenets of scientific socialism. He broke very little new ground, but, in his own lucid manner, he did offer a reaffirmation and to some extent a simplification of what Marx (and he) had been saying all those years.

In *Anti-Dühring*, Engels categorically reaffirmed the primacy of economic relationships and the importance of historical determinism, even implying that capitalism was a progressive force *at a given stage of history*, although it was destined to become obsolete and repressive. He downgraded the importance of the state, noting that the proletariat would not devote its efforts to its abolition, but rather that the state would wither away of its own obsolescence. Years later V. I. Lenin, the leader of the Russian Revolution, would seize on *Anti-Dühring* for an important rationalization of his own tactics, but at the time of its appearance Engels's work appeared to be little more than a distillation of existing Marxian theories. It was, however, eminently readable, and, despite an initial lack of interest, in its abbreviated form it eventually became one of the most widely read of socialist works. Though not immediately realized, with the

---

[4]Engels's better-known work, *Socialism: Scientific and Utopian*, is actually an excerpt from *Anti-Dühring*.

publication of *Anti-Dühring*, Engels had replaced the ailing Marx as the leading expounder of scientific socialism.

Outliving Marx by a dozen years, Engels devoted much of his efforts to editing and refining Marx's writing, especially the second volume of *Capital*. In 1884 he published his own study, *Origins of the Family, Private Property and the State*, in which he stressed more openly than Marx ever had the analogy between historical determinism and Darwin's ideas on evolutionary development.

Whereas Marx wrote profoundly, Engels wrote clearly. Only the really well-educated could delve into Marx's theories and follow his philosophical exposition. It was the more lucid, if more simplistic, presentation of Engels's work that evoked visions of a socialist millennium, achieved as the capstone of the historical progression outlined by Marx, something which people began to refer to in the last two decades of the nineteenth century, as Marxism.

The emergence of Marxism as a mass movement barely a decade after Marx's death owed much to the arduous labors of Liebknecht and Bebel, as well as to their peers in other countries. One should stress, as well, the unfailing diligence of Engels in continuing to uphold the essential nature of Marxism in his writings and in serving as Marxism's most formidable and lucid propagandist. Very little original theory has been attributed to Engels; one could speculate that this was the result of his deliberate subservience to Marx, or even that he may have ascribed to Marx ideas that were essentially his own. In any case, as a founding father of modern-day Marxist socialism, Engels is second only to Marx himself.

# SELECTED READINGS

LOUIS ALTHUSSER, *For Marx* (New York: Random House, 1969).
Althusser takes issue with the notion that there is a continuous line of development from the young Marx to the mature Marx and presents the case for a clear break between the two.

SHLOMO AVINERI, *The Social and Political Thought of Karl Marx* (New York: Cambridge University Press, 1971).
Avineri makes the case for a continuous development of Marx's thought from his responses to Hegelian ideas to his own theory of scientific socialism.

LUCIA COLLETI, *Marxism and Hegel* (New York: Schocken Books, 1978).
Colleti offers a new interpretation of Marx's debt to Hegel and the philosophical bases of Marx's ideas.

ERICH FROMM, *Marx's Concept of Man* (New York: Frederick Ungar, 1969).
Fromm not only reprints the famous "1844 Manuscripts" but also offers a long and thoughtful essay on their importance to the development of Marx's ideas.

DAVID MCLELLAN, *Friedrich Engels* (New York: Penguin, 1978).
This is an extremely brief but cogent biography of Engels which serves as an admirable introduction to his work.

STEPHEN MARCUS, *Engels, Manchester and the Working Class* (New York: Random House, 1974).
A complex work involving psychohistory, this book offers a unique view of the impact of Manchester's industrial life in shaping Engels's values.

FRANZ MEHRING, *Karl Marx* (Ann Arbor: University of Michigan Press, 1972).
Mehring's biography was first published in 1910 and is obviously dated. Yet it offers an interesting perspective of the founder of Marxism.

SAUL K. PADOVER, *Karl Marx: An Intimate Biography* (New York: McGraw-Hill, 1978).
Padover's book incorporates recent scholarship to offer a sympathetic but incisive critique of Marx's life.

ROBERT TUCKER, *The Marx-Engels Reader*, 2nd ed. (New York: W. W. Norton & Co., Inc., 1978).
A good anthology of the major writings of Marx and Engels

with well-written introductions. No anthology can ever offer enough of Marx and Engels' works, but this book serves as a useful beginning.

EDMUND WILSON, *To the Finland Station* (New York: Doubleday, 1970).

A brilliant, erudite, and polemical historical overview of the development of socialist ideology through history, using Marx as the pivotal figure.

# 3

# Anarchism and Other Non-Marxist Movements

It should not be assumed that once Marx and Engels developed their theories of "scientific socialism" that all alternative approaches to socialism disappeared or were merged into the Marxist milieu. Quite to the contrary, throughout Marx's lifetime, "scientific socialism" was accepted by only a small retinue, and even after his views began to increase in popularity in the 1880s and 1890s, competing theories not only persisted but in some cases thrived as new doctrines and ideas emerged. Perhaps it is in the nature of socialist movements that unity is elusive; the history of socialism has certainly produced more divisions than other social or political movements. Though there were many who were impressed by the thoroughness of Marx's work, and even more who admired Marx's ideas as recast by Engels, there still remained substantial numbers of socialists who continued to wonder whether a movement more oriented toward immediate action would not be better suited to the quest for the social and economic justice denied by capitalism.

## THE ANARCHIST MOVEMENT

The most visible, and probably the most controversial of these various groups were the people who proudly called themselves *anarchists*. Unlike the Marxists, they were a loose association of individuals rather than a clearly defined organization. Their relationship to socialism was never precise: an American anarchist once proudly claimed, "Every anarchist is a socialist, but not every socialist is an anarchist."

What distinguished the anarchists from other socialist groups was the priority they assigned to the destruction of the state.

Although Marxists were hardly defenders of the state—especially of the bourgeois capitalist state—they tended to stress economic relationships as the critical element in society and considered the state a reflection, not the cause, of these distorted relationships under capitalism. Moreover, Engels had persuasively argued, in *Anti-Dühring*, that with the socialist triumph over capitalism the state would "wither away."

To anarchists, on the other hand, the state was chiefly to blame. In their fixation upon the state as the primary evil in society, the anarchists laid claim to the ideas of Rousseau. Although Rousseau had argued for the corrupting influence of the state upon natural man, he had not, in fact, directly attacked the state as the basic form of social organization. The notion of the state as the primary evil is more appropriately traced to William Godwin, one of the earliest of the Utopian socialists. Godwin envisioned a completely unfettered society in which all authoritarian restraints, including those of the family, would be absent. However, Godwin had been so repelled by the excesses of the French Revolution that he refrained from advocating any move against the state. Whereas he spoke forcefully against all forms of social institutions, he refrained from advocating any tactics for their removal, leaving the problem to future generations. The anarchists of the late-nineteenth century, seeking a theoretical base for their movement, hailed Godwin as their prophet, deliberately overlooking the fact that he in no way had been a revolutionary activist in his own time.

A more discernible influence upon the anarchist movement was the life and theories of the French socialist, Pierre Joseph Proudhon (1809–1865). Proudhon, an associate of Marx during his stay in Paris, had had contacts with almost all of the major socialists of his time. In 1840 Proudhon had published the provocative work *What is Property?* and had answered his rhetorical question with the simple answer: "Property is theft!" The work was hardly more than a pamphlet, but its clever phraseology brought him some instant recognition amongst radicals, and even the young Marx sought to work with him during the 1840s.

There really was no sound basis for collaboration between Marx and Proudhon. Even at that early stage of his career, Marx, as a Hegelian, prized logical thought and a systematic approach to social analysis, whereas Proudhon recognized no such contraints. The collaboration broke down in the late 1840s when Proudhon produced his work *The Philosophy of Poverty* and Marx demolished it in a caustic review/essay entitled "The Poverty of Philosophy." Not without justification, Marx accused Proudhon of being an unsystematic philosopher and of misunderstanding the meaning of Hegel. This marked the end of the relationship between them, and Marx and Proudhon went their separate ways.

Proudhon, in search of principles upon which to build a free society, began to focus his attacks on the state as the instrument of the denial of human liberty. He used the term *anarchism* to describe the stateless society he envisioned, thereby introducing it into the political lexicon. There were limits, however, to Proudhon's libertarianism. Unlike Godwin, he championed the institution of the family, which he considered the ideal example of human association rather than a source of repression. In his personal life, Proudhon was puritanical, sexist, and even racist. His public attraction was largely the result of his skillful turning of phrases—"government of man by man is slavery," "God is evil," "property is theft," and so on—which caught the imagination of dissatisfied worker groups, to the extent that the Paris Commune of 1871 was marked by his influence and rang with his words, even though he had died several years earlier.

## ANARCHISM AND THE USE
## OF POLITICAL TERROR

From Proudhon, the mantle of anarchist leadership shifted to the wandering Russian exile Mikhail Bakunin (1814–1876). Although reasonably well educated, Bakunin had nowhere near the training and understanding of political philosophy of a Proudhon, let alone a Karl Marx. He was much more oriented toward revolutionary activism, and his participation in the 1848 uprising in Dresden had earned him a death sentence. Instead of execution, however, he was deported to Russia, where he served a term of penal exile until he managed to escape and wend his way back to Europe. After involvement in a number of escapades, notably in Italy, he came into contact with Marx through the First International. Initially Marx seemed intrigued by him, especially after Bakunin promised to translate some of Marx's work into Russian; moreover, the fact that he did not challenge Marx in the realm of philosophy and economic theory led to a brief rapport between the two men.

Bakunin was not a political theorist, but he was a political activist. His association with the Russian exile Sergei Nechaev—an open advocate of political terror—led him to accept, at least in principle, the necessity of such terror as a weapon in combatting the state. His contacts with Nechaev, although brief, were critical in introducing a new element into the political program of anarchists: indiscriminate terror as a justifiable tactic against a heinous enemy.

The use of random terror as a revolutionary tactic was completely unacceptable to Marx. But even before this issue arose between Marx and Bakunin there were strains in their relationship, and to some extent, given the very real differences in their personalities and outlooks, a rupture was inevitable. Ideologically as well, they had fundamentally different approaches to socialism. Marx saw socialism as the historically inevitable result of advanced capitalist societies; Bakunin saw it as originating in lesser developed societies, where people had less to risk in seeking revolutionary change. Under these circumstances, what is surprising is not the break between them but the bitterness of their split. To his dying day Bakunin found himself denounced by Marx in terms that were not only exaggerated but even untruthful. Yet his verve and commitment to activism had caught the imagination of young radicals who found Marxism too tame and Marxists too unwilling to confront the state, and perhaps too content to wait for the forces of history to bring about socialism. The message from Bakunin seemed clear: socialism, or at least the anarchist variety, could be achieved only by action, not by theoretical hair-splitting. From Bakunin's day on, anarchists were openly associated with tactics of violence, confrontation, and most spectacularly, of terror.

The death of Bakunin in 1876 found the anarchist movement still disorganized and uncertain of its goals. Bakunin, who had not been a systematic theorist, had based his leadership more on personal dynamism than on any persuasive ideology. Yet his persistent, even if erratic, involvement in revolutionary situations had fired the zeal of many radicals who were looking for a movement with immediacy as its hallmark. The movement had few adherents in countries such as Germany where the newly constructed and obviously solid German Empire seemed the antithesis to the stateless society championed by anarchists. In countries such as Italy or Spain, where the state was far less admired, anarchists were more likely to proliferate, often citing Bakunin as their inspiration, particularly in Italy. There the youthful Enrico Malatesta (1853–1932) urged the utter destruction of the rotten existing society and specifically the destruction "of every obstacle that now stands in the way of free development of social law [i.e., anarchist society]."

Such a goal, of course, was rhetorically effective but unlikely to be achieved. Instead anarchists directed their efforts toward isolated acts against authority under the premise, which they had inferred from Bakunin, that revolutionary deeds, even if executed by individuals or small well-trained groups, would undermine the existing order in their cumulative effect.

Malatesta led a disorganized march in 1877 in the countryside around Naples, promoting actions of civil disobedience: the burning of property records, the proclamation of disloyalty to the monarch, and so on. Fortunately, his group was singularly inept, and, when caught, they were treated rather leniently by authorities who did not take them very seriously.

There were, however, more dangerous extrapolations from Bakunin's legacy. One such notion was known as "propaganda by the deed." This simply meant that a great deed, which to an increasing number meant an act of terror, did more than anything else to advance the cause of anarchism. As the Russian anarchist Kropotkin put it, "A single deed is better propaganda than a thousand pamphlets!" For some, the "deed" most easily achieved was political assassination, since it required only one victim and often only one perpetrator.

There were several unsuccessful attempts on royalty in the late 1870s, and then, in 1881, both the tsar of Russia, Alexander II, and the president of the United States, James Garfield, were assassinated. In the case of Garfield, anarchists were in no way involved, for he was shot by a disappointed office-seeker. In the Russian case, however, a group of Russian populists had resorted to murdering the tsar after their policy of propagandizing the peasantry had been frustrated by the hostility of the peasants themselves. The murder of two heads of state caused a great stir of excitement, particularly in the Russia where it had been carried out in the name of revolution.

The anarchist association with terror was further enhanced by events in America. In May 1886, at a labor demonstration in Chicago's Haymarket Square, a bomb was thrown into police ranks, killing seven policemen. Exactly who threw the bomb has never been discovered. However, because several Chicago anarchists had called for militant action in connection with the demonstrations, they were assumed to be the culprits. Eight anarchists were charged with the crime, and four of them were eventually executed. For both the anarchists and the authorities, the Haymarket Square bombing became the symbol of the implacable war between anarchists and officialdom.

In the 1890s "propaganda by the deed," or political assassination, gave the anarchists international notoriety. Assassinated by anarchists were two prime ministers of Spain, the empress of Austria, President McKinley, the president of France, and the king of Italy. None of these acts promoted socialism or weakened capitalism. What they did do was firmly entrench in the public's mind, and in the mind of most nonanarchist socialists, the notion that anarchism and terror were synonymous. Indeed, so pervasive did the association become that most other socialists took great pains to separate themselves from the anarchists, lest they too be tainted.

Most anarchists, however, did not embrace terror as part of their ideology but instead rationalized its use as a tactic born of desperation. After Bakunin's death, the mantle of leadership fell to the Russian nobleman Peter Kropotkin (1842–1921). Kropotkin was a gentle man—one of the few anarchists whom Marxists accepted as part of the socialist movement—whose goal was to promote anarchism as a movement in harmony with nature. He believed that humankind would behave in a moral fashion once evil—the state, capitalism, and so on—was conquered. Toward this goal Kropotkin often called for action against oppression, interpreted by some as a call for terror.* He himself never participated in any such acts, and his persuasiveness in presenting a "moral" case for anarchism was such that he was accepted as anarchism's spokesperson in nonanarchist circles. In 1910, when the Encyclopedia Britannica published its most celebrated edition, Kropotkin was asked to contribute the article on anarchism. So reasonable was the case for anarchism he presented that the publishers, aghast that they might be printing effective anarchist "propaganda," appended a long list of anarchist acts of terror lest the public forget that the two terms were supposed to be inseparable.

The list of anarchist acts of rebellion, real and imagined, is a long one; the list of anarchist successes is quite short. Rarely did anarchists manage to produce a Kropotkin, a man whose sense of morality and breadth of vision earned respect from other socialists. In Europe, anarchists seemed to have an appeal directly inverse to the level of socioeconomic development of the country. Of the major powers, only in France did they receive some level of serious consideration, but even there an occasional bomb-thrower could discredit the entire movement, relegating them again to the lunatic fringe of the Left.

Anarchism did have some vogue in the United States at the end of the nineteenth century. Although the Haymarket Square bombing had raised the spectre of anarchist terror, the basic unfairness of the trials and executions that followed elicited considerable Leftist sympathy for the anarchists. Furthermore, among the anarchist leadership were a number of appealing and dynamic new figures, such as Emma Goldman (1869–1940), a remarkable young immigrant from Russia, who increased the appeal of the anarchist movement by injecting a number of social issues into its program. However, her close associate, Alexander Berkman (1870–1936), also an immigrant from Russia, became caught up in the propaganda-by-the-deed movement. In 1892, outraged by the use of violence against striking workers in Homestead, Pennsylvania, he made a clumsy assassination at-

---

*Kropotkin never defined what he meant by "acting against oppression" and certainly never espoused any *specific* action of terror. Yet he consistently paid tribute to those convicted of acts of terror, thus retroactively condoning, if not approving, their action.

tempt upon the steel magnate Henry Frick. Even though Berkman, some years later, spoke against terror as counterproductive and included his own effort, the public's linking of anarchists with terrorism persisted. In 1901, when President McKinley was assassinated by Leon Czolgosz, it was claimed that Emma Goldman had incited the act, and she was arrested although not tried. The resulting popular revulsion against such wanton terror vitiated any appeal the anarchists might have achieved amongst some socialist circles.

## THE SYNDICALIST MOVEMENT

At the turn of the century anarchist strength persisted in Italy and Spain but waned elsewhere in Europe. In France, some of the fervor that might have gone into the anarchist movement was instead directed into a new movement known as "syndicalism." The term emanated from the French word *syndicat*, meaing trade union. Basically the movement sought to develop worker activism through worker organizations. Its founder was the young labor organizer Fernand Pelloutier (1867–1901), who used a job-placement agency known as the Federation of Labor Exchanges to disseminate propaganda about his ideas to workers. Pelloutier envisioned a society organized by syndicates; each syndicate was to be an amorphous association which workers would be free to enter and leave and which would have no permanent officials. The rationale for the syndicates was to rally the workers to direct action by use of their most powerful weapon, the general strike.

Pelloutier did not live to guide this development, and after his death the leading figure of the movement became the volatile Georges Sorel (1847–1922) who, after a brief involvement in Marxist socialism, came to the conclusion that only a movement based on immediate action made any sense. Declaring that socialism was finished as a political movement—at least Marxist socialism—he turned to the syndicalists. Of his many published works, the one best remembered —and often cited as a syndicalist credo—is his *Reflections on Violence*, in which he called for the revolutionary general strike to replace the ineffective "propaganda by the deed" espoused by anarchists. Only when the working class had thus demonstrated their power, he argued, could they then move to overthrow capitalism. The syndicalists, however, proved to be more articulate speakers than able organizers. They did get some following from erstwhile anarchists and at various times were able to revive the call for a general strike, but they were never really successful. Though the French workers had cause for unhappiness and were often prey to syndicalist arguments, they were nowhere near as alienated from the French Republic or industrial society as Sorel maintained they were.

## BRITISH REFORM SOCIALISM

For some socialists, the radical approaches of both anarchism and syndicalism were out of keeping with their objectives. They were interested in a socialist movement less at war with established society and more reconcileable to benevolent change. In mid-nineteenth-century England, in particular, there was little sympathy for movements oriented toward violence; as a road to social justice, insurrection was generally denounced. The great Chartist movement of the late 1830s had sought to force social changes through the vehicle of a Charter of Rights, signed by millions of petitioners. Yet when Parliament rejected the Charter, only local demonstrations resulted and not the general strike or worker uprising that some had predicted. The Chartist movement continued to pressure Parliament for social and political reforms—in some instances successfully—but without the coercive threat of rebellion.

English reformers, socialists among them, although appalled by factory conditions and the exploitation of the workers, still sought remedies which avoided the overthrow of the system or of British society. Their intention was not to destroy society but to humanize it. There were, of course, British zealots who did call for the most radical of solutions, among them worker insurrection, but they tended to be isolated individuals who were rarely taken seriously.

After the decline of the Chartist movement in the 1840s, a

strong voice for an end to poverty and a new commitment to social justice arose from a group of young Anglican clergy, who charged that the established Church had closed its eyes to the misery of much of the population. These clergy called upon the Church to desist from its practice of threatening the workers with damnation for insubordination to their employers, demanding instead that the Church use its influence to bring about an end to exploitation.

Among the prominent members of the clergy who adhered to this doctrine was Charles M. Kingsley (1819–1875), who stood out among them for his commitment to a socialist solution. Kingsley's "socialism" owed little to the "scientific" or "determinist" rationales of Marx but a great deal to the social message of the New Testament, which he claimed denounced class exploitation. In 1850, together with the somewhat less-radical Frederick Maurice, Kingsley founded a weekly journal entitled *The Christian Socialist* in which it was argued that Christianity and socialism were interdependent and that neither could survive without the other. Although *The Christian Socialist* lasted only a few years, it did succeed in raising the social consciousness of some clergy. The movement itself faded after 1855, but for the next century there were recurrent revivals of Christian socialism, always seeking to unite church and socialism in a common cause.

However sincere its goals, Christian socialism never became a mass movement nor, considering the political realities of nineteenth-century England, could it have expected to do so. Likewise, Marx's ideas did not fare much better. His theories were known to some British intellectuals, and even to some worker groups, but Marxism seemed alien to the British experience and hard to purvey as the British road to social justice. Marx's major disciple in England, Henry M. Hyndman (1842–1921) had attempted to propagate the Marxist idea but, recognizing the British leeriness of Marxism, did so only indirectly. Thus, in 1881, when Hyndman published his short but provocative tract *England for All*, he carefully avoided even mentioning Marx by name, a tactic for which Engels never forgave him. Throughout the 1880s Hyndman engaged in all sorts of attempts to develop a British Marxist movement, most importantly through the Social Democratic Federation in 1883. Yet he could not establish the organization on a firm footing, and it continued to be fragmented and uncertain of its following.

## THE FABIAN SOCIETY

Of considerably more durable impact was the group of London intellectuals who in the 1880s formed a socialist organization known as the Fabian Society. The group was not Marxist—in fact, in many ways it was anti-Marxist: it specifically renounced the tactics of insurrection or revolutionary confrontation, and it was so committed to "the inevitability of gradualness" tht some felt the Fabians could not be included within the framework of socialism. Yet the Fabians attracted some of the finest minds of their generation, and, although their numbers were always small, their influence was not.

The very choice of their name, the Fabian Society, evoked their philosophy of gradual change. The historical allusion was to the Roman general Quintus Fabius Maximus, who had earned the title of "the delayer" because, refusing to fight for the sake of fighting, he had instead followed tactics of prudence and realism. The Fabians constantly stressed a gradual move toward socialism and rejected the class warfare inherent in Marxism—to say nothing of the more direct activism of the anarchists. They considered the tactics of insurrection incompatible with British values, as well as unnecessary given the realities of British politics and the opportunities offered therein.

When the Fabian Society underwent formal organization in 1884, their most-articulate spokesperson was the playwright George Bernard Shaw (1856–1950). From the very beginning Shaw wrote, and encouraged others to write, the kind of tracts that would spread the Fabian message. His "Manifesto" composed in 1884 did not agitate for the class warfare that dominated Marx's *Communist Manifesto* of 1848. Shaw presented serious social and political objectives, but his urbane style attracted other intellectuals who were put off by the humorlessness and apocalyptic obsessions that marked the work of Hyndman and others of the Social Democractic Federation. Over the next several years, Shaw solicited essays from numerous British intellectuals on the future of British socialism, and in 1889 he published them in a collection called *Fabian Essays*, which remained the handbook of Fabians for several generations.

The Fabians never recruited great numbers to their ranks, but the prestige of those who did associate with the society was enormous. A sampling of their numbers suggests the very best minds in England: Sidney and Beatrice Webb were amongst the earliest and most-important publicists of the new group. At the turn of the century the historian H. G. Wells did much to publicize the society's aims. Later adherents included the noted philosopher-mathematician Bertrand Russell, the political scientist Harold Laski, the economist R. H. Tawney, the sociologist Graham Wallas, the novelist John Galsworthy, and other famous intellectuals. In terms of sheer intellectual stature, the Fabian Society has never been matched in or out of the ranks of socialism.

What the Fabians never accomplished, and indeed never sought to, was the formation of a broadly based political party. Their goals were far more modest, since they were keenly aware that their strength was in the written word and not in organizational genius. Through careful exposition of their doctrines they sought to influence other political parties to adopt the Fabian program for social justice, which they considered a form of socialism compatible with the British experience. As Shaw bluntly admitted: "All Fabians have their price, which is the adoption of Fabian measures, no matter by what party."

It is easy to write off the Fabians as intellectual snobs who avoided dirtying their hands with worker organizations. In fact there is some justification for such a description. The Fabians always kept their numbers small, were almost exclusively London-centered, and recruited new members only amongst the few they considered their intellectual peers. Moreover, they failed to appreciate the importance of the trade unions as a political base for Fabian ideas. When the forerunner of the British Labour Party, the Independent Labour Party (ILP), was formed in 1893, it was done without any input or participation from the Fabians, and the ILP's initial militant statements seemed at odds with the Fabian policy of patience. Over the years, however, the ILP mellowed, and the ideological influence of the Fabians became quite important. Indeed, the British Labour Party of the twentieth century became a curious amalgam of trade-union militancy and Fabian "gradualness." Capitalizing on the Fabian idea of penetrating existing political parties, Labour was able to use the Liberal Party, which needed its vote, to promote worker-oriented legislation. In time, as the Liberals declined, the Labour Party replaced them as one of England's two major parties. After 1945, Labour as often as not won the national elections, and it proceeded, in the best Fabian tradition of "gradualness," to effect socialist and parasocialist changes in British life.

The ultimate success of socialism in England was not predictable in the nineteenth century. Instead the mantle of world socialist leadership fell to the well-organized and overtly Marxist German Social Democratic Party, to whom British, French, and other socialists turned, if grudgingly, at the end of the century.

# SELECTED READINGS

ANN FREMANTLE, *This Little Band of Prophets* (New York: Mentor, 1963).

Fremantle offers an affectionate yet perceptive group portrait of the men and women who built the Fabian Society.

J. HAMPDEN JACKSON, *Marx, Proudhon and European Socialism* (New York: Collier, 1966).

This short study illustrates why the collaboration of Marx and Proudhon was so brief and why each developed his ideas in different directions.

JAMES JOLL, *The Anarchists* (New York: Harper & Row, Pub., 1970).

Joll offers an overview of anarchism's development as well as vignettes of its major leaders.

MARTIN MILLER, *Kropotkin* (Chicago: University of Chicago Press, 1976).

Miller develops an in-depth analysis of the major thinker of anarchism and his commitment to a libertarian conception of socialism.

BARBARA W. TUCHMAN, *The Proud Tower* (New York: Bantam, 1966).

This book is primarily a social history of Europe in the generation prior to World War I. It has an excellent chapter on anarchism and its association with terror as well as useful reconstructions of Fabianism and other forms of turn-of-the-century socialism.

GEORGE WOODCOCK, *Anarchism* (New York: New American Library, 1962).

In the author's words, anarchism is viewed (sympathetically) as a history of libertarian ideas.

# 4

# The Second International (1889–1914)

# THE EUROPEAN SOCIALIST PANORAMA

The Marxist socialist movement that emerged in Germany in the 1880s had developed through the efforts of Liebknecht and Bebel into a viable and dynamic organization, capable of meeting repression and thriving in spite of it. Liebknecht and Bebel, ever true to Marx's teachings, had labored heroically to keep the new German Social Democratic Party committed to an opposition program, if not a revolutionary one, and to use the antisocialist policies of Chancellor Bismarck to enhance the commitment of the Socialists to their cause. The effectiveness of their work was mirrored in the progressive increase of the Socialists' representation in the German *Reichstag* and by the Socialists' feat of winning almost one-fifth of all votes cast in the parliamentary elections of 1890. The German Social Democratic Party, popularly known as the SPD, developed into a mass party that Marx himself could never have envisaged and indeed might not have cherished.

To the outside observer, the German Socialists presented a facade of unity incapable of replication elsewhere. In 1891, the SPD adopted its Erfurt Program—so-called after the city in which the meeting took place—in which it spelled out the minimal targets it hoped to achieve as a Marxist party. Further, the SPD sought to exploit its parliamentary strength by adopting the tactic of the bloc vote which required all socialist members of Parliament to vote unanimously on all important issues after a party caucus decided on the position to be taken. These actions seemed to indicate that the German party was above the petty factionalism that seemed to beset socialists elsewhere. In France, for example, dissent and factionalism

were not only in evidence but were even cherished by French socialists as being in keeping with the French revolutionary tradition. A
France which embraced the anarchism of Proudhon, the chronic activism of Blanqui, and the Utopianism of Saint-Simon and Fourier, to
say nothing of the dethronement of kings and emperors, was not easily
convinced of the blessings of a unified party.

The most important figure in French Marxism was Jules Guesde.
He founded a Marxist party in 1879, the *Parti Ouvrier Francais,* and
then went to London to report to Marx that France had joined the
fold. Mindful of Marx's critique of the Gotha program, Guesde flat-
tered the old man by soliciting a critique of the new party's program
and duly accepted the master's revisions. These were empty gestures,
however, because the unity of the new French party was superficial.
France had suffered too much internal strife, particularly the episode
of the 1871 Paris Commune, to accept a single doctrine as the course
to political salvation. Although Guesde continued to be a relentless
advocate of Marxism, factionalism beset him at every turn.

The most important of these factions was the *Fédération des
Travailleurs de France*, founded in 1882 by Dr. Paul Brousse.
Brousse was appreciative of the potential of Marxism but found its
strictures too inflexible. Unlike Germany, France was a highly volatile society; challenges to the regime, the shaky Third Republic, were
almost *de rigeur*. In such circumstances, Brousse thought that socialists had to be prepared to respond to any challenge, whether they appeared to be directly related to Marxism or not. Brousse's faction,
known as the "Possibilists" for their willingness to cooperate with
various groups in various situations, entered into the major disputes
of French political life—for example, the threat of a right-wing coup
against the Republic by General Boulanger in the 1880s—and derided
the Marxists for their ostrichlike refusal to become involved in everyday political strife.

There were other important factions active in France. The
anarchist tradition of Proudhon continued to attract followers who
spurned what they considered to be the dogmatism of Marxists. Syndicalist sentiments ran high amongst many of the trade union leaders.
The survivors of the Commune were constantly pressing for a commitment to revolution. They revered the memory of Blanqui, and after
his death in 1881, rallied around the excommunard Edouard Vaillant,

who preached a revolutionary activism which many considered to be in harmony with the Marxist ideas of class conflict.[1]

Of course, France and Germany were not the exclusive preserves of Marxist growth. Yet initially at least, in these two countries alone did movements of any size and consequence emerge. In Austria and Italy early Marxists found their numbers vitiated by competing political attractions—national causes in the former, and more radical approaches such as anarchism in the latter. Russia had Marxists, most notably Georgi Plekhanov and Pavel Akselrod, but it had no Marxist organization and little prospects of attracting substantial membership. In Great Britain, the articulate and forceful propaganda of the Fabians presented a case for socialism in England but in a manner relevant to the British experience and divorced from the universal claims of Marxism. In Belgium, Holland, and a number of other countries, Marxism attracted noteworthy groups of intellectuals and labor leaders, but their numbers were too small to make serious inroads on the Franco-German domination of the Marxist movement.

## THE SECOND INTERNATIONAL

Such was the panorama of Marxism as the year 1889 arrived. For the French, that year was the equivalent of a political millenium—the centennial of the great French Revolution (and in many ways the great European revolution). For socialists, 1889 was particularly commemorative; the events of 1789 had begun the process whereby the economic remnants of feudalism were dissipated and the class consciousness that made nineteenth-century Marxism possible was launched. French socialists therefore planned to celebrate the centennial in a manner befitting the occasion: both the Possibilists and the Marxists issued calls for international socialist meetings to gather in Paris on July 14, the anniversary of the storming of the Bastille. Efforts by Liebknecht and other foreigners to reconcile the two factions only seemed to stiffen the claims of each that it alone was the true socialist organization.

[1]In fact, the French socialist tradition claimed Marx himself through two of his sons-in-law, Paul Lafargue and Charles Longuet, the latter to become a major figure in the nascent Marxist movement.

When summer came, the Possibilists and the Marxists each held a separate congress in Paris; with various foreign socialists uncertain which to attend, some resolved the dilemma by commuting between the two congresses.

Liebknecht worked tirelessly in Paris, attempting to achieve a rapport between the two groups. When it appeared that the Possibilists simply were not interested, his strategy moved from unification to attrition. Foreign delegates were induced to abandon the Possibilists' congress and convene with the Marxists', until the Marxists became an international assembly of socialist leaders, while the Possibilists' meeting became almost exclusively French. Savoring their evident triumph, the Marxists declared their meeting to be the founding congress of a Second International, the successor to Marx's 1864 assemblage in London of the International Workingmen's Association, which retrospectively they viewed as the First International. The congress founding the new International was contentious to say the least, with all sorts of delegates from everywhere offering a bizarre melange of doctrines.

From all the confusion there did emerge unity on one tactic: that the founding of the new International be heralded by a worldwide, one-day strike of the proletariat. The simple act of withholding labor would be a symbol of proletarian power and solidarity, while at the same time it would call attention to the universal demand for an eight-hour working day, among other things. Although practical problems in individual countries necessitated certain adjustments, the International voted to accept the proposal of the French delegation that May 1, 1890, be the day of the general strike.

This "May Day" proved to be a major landmark in the development of Marxism, even though not all of the demonstrators who took part were Marxists. In the United States, for instance, the distinctly nonsocialist American Federation of Labor participated enthusiastically in the strike. In some cases, less militant tactics such as rallies and demonstrations were substituted for work stoppages. Equivocation over May Day was most marked in England where the first Sunday in May was substituted for the working day set aside elsewhere in order to preempt any confrontations between workers and owners. Other demonstrations were marred by violence, particularly where anarchists became involved. Yet, taken altogether, May Day became the touchstone on which the Second International proved its existence.

## THE PATH TO SOCIALISM

The Second International as it emerged from the confusion of 1889 in Paris presented its followers with both a rallying point for socialist unity and action, and a forum for deliberation. Although the founding congress had been dominated by Marxists, there was clearly no unanimity or even majority opinion on the organization's mandate or function. Was it mainly an advocate of workers' rights, or was it a revolutionary organization committed to oppositionist and, if necessary, illegal activism? Between word and deed, between apocalyptic pronouncements of the workers' destiny and active confrontation with civil authorities, there was a large gap, and few of the early members were entirely certain just where the organization stood on such critical matters.

There was a basic problem of legality. Could a Marxist organization, professing its commitment to the overthrow of the existing capitalist system, eschew illegal or violent tactics? The rhetoric of Marxist literature, especially the *Communist Manifesto*, spoke unambiguously for revolution and confrontation, but did Marxism expect this rhetoric to be translated into action? The arguments against mounting the barricades were numerous and persuasive.

First and foremost there was the issue of whether such a call might be heeded. By and large, the delegates who formed the Second International were not leaders of disciplined constituencies. Although the call for May Day demonstrations in 1890 had met an impressive response, this call had been keyed to a specific worker issue: the eight-hour day. Would the same workers rally together in the name of insurrection? In most places, and certainly in Germany, this was not even a remote possibility. The memory of the Paris Commune and its bloody aftermath was as much a deterrent as an inspiration to revolutionary action. There was also the consideration that most Marxists regarded themselves as Social Democrats and therefore committed to certain doctrines of political liberalism which precluded the use of violence. Even those Marxists most articulate in revolutionary rhetoric backed down when the actual use of force was anticipated.

So it was that the leaders of the Second International spoke in revolutionary terms but, in practice, concentrated their real efforts on formulating responses to the practical matters of the day. They tended to regard the extremist elements in the movement as almost as great a danger as the regimes in power. Their great fear was that these extremist elements might launch revolutionary adventures that would bring the wrath of the established governments down on the Social Democrats. The anarchists in particular implied such a danger, on the one hand, arguing that they were good socialists, albeit not Marxists, and on the other, being associated in the public mind with terror and violence. It was the wish of many anarchists to reconcile ideological differences between themselves and the Marxists so they might use the Second International as a forum for disseminating anarchist views. This created an embarrassing situation for the Second International since the term "anarchist" was automatically associated with assassination; an organization which welcomed anarchists would appear to the world to be committed to terrorism. Furthermore, the International would be shunned by trade union organizations, who would refuse to join an organization that included anarchists.

Whether or not to include the anarchists in the Second International became a critical issue. The growth of the movement depended on reaching the mass of the workers through the trade unions. Thus if one accepted anarchists, one lost trade union and mass-worker support. In the eyes of Bebel and Liebknecht, the price was simply too high. They saw in the 1890s no imminent revolutionary confrontations with capitalism for which anarchist support might be important. Moreover, many were weary of the anarchist tirades that tended to turn socialist congresses into never-ending exchanges of bombastic language.

At the 1896 congress in London, Liebknecht announced that the choice had been made. Henceforth, the Second International's criteria for membership would welcome the following:

1.  The representatives of those organizations which seek to substitute Socialist property and production for capitalist property and production, and which consider legislative and parliamentary action as one of the necessary means of attaining that end.
2.  Purely trade organizations, which, though taking no militant part in politics, declare that they recognize the necessity of legislative and parliamentary action: *consequently Anarchists are excluded*. [italics added]

With the exclusion of the anarchists, the Second International had made a greater commitment toward legality than it realized. The sanction of parliamentary activity was in itself a sanction of existing democratic institutions. Once the Social Democrats had committed themselves to seeking representation in these institutions it would become increasingly difficult, should electoral success follow, to reject responsibility for defending these institutions, a responsibility that was to confront the Social Democrats much sooner than they might have envisaged.

There were other pressures on the Second International to turn toward legal tactics and eschew revolution. There was Marx's inaugural address to the First International, which was an implicit mandate for a social democratic movement rather than a revolutionary one. There was also the philosophical argument that historical determinism made socialism an inevitable consequence of capitalism, therefore there was no necessity to undertake illegal activities in pursuit of a goal that, regardless, could not fail to occur. It was this very premise of historical determinism that had lured trade unions into the Social Democratic camp.

In any case, simply because the *Communist Manifesto* and other Marxist literature spoke of the workers' revolution, did that mean that no other path to socialism existed? Marx was not a biblical prophet, and a growing number of Social Democrats began to chip away at the notion that scriptural adherence to Marx was necessary for a Marxist movement. Marx was for them the great man who had unlocked the secrets of past history and provided the tools for understanding the future and the inexorable march to socialism. This did not mean that every nuance, every projection, and every extrapolation of Marx had to be slavishly accepted when it contradicted the evidence of one's own experiences and evaluations. Even Engels, who remained a force in the movement until his death in 1895, stressed gradualism as essential to the development of socialism. Creating a parallel between Darwin's explication of the laws of biological development and Marx's historical determinism, in his funeral oration for Marx, Engels said, "Just as Darwin discovered the law of development of organic nature, so Marx discovered the law of development of human history." The Implications Engels's words on this occasion, as on others, was clear: Marxism stressed evolutionary development, not revolutionary confrontation.

## THE BEGINNINGS
## OF MARXIST REVISIONISM

The idea of "revising" Marx is almost as old as the existence of Marxists. There were any number of socialist theorists who chipped away at specific elements of Marx's writings—the posthumously published third volume of *Capital* provided one such opportunity—but the revisionist movement as a force in Marxism dates primarily from the work of the German Social Democrat, Eduard Bernstein (1850-1932).

Because of the harassment of socialists during Bismarck's heyday, Bernstein had spent much of his early career in England. There he had established a fine rapprochement with Marx and Engels, apparently impressing Marx favorably. He became the editor of *Sozialdemokrat*, a German-language Marxist publication that had to publish abroad to survive. Although he edited the paper for several years in Switzerland, German diplomatic pressure caused the Swiss to expel him in 1888, and he returned to London.

In his renewed London residence, Bernstein not only reestablished contact with Engels but came into frequent contact with the British Fabians. He could not help but be impressed by the intellectual competence of the Fabians, and even more by their commitment to democratic change and their rejection of the tactics of violence. Although he refrained from any public utterances on the subject for as long as Engels lived, Bernstein continued to wonder whether Marxism had overlooked some important considerations, particularly the prospects of achieving social change through nonrevolutionary means. He began to challenge the assumptions of other Marxists that revolutionary confrontation was inevitable and necessary. In a series of writings, of which the most notable was *Evolutionary Socialism*, Bernstein paid deference to Marx as the father of social democracy but declared that it was necessary to "revise" Marx in view of the developments of the times. Whereas Marx had preached the continuing impoverishment of workers under capitalism, Bernstein demonstrated that the experience of his generation was the reverse. Workers of the 1890s were getting better wages, better working conditions, and through the Social Democrats an increasing voice in political activity. Furthermore, he noted, the improvement of the workers' status was concurrent with the continued growth of capitalist strength. The crisis of capitalism, foreseen by Marx, seemed further away than ever.

Bernstein did not relent in his criticism of capitalism, nor did he deny capitalist exploitation or any of the other fundamental tenets of Marxism. What he did find objectionable was that the Social Democratic leaders, presumably out of misguided fidelity to Marx, talked of barricades when neither the possibility nor the desirability of revolution by force existed. Bernstein summed up his views this way: "What is generally called the goal of socialism [proletarian revolution] is nothing to me; the movement, everything." Simply stated Bernstein had proclaimed the validity of the Second International but not of revolution.

The impact of Bernstein's new theories was immense and immediate. The leaders of the Second International saw his views as nothing less than heresy. Most considered him a convert to Fabianism; Karl Kautsky even went so far as to suggest that Bernstein remain in England where he belonged rather than contaminate German Marxism. At Kautsky's behest the German Social Democratic Party censured Bernstein and rejected his views as incompatible with Marxism.

Bernstein, although hardly the first revisionist, was the most articulate and forceful of those who attempted to revise Marx. When he returned to Germany in 1901, he instantly became the leader of Social Democrats who associated themselves with a revisionist viewpoint. His views also inspired the growth of a reformist movement, which consisted of socialists who were less concerned about Marxist theory than were revisionists but who sought to commit the Social Democrats to a program of reform and social progress for the German workers. This latter group attracted trade union leaders who saw in "evolutionary socialism" an appreciation of their own role and a downgrading of doctrinaire revolutionaries. Revisionism in its several forms may have lacked the votes to carry the SPD congresses, but it found a ready-made following throughout the ranks of German socialism.

In France, the growth of revisionism had more dramatic origins. Many French leftists felt that in a democratic republic socialists should seek to defend the republic, not conspire to overthrow it. They disavowed Marx's famous statement that "the proletariat has no fatherland" and proceeded to define themselves as Marxists, French citizens, and republicans, with none of the categories mutually exclusive. Yet Guesde and other French leaders still promoted orthodox Marxism and tended to ignore or at least play down those who asserted their French nationalism.

It was the renowned Dreyfus Affair of the 1890s that forced French Marxists to define their position at last. In 1894 Alfred Dreyfus, a French captain, was imprisoned for apparrently selling military secrets to the Germans. Proof began to accumulate that Dreyfus was innocent and that the charges against him were motivated by anti-Semitism and backed by forgeries condoned by the army. At first the case seemed grossly irrelevant to French socialists. Dreyfus was the scion of a wealthy Alsatian family and a devoted supporter of the military. If he was unjustly dealt with, it was but one more proof of capitalist immorality, and at least in this case the victim was a capitalist himself.

The Dreyfus Affair, however, far transcended the fate of a captain on the French generals staff. The issues of anti-Semitism, clericalism (policy of promoting church power and influence), the role of the military, antirepublicanism, and even the question of who should be considered a Frenchman intruded. It soon mattered little whether or not Dreyfus was vindicated; at stake was the very survival of the republic. By 1898 feelings had run so high that the entire nation was divided between *Dreyfusards* (those who supported the Republic) and anti-Dreyfusards (monarchists and other antirepublicans). Even families were divided on the issue. Emile Zolà, one of France's greatest writers, had to flee the country after his dramatic defense of Dreyfus.

In such circumstances, the socialists could no longer stand aside pretending that the Dreyfus case was an intramural dispute between capitalists. To establish any sort of rapport with the French workers, they had to choose, and, faced with a choice between a republic and a monarchy, they naturally chose the former. Socialist leaders openly rallied to the support of republican leaders and fought for the reopening of the Dreyfus case. This contributed to his eventual vindication. One socialist, Alexandre Millerand, was so convinced of the stakes involved that he agreed—without consulting any of his fellow ists—to join the French cabinet (as Minister of Commerce and Industry, no less) so as to help rally support for the republic.

Guesde and others denounced Millerand as a defector to capitalism. Others, most notably the historian Jean Jaurès, supported Millerand. Jaurès, who was just now emerging as the major figure in French socialism, argued that Millerand's actions had to be viewed as a tactic to cope with the crisis of the moment, no matter how unpleasant it was to defend a capitalist government. Millerand himself announced that he would use his new post to further reforms that benefited the worker. That he later abandoned the socialist cause is quite beside the point; when he joined the French cabinet in 1899 he did so as a socialist, convinced that he was making as much a contribution to the cause of socialism as to the French republic. Moreover, he had forced Jaurès and like-minded socialists to acquiesce, however reluctantly, in downgrading their aspirations from revolution to developing tactics for bringing about the reform of the republic. Although the words, the rationalizations, and the political causes were different, what happened in France paralleled the results in Germany: an increasing number of French socialists in the twentieth century turned away from revolutionary ideology and theory and turned to tactics and goals that were compatible with parliamentary democracy.

Revisionism spread from Germany and France until it became a major international force, particularly in countries where the role of the trade unions in the socialist movement was important. As socialist visibility in parliaments increased, so did the strength of revisionists and reformists. The result was a substantial increase in the membership of the Second International.

## ROSA LUXEMBURG

"Orthodox" Marxists regarded revisionism and reformism as nothing less than heresy; they considered the effect to be a weakening of the movement. Bebel and Kautsky, although successful in leading votes of censure through the congresses of the SPD and the Second International, were only too well aware that the revisionist movement was growing constantly. Liebknecht died in 1900 just as the controversy came to a head, and his considerable prestige was sorely missed by the more orthodox Marxists as they sought to fend off the heretics.

Karl Kautsky's articulate defense of revolutionary Marxism in the socialist press and the various socialist congresses confirmed his reputation as the "high priest" of revolutionary Marxism. In the long run, however, it was not Kautsky who was the most influential and important foe of revisionism but a young emigré from Russian Poland, Rosa Luxemburg. Born in 1871, in the Polish city of Zamość, she could not claim, as could Bebel or Bernstein, to have worked with Marx himself. Nor could she claim a mandate or constituency in Russian Poland, since she was a Jew; in fact, when she first appeared at the congress of the Second International in 1893 she really represented only herself. Within two decades, however, she became the voice of revolutionary Marxism, speaking for revolution not in the vague and distant future but as a tactic for the present with a cogency that no other Marxist, not even V. I. Lenin, could match.

Luxemburg had gone to Switzerland for her advanced education and had earned a doctorate in economics at the University of Zurich. Although she was a strong student at Zurich—one who perennially challenged her professors—what was most important about her years there was her introduction into the arena of emigré socialist politics. Switzerland was traditionally a haven for outcast revolutionaries, the great majority of whom were from East Europe. There she met Georgi Plekhanov—by then the acknowledged leader of Rus-

sian Marxism—as well as a substantial contingent of Polish socialists. She became especially active in the latter group, particularly in
the new antinationalist faction of Polish socialism being formed
under the leadership of Julian Marchlewski.

Rosa was sharply critical of the priority assigned to the resurrection of the Polish state by most Polish socialists. She felt that a na-
tional-independence movement for Poland, which had been divided
for nearly a century amongst three empires and had developed within
their borders quite different political and economic systems, was
both irrelevant to the socialist cause and historically regressive. She
joined with Marchlewski and a small group of radicals who argued for
abandonment of the fight for Polish independence in favor of organizing the workers for the struggle against capitalism.

There were inherent limits to how much activism could be generated amongst emigrés in Switzerland, so in 1898 Luxemburg emi-
grated to Germany—using a false marriage to a German citizen to
gain German citizenship—for the express purpose of entering the
politics of the large and active German socialist movement.

In Germany Rosa Luxemburg became the voice of revolutionary
socialism. She did not fear police repression; on the contrary, she
went to jail several times on charges ranging from sedition to insult-
ing the emperor. By her overall commitment to activism, she did
much to spark the small remnant of active revolutionaries in Germany, even goading Kautsky with the taunt that the leaders of the
Second International ought to be preparing for revolution and not
merely talking about it. There was always the apocryphal story of
how when she arrived, together with her friend Clara Zetkin, quite
late for a meeting with Bebel and Kautsky, the two men jokingly voiced
fears that reactionaries had assassinated the women. Whereupon
Luxemburg bitterly retorted that then the SPD could have erected a
tombstone for them inscribed: "Here lie the last two men in German
Social Democracy!"

As impatient as Luxemburg was with the excessive caution of
Bebel and Kautsky, she had no toleration at all for revisionism. The
revisionists, she felt, had betrayed the movement, not only by attempting to deradicalize the workers, but by corrupting them. In one of her
most famous works, *Social Reform or Revolution*, she accused Bernstein and his friends of abandoning the quest for worker power in re-

turn for meager limits to capitalist exploitation, and of decreasing the workers' class consciousness by winning them placebos in the form of small wage increases; democracy, or at least bourgeois democracy, she contended, did nothing about "wage slavery." The main thrust of her argument was that revisionism was a bourgeois tactic which attracted the faint of heart in the socialist camp. Such socialists, she asserted, should be read out of the movement.

Rather than be co-opted into the bourgeois system, workers ought to be organized to disrupt and cripple it, Luxemburg argued. What she wanted was not strikes against specific factories or even a specific industry, but the use of the political mass strike as a tactical weapon to paralyze capitalist society. Such a strike would be a true expression of revolutionary Marxism; it would satisfy, as well, the need for worker participation in the revolutionary process. Luxemburg was no supporter either of the elitist activism being developed by some of the Russian socialists, most notably V. I. Lenin, or of the symbolic (rather than tactical) "general strike" increasingly proposed by syndicalists. Her position was made more credible by the success of the 1905 mass strike in Russia, where a hitherto presumably weak proletariat had been able to force concessions from the government.

In the euphoria induced by the Russian upheaval of 1905, it briefly appeared that Luxemburg's advocacy of the mass strike had genuine prospects. In that year, in fact, the SPD even agreed to adopt the mass strike as a tactical weapon. Once the impact of the Russian Revolution wore off, however, the SPD backtracked, setting up so many qualifications to the employment of mass strikes that they in effect disowned them.

Luxemburg's approach to revolution was distinctive in another way: she insisted that there must be moral premises for revolutionary action. She was no bloodthirsty Blanquist who favored insurrection for its own sake; she sincerely believed that the class consciousness of the workers would lead them to confront the evils of society—in this case bourgeois capitalism—and by their spontaneous activism create a new society that was both democratic and socialist. She had an unshakable belief in the inherent morality of the working masses, and she believed that, if properly guided, they would follow their instincts for mass action against capitalism. She had little tolerance for elitist coups or repressive methods in the name of revolution. In later years she was critical of the Russian Revolution of 1917 on these grounds.


## NATIONALISM VERSUS INTERNATIONALISM


The debates between Luxemburg, Jaurès, Kautsky, Bernstein, and others, enlivened the activities of the Second International. They were for all practical purposes, however, shadow-boxing. Except for the Russian event of 1905 no revolutionary potential appeared on the European scene. Governments in general were stable. Where threats of overthrow existed, they were political, not of the class-versus-class variety. To be a revolutionary in the decade after 1905 was in essence to live in a semiromantic world of class conflicts that existed in Marxist theory but not in reality.

If there was an evident peril on the European scene, it was not class upheaval but international war. International crises, many of them emanating from imperialist rivalries, kept bringing major powers to confrontations on an almost annual basis. Miraculously, it seemed, each crisis was resolved at the last moment: flare-ups such as the Anglo-French confrontation at Fashoda on the Nile, the Franco-German disputes in Morocco, the Austrian-Russian arguments over Bosnia, and others were all stopped before the conflicts spread. Although each crisis was successfully negotiated, thus avoiding war, the international tensions that had produced these crises remained. The continually escalating arms race of the major European powers, led by the unswerving German commitment to the building of a major navy, was a distressingly ominous challenge to the preservation of peace.

For most orthodox Marxists, the aggravation of international tensions by imperialist rivalries signaled the natural denouement of capitalism. They explained that capitalism, having exhausted its own internal markets, was now driven to colonial expansion as an outlet for its products as well as a source of materials at low labor costs. This process, the theorists argued, which might appear to succeed at first, was actually an illusion. Some revisionists claimed that the workers' lot had improved under contemporary capitalism. Some argued that "benevolent colonialism" raised the standard of living of both the colonial peoples and the workers of the home country. The orthodox Marxists argued that such "progress" was at best ephemeral and certainly immoral. In the long run, they believed, the colonial market was inherently limited; imperialist rivalries were inevitable, as were the international crises they engendered. Eventually there would be an impasse which would result in an international war. These ideas were drawn together by Lenin during World War I in *Imperialism: The Highest Stage of Capitalism*; but the original discussion had been carried on by many Marxists, including Luxemburg, since the end of the nineteenth century.

All socialists were horrified at the prospects of war. Not that there had been any absence of imperialist wars during the tenure of the Second International: there had been the Boer War of 1900 between the British and the Dutch-descended Afrikaaners for supremacy in South Africa; and there had been the Russo-Japanese War (1904–1905), resulting from imperialist rivalries in Korea. In the latter case, the Second International made an ostentatious display of nonparticipation: at the 1904 Congress of the International in Amsterdam, the Russian Marxist Plekhanov shook hands at the rostrum with Sen Katayama of Japan to symbolize that socialism did not accept the war. The fact that neither had any sizeable following in their respective countries was quite beside the point.

Socialists were eager to commit themselves to averting war, but they were uncertain as to how this might be done. Using their political power in their respective countries, they opposed without any great success the imperialist policies of their governments, voted against military appropriations, promoted the idea of a national militia in place of a standing army, and even entertained the idea of using mass strikes to demonstrate their pacifist convictions. At virtually every meeting of the International, the topic of war dangers ranked high on the agenda, but the tendency of many socialists to see aggression as coming only from other countries clouded the issue.

At Stuttgart in 1907, the Second International finally sought to face the problem head on. After much wrangling, a statement was adopted not only condemning war but committing the Second International to action against it. The more radical socialists, led by Luxemburg and Lenin, not only succeeded in committing the International against war but also won unanimous adoption of a militant resolution: should the war come, the International would fight to end both the war and capitalism as well. The statement clearly implied revolutionary insurrection, although few of the delegates supporting it had any such intentions.

The Stuttgart resolution, although laudable in intent, was devoid of any tactical conceptualization. Socialists could content themselves knowing they had done the right thing by voting against war, but they did not know what they could effectively do to prevent war from breaking out. Ironically, although socialists generally felt powerless in the face of the impending crisis of a war, in fact, there was a marked increase in socialist strength at the polls. In 1912, for instance, the German elections gave the SPD 110 seats in the *Reichstag*, or parliament. Such electoral successes tended to downgrade revolutionary tactics and seemed to confirm the hopes of the revisionists for a peaceful penetration of capitalism. Though the French socialists could not equal the Germans' parliamentary strength, they had, since the Dreyfus case, become more and more of a factor in French parliamentary politics. The presence of so many socialists in parliaments was auspicious, and many socialists hoped that the pressure of socialist politicians in France and Germany might preclude war. Indeed, there were numerous demonstrations of solidarity between the socialists of the two powers.

The Balkan Wars of 1912 between the Ottoman Empire and the small states of Southeast Europe threatened to ignite an all-European war as a by-product of the vicarious confrontation of Russia and Austria in the area. To cope with the crisis, an emergency congress of the International was convened in Basle, Switzerland. The solidarity of the socialists, particularly in France and Germany, was reaffirmed. August Bebel, the sole surviving founder of Marxism, then in the last year of his life, presided over the meetings, exhorting the delegates to commit themselves to implementation of the Stuttgart Resolution. But resolutions, however noble, had little effect on the subsequent course of events.

The war that finally came in the summer of 1914 caught the socialists by surprise, as it did everyone else. There was no reason to expect that the assassination by Serbian terrorists of the Austrian crown prince in Austrian-held Bosnia would spark a war. Assassinations of royalty were by no means rare, but this time the event became the pretext for the Austrian military to prepare a punitive expedition against Serbia. In the month of recriminations that followed, international treaties were invoked, old rivalries resurrected, and intractable diplomatic and political postures developed. The net result was that by the end of July most of the major European powers were on the brink of war: Austria was committed to punishing Serbia, Russia determined to preclude such an event, Germany ready to defend Austria against a Russian invasion, France committed by treaty to aid Russia against German attack, and so on.

A situation had sprung up which threatened war on a scale not known since Napoleon's day. For the Second International, the moment of action was at hand. If the German Social Democratic Party voted against government war credits, there was a chance that the phenomenon of over a hundred Reichstag members denying financial support to the war might cause the government to rethink its actions. If the French socialists could then follow with a similar action, the International might have a chance at aborting the war. The likelihood was slight, but many socialists believed that it was a genuine possibility. The situation in France, however, became less hopeful when Jean Jaurès was assassinated by a nationalist fanatic, thus depriving the French socialists of their acknowledged leader. Traumatized by the death of Jaurès at the hour of crisis, the French socialists looked to their German colleagues for leadership.

The SPD's situation was, to say the least, difficult. During the crisis month of July 1914, the SPD had remained faithful to the anti-war program of the Stuttgart Resolution, denounced the aggressiveness of Austria, organized antiwar demonstrations, and even sent a mission to consult with the French socialists. Within the ranks of the SPD leadership, however, there were serious doubts about the anti-war policy once the international situation had so deteriorated. For one thing, they were loath to expose Germany to what they genuinely considered to be a threat of aggression from Russia. Of more importance though was the disturbing evidence of an increase in worker support for a war. Antiwar demonstrations were faithfully scheduled by the SPD, but many socialist leaders received avowals from the workers in their constituencies that in their opinion loyalty to nation took precedence over international class solidarity.

As it turned out, the SPD was by no means as radical as the rhetoric of its antiwar proclamations implied. The years of participation in parliamentary politics had entrenched the SPD far more firmly in the German body politic than it ever admitted. A Rosa Luxemburg could still call for the mandate of proletarian internationalism, but then the point could be made, and often was, that she was not a German anyway. The German workers wanted their nation defended, and their parliamentary representatives by and large shared this sentiment. On August 4, 1914, after several tumultuous caucuses, the SPD chose the German nation over the Second International. The SPD, which had always voted as a bloc on major issues in parliament, now did so on the critical issue of war credits which they now supported; those opposed to the war credits went along with the majority in the name of party unity.

Throughout Europe the scene was much the same: as nation after nation issued its declaration of war, the socialists of Western Europe lined up solidly behind their governments, in some cases becoming government members to emphasize the loyalty of socialists to their homeland. Lenin, making his way to Switzerland after being briefly interned in Austria, bitterly but correctly observed that "overwhelmed by opportunism, the Second International has died."

# SELECTED READINGS

AUGUST BEBEL, *Woman Under Socialism* (New York: Schocken Books, 1971).
Although Bebel's views seem antiquated by present standards, he does reaffirm socialism's commitment to remedy sexism.

EDWARD BERNSTEIN, *Evolutionary Socialism* (New York: Schocken Books, 1963).
Bernstein sums up his revisionist approach to Marxism and revolutionary activism.

JULIUS BRAUNTHAL, *History of the International*, vol. 1, 1864–1914 (New York: Praeger, 1967).
An extremely detailed examination of the development of a Marxist international movement, beginning with Marx's own involvement in the First International and continuing into the Second International and its complex history.

PETER GAY, *The Dilemma of Democratic Socialism: Eduard Bernstein's Challenge to Marx* (New York: Collier, 1962).
Essentially an intellectual biography of Bernstein, Gay's book is also a fine study of the origins of the revisionist movement and of the response to the movement.

NORMAN GERAS, *The Legacy of Rosa Luxemburg* (Atlantic Highlands, N.J.: Humanities Press, 1976).
Geras seeks to bridge the differences between Luxemburg and Lenin and to "reinterpret" her tactics.

DICK HOWARD, ed., *Selected Writings of Rosa Luxemburg* (New York: Monthly Review Press, 1971).
Of the several Luxemburg readers, this anthology seems to offer the fullest selection of her works.

JAMES JOLL, *The Second International, 1889–1914*, 2nd ed. (New York: Harper & Row, Pub., 1975).
Just as Braunthal's book, cited above, is perhaps too long and too detailed, Joll's work might seem too brief and lacking details. It is, however, a fine concise history of the rise and fall of the Second International, properly highlighting the major leaders and major issues.

KARL KAUTSKY, *The Class Struggle* (New York: W. W. Norton & Co., Inc., 1971).
Written when Kautsky was emerging as the leading theoretician of the new Second International, the book is in Kautsky's words, "a catechism of Social Democracy."

J. P. NETTL, *Rosa Luxemburg* (New York: Oxford University Press, 1969).
 An excellent biography of one of the major figures of the Second International, examining both her dynamism and her failings. There is a more-detailed two-volume version by the same author (New York: Oxford University Press, 1966).

CARL E. SCHORSKE, *German Social Democracy, 1905–1917* (New York: John Wiley, 1965).
 A lucid and scholarly presentation of the complex history of the major socialist party of early twentieth-century Europe which not only reads well but informs too.

# 5

# The Origins
# of the
# Russian Socialist
# Movement

Socialists of the nineteenth century rarely included Russia in their grand schemes for rebuilding society. Few had ever visited Russia, nor did most consider such a visit relevant to socialist goals. They generally regarded Russia as a backward feudal land of enormous size beset by a harsh climate, a harsher political system, and a population made up largely of illiterate peasants. A country that had abolished serfdom as recently as 1861 scarcely seemed to offer prospects for the development of socialism. When socialists encountered Russian emigrés in Western Europe, they sometimes welcomed them individually as comrades, but they rarely regarded them as representing any particular movement or organization within Russia. Some socialists, Marx included, never really were able to accept Russians as peers, and personal relationships were often strained. There were a number of Russian emigrés, Bakunin and Kropotkin for example, who had enormous influence on the anarchist movement, but their importance was as individuals rather than as representatives of any group in their homeland. Till the beginning of the twentieth century, the influence of any Russian on Marxism and the Second International was negligible.

## THE POLITICAL STAGNATION
## OF NINETEENTH-CENTURY RUSSIA

The stereotypes of Russians held by Western socialists were exaggerated but did have elements of truth. To a great extent, Russia in the first half of the nineteenth century was a closed society—closed to new ideas as well as to any political or social intrusions from the outside world. Under Tsar Nicholas I (1825–1855) the regime had so succeeded in cutting off Russia from European thought and activity that not only was Russia able to escape the revolutionary wave that swept the rest of the continent in 1848, but Nicholas was even able to use his army to march into Hungary and squelch the nationalist revolution there.

The social challenge of urban industrial society, which had spawned the rudimentary beginnings of socialist thought in the West, was largely absent in Russia. There were a very small number of Russian intellectuals who knew of Hegel's work—since Hegel was a monarchist, his work was permissible—and they were much impressed by his approach to history; the young Bakunin was one of these people. Most Russians who knew Hegel were impressed by his logic, by his appeal to Christian values, and by the comprehensiveness of his undertaking. The interpretations they derived from Hegel's work were far less radical than those of the "Young Hegelians" at the University of Berlin; Bakunin was a notable exception to the rule.

To be an intellectual, probing for an understanding of the human condition, was a far more difficult task in midcentury Russia than elsewhere in Europe. The greatest deterrent was the overpowering influence of state censorship, supervised almost directly by the Tsar himself. To be a dissident, or even to traffic in controversial ideas, was dangerous. An excellent example of just how dangerous such inquiry could be was the fate of the Petrashevsky Circle, a harmless group of intellectuals who merely discussed the ideas of Fourier and other Utopians. For examining proposals for social and political change, fifteen of its members, including the future great novelist Fyodor Dostoyevsky, were sentenced to death. The sentences were eventually commuted to forced labor in Siberia, but the severe treatment of the group, which was not at all conspiratorial, was not lost on other potential dissidents.

Police surveillance was far more easily carried out in Russia than in the West because educated people constituted a far smaller fraction of the population. The situation forced some dissidents into exile in western Europe, where they were usually safe from imprisonment but unable to rally other Russians to their ideas and proposals.

A significant number of those who remained in Russia were either sufficiently coerced by the regime to remain silent or simply closed their eyes to the repressive society around them, resolving the moral dilemma by becoming cogs in the bureaucratic apparatus of the state. They ignored or excused serfdom, the autocracy, and other unpleasant realities of Russian life, fleeing into and becoming part of the bureaucracy, which was large enough to accommodate them. The pages of Russian literature are replete with depictions of these people who emerge, sometimes without the authors so intending, as intellectual refugees from reality.

Even under such conditions there were people who through their education and experience recognized the unsatisfactory state of affairs in Imperial Russia. These disgruntled intellectuals, some of whom had the opportunity to travel or study abroad, formed an acknowledged stratum of the educated populace known as the *intelligentsia*, a term used to denote people who were caught up in the world of ideas. The existence of such a class was not peculiar to Russia; what was unique was the reaction of the Russian regime, which regarded intellectualism as dangerous and intellectuals as potentially disloyal. By no means were the intelligentsia inherently subversive; however, the regime's practice of treating them with suspicion had the effect of turning many of them toward radical and socialist ideologies.

## THE RUSSIAN POPULIST MOVEMENT

A prime example of the alienated intelligentsia was the writer and political essayist Alexander Herzen (1812–1870), who was educated under the repressive regime of Nicholas I. In 1847, disgusted with the political stagnation of Russia, he emigrated abroad, eventually settling in London. There he encountered numerous socialists, including Marx and Engels, and gradually he began to wonder if only a drastic solution would cure Russia's ills. At first he addressed himself to reform within the system, applauding in 1861 the new tsar, Alexander II (1865–1881), for eliminating serfdom and initiating other badly overdue reforms. However, it soon became apparent that the tsar's zeal for social change had its limits; after 1866 the regime returned to repressive measures, though on a lesser scale than under Nicholas I.

Disappointed by the failings of the "reform Tsar," Herzen began to consider revolutionary socialist change as essential for Russia. He rejected the theories of Marx as irrelevant to Russian conditions, since Marx's stress on the industrial proletariat as prime mover of socialist revolution was clearly inappropriate. The domination of the agrarian sector in the Russian economy, and the low level of Russian industrialization, suggested to Herzen that Marx's criteria would not yield socialism in Russia for centuries.

Herzen also rejected Marx and Engels' thesis, accepted by most socialists of that time, that societies had to experience capitalism as a prerequisite to socialism. In the case of Russia, Herzen considered capitalism an unnecessary trauma which the Russian peasant could be spared. In fact, Marx himself later equivocated on the question of whether Russia would indeed have to experience the full development of capitalism, although he never went further than a suggestive sentence, elicited by persistent questioning of Russian emigrés.

Herzen argued that the peculiar institution of the rural commune in Russia, the *mir*, provided the basis for building socialism in Russia without experiencing capitalism. The *mir* was an old Russian institution which for lack of more-sophisticated forms of village government had undertaken to redistribute peasant lands on the basis of equity, collect taxes, and see to the fulfillment of other peasant obligations. Herzen considered the *mir* as symbolic of the Russian peasant's yearning for a collective or socialist mode of social and political organizations. Now that the serfs were emancipated, he anticipated the peasants turning to the *mir* to settle their interpersonal relationships and developing thereby an awareness of the benefits of communal association. Herzen refrained from attempting to develop a complex scheme for the building of socialism on the Marxist model. Russia's needs as he saw them were simple: as a society in which the peasants were numerically the largest as well as the most-exploited class, Russia should produce a form of socialism based on peasant needs. Herzen himself died before any movement took shape, but his influence on future Russian socialists was immense.

Herzen had to propound his arguments from his far-off exile in England; within Russia itself no such direct discussion of socialism would have been tolerated. There the intelligentsia, frustrated by censorship, either suppressed their criticism for fear of arrest or sought oblique methods to make their feelings known. One method of discussing social and political issues was the use of literature to get past the censor. Even when the writers themselves were apolitical, their works sometimes became the departure point for an analysis of the political, social, or economic life of Russia. Any literary treatment of Russian society in the nineteenth century automatically raised certain issues which, whether or not so intended, made them political tracts. For example, the distinctly apolitical writer Nikolai Gogol (1809–1852) satirized the tsarist bureaucracy in short stories such as *The Overcoat*, in the novel *Dead Souls*, and in the play *The Inspector General*, but he had no wish to be a revolutionary or even an agitator. In fact, he was ignorant of socialism and retreated to deep religious commitment in his personal life when others such as the literary critic Vissarion Belinsky demanded that he face the social issues raised in his writings.

·Other writers, not as talented as Gogol, were more willing to use the novel as a subterfuge for inserting socialist themes into literature. Nikolai Chernyshevsky (1828–1889), influenced by both Belinsky and Feuerbach, began to use his regular column of literary criticism to attach not only the Tsarist regime but moderate reformers as well. Eventually Chernyshevsky fell afoul of the censor and was sent to Siberia, but he still managed to publish the major social novel of his time, *What Is To Be Done?* (1863), a work marked less by literary merit than by social content. His romantic depiction of seamstresses who conquer the owners' exploitation by forming their own producers' association would seem to imply little more than a Utopian approach on the level of Fourier or other early nineteenth-century socialists. However, the novel was also laced with an exhortation for political action, and it produced an image of a strong revolutionary leader in the character Rakhmetov, a political organizer whose dynamism fired the imagination of some readers (and apparently of the censor).

People such as Chernyshevsky and Herzen did not have immediate followings, but their writings served to keep ideological ferment alive amongst the intelligentsia, particularly in the universities where restless students were inspired by the idea of "going to the people" to deliver the messages of socialism and revolution. In the 1870s, "going to the people"—a phrase originally coined by Herzen—meant going to peasant villages and hamlets and arousing the peasantry to their destiny and opportunity. Not only had Herzen urged such an approach, but later leaders such as Peter Lavrov (1823–1900) who had been involved in the Paris commune admonished the intelligentsia that they had an obligation to make the people aware of their revolutionary potential.

The "going-to-the-people" movement, known as *narodnichestvo* (populism), peaked in 1873–1874 as eager youths flocked to the countryside. The young populists, however, were not prepared for the gulf in communication that existed between them and the Russian peasant. The latter, barely a decade out of serfdom, politically as well as functionally illiterate, simply could not, and did not wish to understand the message of revolutionary socialism. The peasants intuitively perceived that, whatever the ideas being peddled to them by the youthful agitators, they were likely to cause trouble. They also perceived that the young populists, by virtue of their education and experience, had never known the harsh life of the Russian countryside: they were as alien as their message. When they came to speak, as often as not the peasants were likely to beat them or to call in the local constable. Thus the populist movement foundered in Russia, not so much because of police interference as because of open hostility from the peasants to whom it was addressed.

For at least one group of erstwhile populists, the experience seemed to suggest the futility of arousing the peasantry; instead they suggested committing the movement to direct action. This group, calling itself *narodnaia volia* (The People's Will) embraced terror as its weapon against the regime and actually succeeded in assassinating Alexander II in 1881. The effect was hardly a popular surge of revolutionary spirit; to the contrary, the peasantry, shocked by the assassination, now approved of new repressive measures taken by the regime against agitators. Revolutionary groups found themselves facing the choice of incarceration or emigration; they had lost any chance to function in Russia. Although not responsible for the terrorist activities, the populist movement was blamed for the assassination and never recovered from both the official and popular reactions.

## RUSSIA'S FLEDGLING PROLETARIAT

In the 1880s there was a new influx of political exiles to the West, many of them by no means terrorists or even insurrectionists. Yet all of them, reflecting on the circumstances that had compelled them to flee Russia, had to reconsider the *narodnichestvo* movement as a tactic for social change, especially in light of the dire consequences the move to political assassination had brought. Both tactics were not discredited, although the former still maintained more adherents than the latter.

One of these exiles, Georgi V. Plekhanov (1857–1918), began to question the validity of raising class awareness amongst "the people." He called upon his fellow exiles to reconsider their assumption that Russia might be able to avoid the capitalist stage of economic development. Speaking in language that echoed Marx and Engels more than Herzen, Plekhanov insisted that capitalism was a necessary transition between feudalism and socialism and could not be omitted from Russia's historical development. He also claimed that Russia was further on the road to capitalism than the populists realized, and the developing proletariat could eventually, after capitalism broke the economic remnants of feudalism, *lead* the peasantry to socialism. Plekhanov was not abandoning the peasants, but he did see political lessons to be inferred from their rejection of the populists as well as from his own brief involvement with the workers of St. Petersburg, whom he claimed were more receptive to doctrines of revolutionary socialism.

· Plekhanov had denounced the counterproductivity of terrorism even prior to the murder of Alexander II, and in his exile he condemned his fellow emigrants who sought to hatch new assassination plots. He issued a veritable torrent of articles, booklets, and speeches, all of them moving closer to Marxism as the only proper course for Russian socialism. His persuasiveness was acknowledged by ever-increasing numbers of the intelligentsia who were impressed by his argument for the validity of historical determinism and his claim that the growing political awareness of the Russian proletariat was the best hope for the future of Russian socialism. Years earlier, the intelligentsia had listened to Herzen, who, obsessed with the problem of serfdom, had rejected the Marxist view of historical development when applied to Russia. That, however, was when Russia still seemed to be in the feudal stage of history. In the late 1880s, Plekhanov could and did argue that Russia's belated program of industrialization and railroad building was finally moving it into the ranks of capitalism and, as an inexorable by-product, producing a class-conscious proletariat.

The number of socialists attracted by Plekhanov's arguments was substantial. Some of his own generation, notably the erstwhile populist Pavel Akselrod, gradually came over to Plekhanov's commitment to Marxism, but his influence was even more marked amongst the exiles of the next decade. The most important among them was Vladimir I. Lenin (1870–1924), a young radical lawyer who, like so many of his generation of intelligentsia, had first dabbled in the populist cause.

By the close of the century, Lenin (whose family name was actually Ulyanov) had given few indications that he would rise to world prominence. Born to a respectable and moderately well-placed family in Simbirsk, he studied law and seemed destined for some modest bureaucratic career, despite a minor interest in revolutionary ideologies. However, the execution of his older brother in 1887 for involvement in plots against Tsar Alexander III led to Lenin's fervent commitment to the revolutionary movement. Even so, he continued his education in law, only occasionally running afoul of the authorities and usually for minor infractions.

Although he trained in law, his major interests were in economics and history, and, as did Marx a half-century earlier, Lenin steeped himself in the literature available to him. He also read as much as he could of the revolutionaries of the period, particularly Chernyshevsky, whose novel *What Is To Be Done?* he read and reread in hopes of finding some guiding principles for his own life. He was much caught up with the book's implied exhortation that the intelligentsia should commit themselves to action. Under the influence of Chernyshevsky, and to a lesser degree Herzen, he briefly turned to populism, and also observed the discredited *narodnaia volia* and their approach to revolution. He apparently was never persuaded, however, of the merits of terrorist tactics.

He was, however, quick to perceive the problems of these approaches and became more and more convinced that the case Plekhanov was making for a Marxist development in Russia was valid, even if it meant the temporary sufferance of capitalism. In 1895 he went abroad briefly, and, after meeting Plekhanov, the conversion was completed.

Returning to Russia as a convinced Marxist, Lenin soon was arrested as a political agitator, and, after a long stay in jail, exiled to Siberia. There he met and married another socialist exile, Nadezhda Krupskaia. Jail and exile convinced him that revolutionary Marxism could not be pursued in Russia at that time, and in 1900 he went abroad again, not to return until the momentous revolutionary year of 1917.

Plekhanov had been singularly successful in recruiting Marxists abroad from the young intelligentsia, and at first it seemed that Lenin was but another of this growing group of alienated emigrés. However, it was not long before Lenin ceased to be merely a precocious convert to Marxism and began to establish his own approach to revolutionary socialism. In later years, Lenin recognized Plekhanov as an important force in developing his appreciation for Marxism and its application to Russia, but he pointed out the important differences in their thinking that precluded his continuation as Plekhanov's disciple. In contrast to Plekhanov, for instance, Lenin was sympathetic to authoritarian, elitist concepts of socialist organization and tactics and somewhat dubious toward the arguments of social democracy advanced by Western Marxists. Specifically, he was attracted by the idea put forth by a minor figure in emigré circles, Piotr Tkachev, that the revolutionary minority had the right to act in the name of the socialist revolution.

## THE RISE OF THE BOLSHEVIK PARTY

In 1900 Plekhanov established an emigrant-Russian Marxist publication called *Iskra (The Spark)*, and Lenin was invited to join several other young Russian Marxists on the editorial board. Lenin found unexpected difficulties in such collaboration, and in 1902 he independently published his own thoughts on revolutionary potential in Russia, a set of views that was permanently to set him aside from many of his comrades. This publication, the length of a short book, was called *What Is To Be Done?*, which was Lenin's way of acknowledging his debt to Chernyshevsky's novel in shaping his views. Lenin's *What Is To Be Done?* was a credo for a new tactical approach to revolutionary Marxism; from the moment of its publication, there existed a distinct "Leninist" blueprint for revolutionary organization.

In *What Is To Be Done?* and subsequent works, Lenin argued that there was little to support the notion that the proletariat had any potential for becoming a spontaneous revolutionary force. What Marxists had overlooked was the desirability of developing a disciplined core of professional revolutionaries, whom he referred to as the *vanguard*, who would organize and lead the workers in revolutionary action. Lenin did not believe that the worker, especially the Russian worker, possessed either the political consciousness or the command of revolutionary theory necessary to effect a socialist revolution; instead he unabashedly championed the mission of the Russian Marxist party—known then as the Russian Social Democratic Labor Party (RSDLP)—to develop a central committee which was to organize revolutionary activity without any serious decision-making involvement from the mass of the workers. Lenin pointed to the danger of infiltration by tsarist police and other tactical considerations as a rationale for his viewpoint, but there was no gainsaying his vote of "no confidence" in the ability of the workers to generate and carry out their own revolution. Furthermore, his approach suggested an authoritarianism that had hitherto been alien to Marxists, who, whatever their nationality, prided themselves on their democratic ideals. This authoritarianism was not immediately perceived by other Russian Marxists, but the following year at the Congress of the RSDLP his departure from traditional Marxist values was clearly noted.

Meeting in the summer of 1903, at first in Brussels and then shifting to London because of harassment by Belgian officials, the Congress soon focused on Lenin's proposal for the development of a vanguard type of leadership. Ostensibly, the specific issue at stake was the criteria for party membership and, by extension, the composition and role of the party leadership, which was to be entrusted to a central committee with broad powers. In such an arrangement, the central committee would become for all practical purposes the party leadership.

Before any real confrontations on the issue could develop, an unforeseen turn of events rescued the day for Lenin. The RSDLP Congress, despite its importance to future socialist history, was really a hastily assembled group of only fifty-five people, few of whom were really mandated by or represented any specific groups or regions. One group which did have a constituency was the *Bund*, an organization of Russian-Jewish workers, which had played a major role in the development of Russian Marxism at the grass-roots level and now claimed the right to be the exclusive organization for Russian-Jewish workers and their activities in the movement. With five delegates at the Congress, this group demanded that the Bund be given special status as an autonomous unit within the RSDLP.[1] When this was denied, the Bund delegates and two of their sympathizers walked out of the Congress in protest. Up until this walk-out, Lenin had only been able to count on twenty-four votes for his policies; the new situation left him with a *temporary* majority amongst the remaining delegates. Seizing the moment, Lenin was able to get a quick vote supporting his selections for the major party-leadership groups and, by implication, for his vanguard policy. Claiming a majority, Lenin's group called themselves the *Bolsheviks* (from *bol'shinstvo*, the Russian word for "majority") and derided their opponents as *Mensheviks* (from *men'shinstvo*, the Russian word for "minority"). The terms have remained to the present day.

Lenin's "majority" lasted only as long as the Congress. When Plekhanov, who had initially been intrigued by Lenin's ideas, realized that Lenin meant to exclude the Mensheviks from all major party positions, including the editorial board of *Iskra*, he rallied to the Menshevik side and invited them and Lenin back into a reunited RSDLP. Lenin, who had not been that disturbed by the split, declined to be-

---

[1] There were far more than five Russian Jews at the Congress but only these five represented the Bund. The other delegates of Jewish descent there (e.g., Trotsky, Martov, etc.) disclaimed any specific Jewish identity and claimed to be leaders of the larger Russian organization.

long to a group in which he would be just another voice, and he persisted in maintaining a separate Bolshevik group, dedicated to the vanguard approach to revolutionary organization.

There were other major differences between the Bolsheviks and Mensheviks, such as a ceaseless debate on what kind of revolution a not-fully capitalist Russia should have, but many Marxists were most unhappy about Lenin's insistence on a centralized and elitist leadership. Rosa Luxemburg, who claimed an interest in the affairs of the RSDLP as a native of Russian Poland, was horrified at the downgrading of worker spontaneity implicit in the vanguard and criticized Lenin for abandoning Marxist ideals of proletarian democracy. Even Plekhanov, who had first suggested that he supported Lenin's ideas, now ridiculed him in a new publication sarcastically titled, *What Is Not To Be Done?*

Critics notwithstanding, Lenin had in essence created a new Russian Marxist party: the Bolsheviks. Attempts to reunite the Mensheviks and Bolsheviks during the next decade were futile, largely because Lenin preferred a disciplined Bolshevik Party to what he considered a too-broadly diffused reunited RSDLP. Bolshevik numbers were never very large, and they shrank further with each feud Lenin provoked with other Bolsheviks, but the Party persisted as a separate entity with Lenin its creator, its leader, and its most visible and influential member.

## THE MENSHEVIKS

The Mensheviks seemed to be politically immature next to the dynamic and ruthless figure of Lenin. Certainly one wonders about the political sagacity of a party which allowed itself to be known by a term that meant they were in a minority. They were, however, led by men of equal intellectual stature to Lenin, similarly knowledgeable in Marxism, the world scene, and other matters. After 1903, Plekhanov himself became a nominal adherent to the Menshevik faction, but their most important leader was a former collaborator of Lenin's on the staff of *Iskra*, Yuri O. Martov (1873–1923). In the years when *Iskra* was being established, Martov had worked closely with Lenin under the sponsorship of Plekhanov. Like Lenin, Martov was in favor of a strong Russian Marxism, but he saw it as embracing all people devoted to the revolutionary cause, and he was suspicious that the elitism espoused by Lenin was not only excessively authoritarian but a confession of a lack of faith in the ability of the RSDLP to raise the consciousness of the Russian proletariat.

The Menshevik criticism of Lenin was that he was not as firm a believer in historical determinism as Marxist philosophy required. Marx had taught that capitalism's exploitation inevitably made an enemy out of the proletariat it spawned. This was the inherent contradiction of capitalism. Marx believed that inevitably the proletariat would rise against the system that was its exploiter. Lenin, by his own subsequent admission, had little faith in the proletariat to "develop anything higher than a trade union mentality"; only the vanguard, the highly centralized leadership, could author a revolution. This dispute was of fundamental significance, involving not only the organization of the RSDLP and the mandate of its leadership but, in the Menshevik view, faith in the entire Marxist idea. Plekhanov pointed out that Lenin's position negated Marx's teachings if he insisted that capitalism drove the proletariat only as far as trade unionism and no further. With considerable support from major figures in the Second International, the Mensheviks came to regard themselves as the true Russian Marxists and the Bolsheviks as elitists of wavering faith.

## THE IMPACT OF THE 1905 RUSSIAN REVOLUTION

Lenin's dismissal of the proletariat's potential revolutionary commitment and consciousness was irreconcilable with the faith in the proletariat of Mensheviks such as Yuri Martov and Pavel Akselrod. Mensheviks and Bolsheviks, particularly Lenin and Martov, began to assail each other in *Iskra* and elsewhere. The bickering was trivial, however, compared to events that developed at the beginning of 1905.

Angered by the tsarist government's blundering into a war with Japan and the resultant hardship on the population, Russian workers had demonstrated against the war and voiced demands for reform. On January 22, 1905, thousands of workers staged a massive demonstration at the Winter Palace in St. Petersburg, so unnerving the palace guard that they fired into the assemblage, causing hundreds of casualties. The massacre, known retrospectively as Bloody Sunday, sparked worker demonstrations throughout the Russian Empire, and violent peasant demonstrations as well. It was the wave of strikes and demonstrations by the urban workers that caught the imagination of the socialists, especially an October 1905 general strike that paralyzed the country and forced the tsar to promise concessions.

Socialists outside of Russia were heartened by the apparent rising of the Russian worker against oppression and exploitation. If the relatively unorganized and politically undeveloped Russian proletariat could use the general strike to bring a repressive regime to its knees—so went the reasoning of Rosa Luxemburg and her friends— how much could be achieved by the more politically sophisticated Western proletariat! The Russian Revolution of 1905 was a badly needed tonic for the languishing radicals in the Second International.

Russian socialists within the country were less interested in the emotional aid their revolution gave the Second International than in the prospects for substantial change in Russia. Under the euphoria of events, Bolsheviks and Mensheviks there patched up their doctrinal differences and combined their effort in the common cause, particularly in support of the general strike. Lenin, however, in exile abroad, refused to be reconciled with his Menshevik rivals, although he too was caught in the excitement of the moment and spoke of the activities of the workers with evident exhilaration.

In St. Petersburg, the capital of imperial Russia, the workers and their Menshevik sponsors coalesced in a coordinating organization known as the Soviet. (The Russian word *soviet* simply meant "council.") The convening of such an organization in 1905 brought a new possibility to the socialist scene, particularly when other soviets appeared in cities where strike activities were taking place. Lenin and the Bolsheviks recognized the potential use of the Soviet as a tactical and organizational weapon, despite its Menshevik origins, and in 1905 the Soviet enjoyed full support from both groups.

The Revolution of 1905 engendered much excitement, but it was not a socialist triumph. It led to the tsar's reluctant concession of a parliament (the Duma) with limited powers, but a parliament had not been a socialist goal for Russia. In the major cities, especially in Moscow, the army had proved its loyalty to the tsar by breaking up worker strikes and pacifying both cities and countryside with un-abated ruthlessness. By the end of the year the soviets were dissolved and their leaders arrested. It seemed that Russia had undergone an experience similar to that of the Western countries in 1848: a period of demonstrations, rebellions, and demands, which in the end had yielded to the survival of the existing regime.

From the socialist viewpoint, however, the year 1905 had resulted in very real accomplishments. Bloody Sunday had finally sundered some of the Russian workers' and peasants' mindless loyalty to the tsar. The Russian worker had displayed a radical zeal and class consciousness that few besides Plekhanov had believed was there. No longer could the Russian worker movement be cavalierly dismissed in the councils of the Second International. By spontaneously convening soviets to deal with a crisis, the Russian workers had introduced a new revolutionary weapon which could be employed by socialists in and out of Russia at a future date. The highly politicized general strike of October 1905 gave renewed credence to the demand of Rosa Luxemburg that mass strikes become an approved tactical weapon in the Marxist arsenal. On the other hand, the failure to maintain the momentum of the strike once concessions began—except in Moscow[2]—suggested that some of Lenin's observations on the special role of vanguard leadership were well taken.

During the hectic year of 1905, and thereafter, Lenin resisted pressures on him both to reunite with the Mensheviks into one party and to return to Russia and become personally involved in the events taking place there. Unpersuaded, he remained abroad and concentrated on building the Bolshevik faction into a party in its own right. Total capitulation by the Mensheviks was the only basis for reconciliation that Lenin would consider, and this the Mensheviks were unwilling to do. The two groups proceeded in separate directions, be-

---

[2] In Moscow, the Soviet succeeded in reviving the strike in late December 1905, forcing the army to resort to military tactics, including the use of artillery, to suppress it.

coming for all practical purposes two parties, although both paid lip service to the idea of a future reunification.

Within the ranks of the Second International, Lenin's reputation was scarcely enhanced by his intransigence. Some regarded him as a nuisance who unnecessarily divided a Marxist party that desperately needed unity. Even the radicals in the Second International were ambivalent toward him, approving of his commitment to revolutionary activism but always retaining a deep-rooted suspicion of the elitism inherent in his idea of revolutionary leadership. Only once was Lenin able to influence the Second International on any matter of consequence. That was in 1907, when together with Rosa Luxemburg he coauthored part of the International's resolution on war; it called upon socialists to respond to any outbreak of war with actions that would terminate "capitalist class rule." Usually his views were politely ignored, as at the 1910 congress when he tried to dissuade the International from considering a rapprochement with the burgeoning European cooperative movement. Until World War I began, Lenin remained a lonely radical rebuffing all attempts to include him in a reunified RSDLP.

## WORLD WAR I
## AND THE ZIMMERWALD CONFERENCE

When World War I burst upon Europe in the summer of 1914, Lenin was as surprised as anyone else, although he had often prophesized such a war. He found it hard to believe the news that socialists had supported their respective countries' war efforts. Indeed, he suspected that the German government had prepared forged newspapers to announce the vote in the *Reichstag*; surely the SPD, the party of Bebel and Liebknecht, could not be so craven!

Lenin at that time was vacationing in Austrian Galicia where, since Austria was now at war with Russia, he was promptly arrested as an enemy alien. Only the intervention of the Austrian socialists, now in the good graces of their government, persuaded the authorities that Lenin was no supporter of the tsar and ought to be freed. Released, Lenin made his way to neutral Switzerland, where he promptly announced that the Second International, having betrayed the European workers, was dead; the time had come, he declared, to build a new international dedicated to nothing less than revolution. Whatever justification there was in such an assertion, they were drowned out against the background of cataclysmic events taking place in the war's first months, and few paid Lenin any heed.

The events which led up to World War I were petty and insignificant. (See chapter 4 for additional details on the outbreak of this conflict.) The assassination of an Austrian prince by nationalist terrorists was an important matter, but there had been in the preceding two decades numerous assassinations of royalty and government officials without such serious consequences. None of the powers had really wanted to wage war, but they had been maneuvered into positions that dictated either war or loss of prestige. National pride combined with a complex set of interlocking treaties had most of Europe at war within days of the initial outbreak of hostilities. The regimes rationalized to themselves, and to their subjects, that it would be a quick war, presuming that a decisive battle or series of battles would resolve the issues, determine the victors, and allow European life to continue essentially the same as before. Indeed, all military strategies, planning, and even stocking of supplies, were predicated on a quick victory. None of the European leaders foresaw the four years of slaughter that were to ensue. Socialists were no more prescient than their national governments: in the first burst of patriotic enthusiasm many had acquiesed—or in some cases jubilantly sponsored—their respective governments' war efforts. Cassandra–like statements, such as Lenin's pronouncement on the death of the Second International, were not taken seriously. Only belatedly did the true horror of what had happened to Europe, to socialism, to the idea of internationalism, and to themselves, begin to sink into the consciousness of the socialist world.

With most of the major European countries drawn into the war, Switzerland became one of the few dependable havens of neutrality. Not only Lenin but a variety of socialists of manifold persuasions ended up there. As was to be expected, they began to discuss amongst themselves not only the traumatic events of the war but also the options that existed for socialists in these circumstances.

With the Second International moribund, the socialists in Switzerland, encouraged by socialists in other neutral countries, called for an antiwar conference to convene in the summer of 1915. Lenin, although not involved in the original planning, was quick to perceive the opportunity that the meeting presented for reasserting the demise of the Second International and for building a new revolutionary organization in which the Bolsheviks might predominate.

In September 1915 the group finally assembled at the village of Zimmerwald outside the Swiss capital of Berne. For Lenin there were certain advantages in the smallness of the group, which numbered less than a few dozen, such as the uncertainty of their mandates and especially the fact that none of the major figures of the Second International were in attendance, not even the radicals.[3] In the old Second International, a person like Lenin had seemed inconsequential next to a Kautsky, a Bebel, a Luxemburg, or a Jaurès. No such luminaries were at Zimmerwald because most governments deterred their nationals from attending antiwar conferences. Such major socialist parties as the German, Austrian, and French were represented by nondescript delegations that belied their past reputations.

As expected, the Zimmerwald meeting drew up an antiwar manifesto and called for an immediate end to hostilities. For Lenin, this was a singularly inadequate program for such a meeting. If all the antiwar socialists could aspire to do was to stop the war, this would amount to a betrayal of the workers who had borne the brunt of the casualties, for simple peace allowed the capitalists to escape the consequences of the war and resume capitalist domination of Europe. Coining the slogan, "Not civil peace but civil war!" Lenin attempted to rally the more radical members present to an overtly revolutionary position. Even amongst such an undistinguished group, however, Lenin was unable to prevail. The Zimmerwald Manifesto called upon the workers "to reorganize and start the struggle for peace" but hedged on any call for revolution.

Only a handful of socialists supported Lenin and joined with

---

[3] Rosa Luxemburg was in jail in Berlin, facing charges of high treason. She was, however, quite interested in the Zimmerwald meeting and even wrote a statement of principles for the conference, a statement she could not get delivered to the meetings.

him in the formation of a Zimmerwald Left, which urged that the war be converted into proletarian revolution. Amongst this handful was the Polish-German journalist Karl Radek (1885–1939), a flamboyant and articulate Leftist member of the old Second International. Radek and Lenin had known each other for years, but only in the wartime exile in Switzerland did they begin to collaborate in the common cause of revolution.

Radek was a controversial figure in socialist circles, having been expelled at various times from both the Polish Social Democratic Party and the SPD. Yet he was one of the ablest writers in the movement, and Lenin was quite happy to recruit his talents. In a way, Radek's on-again, off-again relationship with Lenin during the war pointed up the gulf that separated Lenin from even the most radical socialists of West Europe. Like many of the young radicals in the early years of the twentieth century, Radek had been much influenced by the work of Rosa Luxemburg. As such he had always been a supporter of proletarian spontaneity and the importance of proletarian self-esteem. While he was not as suspicious as Luxemburg of Lenin's elitism, he was not a supporter of tight party organization either. Moreover, his disagreements with Lenin were not only confined to ideas of revolutionary leadership; they transcended a number of issues, the most important being the question of national self-determination, on which Lenin had made some concessions to its supporters. Lenin recognized the obvious attraction of nationalism although he hedged, by reserving the right of national self-determination to the proletariat and not to the general population. As Luxemburg's disciple, Radek did not agree with Lenin's position. He considered this issue related to the development of capitalism and irrelevant to the future socialist society.

The rapport engendered by their common cause at Zimmerwald was not enough to hold together for long the rigid Lenin and the less-organization-oriented Radek. Within weeks, they were dividing the already small Zimmerwald Left over the same old issues of self-determination and revolutionary leadership. Radek was hardly the peer of Lenin as a revolutionary leader; the opening of the rift between them was but one indication of the thin allegiance Lenin could expect from European radicals at this time. Outside of the Bolshevik Party,

Lenin was neither highly regarded nor particularly admired as a leader, even by those who might have reason to make common cause with him.

The Zimmerwald organization held a second meeting at the town of Kienthal in April 1916, and there the Zimmerwald Left received more backing for their call to revolution. The continuation of the war had won over some recalcitrants, but still Lenin was unable to take control of the organization or even get it to commit itself to a revolutionary program. Even amongst these rump socialist parties Lenin was still regarded as the humorless leader of a faction that had little appreciation or consideration of what it meant to be a socialist in the West. Only when Lenin had his own revolution, in Russia itself, would he be able to attract the attention from radicals and others that he felt was the Bolsheviks' due. That this revolution was barely months away was a prospect of which even Lenin was unaware.

# SELECTED READINGS

ABRAHAM ASCHER, *Pavel Axelrod and the Development of Menshevism* (Cambridge: Harvard University Press, 1972).
> A detailed biography of one of the founders of Russian Marxism which not only explores the development of Axelrod himself but the rationale for Menshevism's claim that it and not Bolshevism was the proper expression for Russian Marxism.

SAMUEL H. BARON, *Plekhanov, the Father of Russian Marxism* (Stanford: Stanford University Press, 1963).
> This is an extremely well-written study of the man who essentially converted the Russian socialist movement from populism to Marxism, although the former survived in the SR. The research is thorough, and the book is marked by graceful prose.

ISRAEL GETZLER, *Martov* (New York: Cambridge University Press, 1967).
> Martov was Lenin's peer in the early years of Marxism and never lost Lenin's esteem.

LEOPOLD H. HAIMSON, *The Russian Marxists and the Origins of Bolshevism* (Cambridge: Harvard University Press, 1955).
> Haimson examines the situation of Russian socialists at the turn of the century, particularly addressing the issues which turned them into Marxists and then divided their loyalties between Bolshevism and Menshevism.

V. I. LENIN, *What Is To Be Done?* (New York: International Publishers, 1977).
> Of Lenin's many works, this one set him aside as an individual tactician and interpreter of Marx.

MARTIN MALIA, *Alexander Herzen and the Birth of Russian Socialism, 1812–1855* (Cambridge: Harvard University Press, 1961).
> This book not only offers a biography of Herzen but explores the issues that alienated a patriotic Russian intellectual and urged him to find a peculiarly Russian approach to socialism.

LEON TROTSKY, *The Permanent Revolution* (New York: Pathfinder Press, 1969).
> Trotsky enunciates here his unique interpretation of the preconditions of revolution and its extrapolation to countries such as Russia.

FRANCO VENTURI, *Roots of Revolution* (New York: Knopf, 1960).
Venturi offers an exhaustive analysis of Russian populism and its problems.

ALLEN K. WILDMAN, *The Making of a Worker's Revolution: Russian Social Democracy, 1891–1903* (Chicago: University of Chicago Press, 1967).
This is an overview of the formation of Russian Marxism prior to the Bolshevik-Menshevik split.

BERTRAM D. WOLFE, *Three Who Made a Revolution* (New York: Dial Press, 1958).
This is a triple biography of the early years of Lenin, Stalin, and Trotsky and their separate, and interconnected, paths to the Russian Revolution of 1917.

6

The
Socia
The
in Ru

## THE FEBRUARY REVOLUTION

The year 1917 opened bleakly throughout Europe. Despite ever-mounting casualties, the war continued to lay waste to the continent with no end in sight. In Russia, the situation was particularly dreary with every indication that it would get worse. Russian war casualties were enormous, almost 4 million in the first year alone, but that was not the only cause for despair. Russia was simply economically incapable of providing the armaments and supplies required by its armies, and the barriers imposed by geography prevented the Western allies from coming to its rescue. Inefficiency and government corruption had compounded the problem so that there were growing shortages in both munitions for the battle front and food for the home front. Morale had been lifted briefly by an apparently successful offensive against the Austrians in the summer of 1916, but it collapsed again in the fall under the force of a German counteroffensive, leaving Russia with hundreds of thousands of new casualties and the feeling that the war would never end.

Confronted with this crisis, the Russian monarchy proved to be inept and irresponsible. The tsar, spending much of his time at the front, left the government in the hands of the Empress Alexandra and her sinister adviser, Grigori Rasputin. The latter, a self-proclaimed holy man, embodied all that was ignoble in the old regime. He was venal, lecherous, and totally unprincipled. The tsar's preoccupation with the war gave Rasputin an opportunity to enrich himself and his friends by advancing the claim that only he could cure the tsar's young hemophiliac son and heir to the throne. The power Rasputin was able to wield was enormous and plainly showed how weak the monarchy had become. The kind of leadership needed to revive popular confidence during a period of war and sacrifice was totally absent.

As the situation deteriorated, even the moderates who had hitherto tolerated the monarchy became outraged. They began to make demands for changes in Russian society, and when their demands were ignored or denounced they withdrew their support and sufferance of the regime. The assassination of Rasputin in December 1916, by a court-hatched conspiracy, failed to mollify dissension, and by 1917 virtually the entire population was alienated from the regime.

Early in March 1917 demonstrations and food riots broke out in the capital—renamed Petrograd during the war—and the city's garrison refused to quell the riots. Within a very few days, popular pressure became so strong that the tsar was forced to abdicate. The Duma, which had been set up as a concession to the insurgents of 1905 but had never become a strong institution, now took it upon itself to appoint a provisional government composed mainly of political moderates.

Socialist participation in the events leading to the overthrow of the monarchy was minimal. Socialists had been caught quite by surprise; the best-known and most-activist leaders were either in exile or in prison, unable to influence in any way the course of the revolution. Overnight, however, Russia became the focus of attention for the remnant of revolutionary socialists around the world who had held out against the war.

For socialists of all countries, the overthrow of the tsarist regime was a cause for jubilation. Nicholas II had symbolized everything socialists detested, and his passing from the scene could hardly be mourned. How to interpret the events that had transpired, and what tactics should now be followed, were the issues upon which socialists now differed. The Social Revolutionaries (known as the SR's), a non-Marxist and exclusively Russian party, served in some ways as the twentieth-century counterpart of the old populist movement. They ostensibly represented the cause of peasant socialism, accepted the Provisional Government, and one of their members, Alexander Kerensky, was recruited into the Provisional Government as a "bridge" between the socialists and the moderates and centrists.

The collapse of the monarchy had also led to the hasty resurrection of the Petrograd Soviet. Though the Soviet was an obvious revival of the revolutionary spirit of 1905, its role was now quite different. It was not the intention of the Soviet to be the Provisional Government's rival for power but a coalition of revolutionary groups whose objective was to protect the gains of the February Revolution.[1] Among its leaders were several SR's and Mensheviks, both of whom were content to let the Provisional Government establish its authority for the time being, although reserving the right to veto any act of the government which they considered to be counterrevolutionary.

Within the Provisional Government, the SR's, by virtue of their long-standing commitment to agrarian socialism, expected to emerge as the dominant party in the promised free elections. This confidence was based on the size of their potential constituency: the peasants, who then constituted upwards of 80 percent of the total population. Policy decisions would then be in the hands of the SR's, even though they were unclear as to what direction they would take (except that, like Herzen, they saw no necessity for building capitalism as a prelude to socialism). Despite able leaders such as Victor Chernov (1873–1952), however, the SR's were not very successful in conveying their message to the peasants, nor were they firmly united on just what the message would be. Throughout the chaotic year 1917 peasants took advantage of the confusion to claim land and declined to wait for the elections to a promised constituent assembly. The latter was in any case a Western institution—historically convoked to develop constitutional governments—which had no meaning to Russian peasants.

For both Mensheviks and Bolsheviks, the February Revolution, while exhilarating, posed an ideological dilemma in terms of its place in the Marxist timetable of historical determinism. The problem was this: if the February Revolution had ended the remnants of feudalism (that is, the tsarist regime), was not a "bourgeois liberal" stage needed to complete the development of capitalism? Such an interpretation, while consistent with orthodox Marxism, also suggested that the

---

[1] Russia observed the Julian calendar, which was then some eleven days behind the Gregorian calendar in use in the West. Thus though the tsar abdicated in March 1917, it was still February in Russia. The Gregorian calendar was finally adopted in 1918.

time was not yet at hand for a proletarian regime in Russia. Thus, the Soviet, at first dominated by Mensheviks, defined its role as preventing historical regression (such as an attempt to restore the monarchy) and eschewed any claims to power for itself or for the workers. It accepted rule by the "moderate" and certainly non-Marxist provisional government so long as that body did not seek to contravene any of the gains of the February Revolution. Even the Bolsheviks in the Soviet initially went along with this policy.

## THE RETURN OF LENIN

In Switzerland, Lenin received the news of the tsar's abdication with a combination of excitement and frustration. He was excited at the revolutionary rising of the people but frustrated that his isolated location left him helpless to participate. After several days of delicate negotiations by Swiss socialists, a carload of emigrés including Lenin was permitted to cross Germany by train and return to Russia. The trip, known to history as the famous "sealed-car" journey, has led to speculation that Lenin was smuggled back to Russia as an agent of the German government. No proof of collusion between Lenin and the Germans has ever been brought forward—and indeed the evidence suggests the contrary—but the possibility has never been entirely eliminated.

Passing through Scandinavia, Lenin paused in Stockholm long enough to organize an "Overseas Bureau of the Central Committee of the Bolshevik Party." Although Lenin's purpose in forming this committee was unclear, it would be of obvious use to have a quickly reached contact point in a neutral country. Karl Radek and Jakob Hanecki, another Pole who had been recruited to the Bolshevik cause, became the *de facto* organizers and leaders of this bureau, while Lenin and his Russian comrades proceeded on to Russia.

Arriving in Petrograd late in the evening of April sixteenth, Lenin received a tumultuous welcome at the railroad station. This reception was headed oddly enough by the Menshevik, Nicholas S. Chkheidze, the nominal leader of the Soviet. The crowd was by no means exclusively Bolshevik, and Chkheidze sought to use the moment for an appeal to socialist unity at this critical juncture in Russian history. Lenin, who had spent more than a decade promoting splits and rebuffing all attempts at reconciliation, was not about to relinquish the unique features of the Bolsheviks at the moment of their greatest revolutionary possibilities. Right there at the railroad station he rejected the Menshevik's offer of reunification, and he denounced as well the Soviet's acceptance of the provisional government.

In the next few days Lenin's position became absolutely clear: by his slogan "All power to the Soviets!" he denied the legitimacy of the provisional government and urged that the Soviet, even if dominated for the moment by Mensheviks and SR's, be converted into the seat of political power. In a collection of policy statements known as "The April Theses," Lenin called for the dissemination of defeatist propaganda in the army to bring about a Russian withdrawal from the war, as well as an end to the toleration of moderates and parliamentarians, whom he curtly dismissed as the exploiters of the population.

Lenin's call for radical revolutionary tactics fired the imagination of some of the younger party members, notably Joseph Stalin (1879–1953) and Vyacheslav Molotov (1890–) who were later to become major party leaders in their own right. By and large, however, most socialists—Bolsheviks, Mensheviks, and even SR's—felt that Lenin had overstated the revolutionary potential of the situation and had proposed theoretical violence to the Marxist interpretation of history by calling for proletarian power before the economic basis of a socialist society was possible. Some Mensheviks even maintained that Lenin had vitiated his role as a leader by espousing irresponsible tactics and downgrading the achievements of the February Revolution.

Lenin was undisturbed by Menshevik and SR rejection of his "April Theses," but he couldn't accept the fact that the majority of his own Bolsheviks, led by Lev Kamenev (1883–1936), believed that he was rushing things by departing from Marxist concepts of revolutionary development. In order to challenge successfully the legitimacy of the provisional government, he realized he had to demonstrate to fellow revolutionaries that Marxist theory would not be violated by a proletarian seizure of power in Russia, even though Russia was one of the lesser-developed countries of Europe. Hitherto, even revolutionary Marxists had assumed that when proletarian revolution did come, it would come in a highly developed capitalist country with a large organized proletariat, such as Germany. Few Marxists had ever claimed that the lesser-developed countries could be the initiators of proletarian revolution, and still fewer had been able to reconcile such ideas with Marxism.


## TROTSKY AND THE THEORY
## OF "PERMANENT REVOLUTION"


The return to Russia in mid-May of the dynamic and controversial revolutionary Leon Trotsky (1879–1940) facilitated a solution to Lenin's dilemma. Trotsky was acknowledged by all to be one of the most brilliant polemicists of Russian Marxism—he was at one time known by the nickname of *pero*, "the pen"—but he was also a difficult person to include in any organizational group. He was sympathetic to the idea of revolutionary activism and had served briefly as the head of the Petrograd Soviet during the 1905 Revolution. He had supported Lenin on some occasions in the early years of Russian Marxism, but for the past decade he had been moving in and out of Menshevik ranks. At Zimmerwald, he had shown some sympathy for the Left's position but had declined to join the group,.eventually going to New York where the February Revolution had found him desperately trying to rally other Marxist emigrants in a regrouping of the American Left. After a difficult return journey to Russia, he joined neither the Bolsheviks nor Mensheviks but formed his own group of "internationalists" who had little impact beyond their own slender ranks. Unable to accept easily the leadership of either Lenin or Martov, who had emerged as the Menshevik leader, Trotsky struck his own course, although he advised Lenin that he was basically in sympathy with the "April Theses."

Trotsky had been developing a theory for some time that might serve as the justification of Lenin's call for a proletarian seizure of power in 1917. Imprisoned by the tsarist regime after the 1905 Revolution, Trotsky had used his enforced leisure to begin to expound the ideas that eventually would become known as the theory of "permanent revolution."[2] When first written in 1906, Trotsky's theory used as examples movements and events that were irrelevant in the context of 1917, but he updated the theory over the years, remaining constant in his assertion that the proletariat had prospects for revolutionary action in Russia.

In his theory, Trotsky suggested that there was no absolute correlation between the numbers of the proletariat and their revolutionary potential; instead this potential was more properly measured in terms of class consciousness and the existence of the opportunity for power. Both of these criteria seemed present in the Russia of 1917. Furthermore, Trotsky offered an alternative means of measuring the maturity of capitalism so that Russia did not seem so far behind. For example, the criterion of the concentration of the ownership of industry in relatively few hands, he noted, was certainly characteristic of Russia at that time because of massive foreign investment and government monopolies. Most important of all, Trotsky's theory made a persuasive case that any revolution that began in Russia could not survive in isolation but required a follow-up revolution in Europe. That the revolution did not interrupt to allow a bourgeois democratic phase was even more startling and, for Marxists, controversial. Trotsky simply proclaimed that the revolution was continuous or permanent, and that it continued without interruption until worker power was established.

As originally presented in 1906 few Russian Marxists, Lenin included, gave the theory of permanent revolution much credibility. Yet Lenin and Trotsky were in many ways not as far apart as their separate careers prior to 1917 might have suggested. Like Lenin, Trotsky believed in vanguard leadership, but he thought of it as the revolutionary element of the proletariat, not as a select, disciplined party organization. Instead the proletariat would continue the revolution until proletarian power was an accomplished fact.

---

[2] Actually the term "permanent revolution" is inaccurate and slightly misconstrues Trotsky's idea. A more accurate translation from the Russian would be "uninterrupted" or "continuous revolution." However, over the years, the theory has been popularly known in English translation as "permanent revolution," and hence the use here.

Both Lenin and Trotsky were quick to extrapolate the concept of permanent revolution to the Russia of 1917. Given the weakness of the Provisional Government, one could argue that the radicalized proletariat, with Bolshevik leadership, was capable of seizing power and holding it. Further, one could rationalize that Marxists were not bound by bourgeois definitions of national boundaries and that, especially given the carnage of World War I, all of Europe was the target and it made tactical sense to attack capitalism at its weakest link: the Russia of 1917. Once the "dictatorship of the proletariat" was in power in Russia, the revolution would be extended to the capitalist countries of Europe, thus fulfilling Lenin's old slogan of "Not civil peace but Civil War!" Presumably the end result would be the establishment of a socialist society on an international basis.

Obviously revolutions do not emanate from ideology alone; Lenin is reputed to have said that theory was no more than a guide to action. Yet Trotsky's ability to adapt Marxist theory to specifically Russian conditions provided Lenin with a much needed ideology. After two months of aloofness from party identification, Trotsky joined the Bolsheviks, convinced that they had proven their worthiness as revolutionaries. The charismatic Trotsky complemented the more intense Lenin to form a revolutionary leadership that proved more than equal to the challenge of 1917. Both men suppressed their obvious personality differences; in any case, the flow of events minimized the amount of direct contact between the two.

## THE BOLSHEVIK REVOLUTION

Even without the provocative activities of Lenin and Trotsky, it is questionable whether the provisional government had a chance to produce parliamentary democracy in Russia. The term was dear to the hearts of Russia's Western allies, as well as to Russian moderates, but it was hardly the aspiration of the suffering masses. The provisional government went through a series of crises and leadership changes, but the determination to develop constitutional government remained unaltered. Finally, on July 21, 1917, Alexander Kerensky, the erstwhile SR, became the prime minister, and he too reiterated a policy of deferring all major decisions, social, economic, or political, until there had been an opportunity to elect a constituent assembly by universal suffrage. In retrospect it might seem that he would have been better advised to have acted forcefully for reforms. At the time, however, he had misgivings about initiating basic changes in Russian life when chaos and war precluded any truly democratic activities.

Kerensky's commitment to Western democracy and its political forms overshadowed whatever remained of his never-too-strong commitment to socialism. A flamboyant orator, he was able to spur the armies into a new, short-lived and ill-advised offensive. When street riots in July 1917 threatened the regime, he cracked down on the Bolsheviks, some of whom were involved, by arresting a few leaders, including Trotsky, and forcing others such as Lenin into hiding to avoid a similar fate. Yet several weeks later, when Kerensky was threatened by a military coup from a disaffected general, he was forced to turn for aid to the socialists and was able to suppress the threat only at the cost of allowing the Soviet to form its own armed units to "protect the revolution." In the fall, he reshuffled the government and released Trotsky and the other Bolsheviks from prison. Whatever his actions, however, they seemed too little and too late. Russia, with political chaos increasing daily and with no end of the war in sight, had become more receptive to radical ideologies than it had been at the time of the abdication of the monarchy. Kerensky's response, more talk of electing a constituent assembly, seemed totally irrelevant to a people who had lost all patience with promises.

Released from jail in September, Trotsky ignored the Provisional Government and concentrated his attention on the Soviet, which under the pressures of the time had become more and more radicalized. This radicalization worked to Trotsky's advantage, since he was now able to use his own oratorical skills to get himself appointed chairman of the Petrograd Soviet. He immediately exploited this position to create a separate base of armed force for the Bolsheviks.   ·

Bolshevik maneuvering for a coup in the fall of 1917 was hardly a secret; however, Kerensky's position was so uncertain that he really could do little about it. The Military Revolutionary Committee of the Petrograd Soviet became in reality the armed guard of the Bolshevik Party. When Lenin slipped back into town from his Finnish hiding place, plans were laid for an armed insurrection. Despite last-minute attempts by the Provisional Government to foil the use of the Military Revolutionary Committee, on November 7, 1917, the Committee announced the overthrow of the provisional government, an event which, despite its enormous consequences, was accomplished with a minimum of fighting and resistance. Only a few military cadets and the "Women's Death Battalion" offered any resistance and, at least in Petrograd, the revolution took only a few hours. At a congress of Soviets meeting in Petrograd, Trotsky announced that the revolution had deposed the Provisional Government and that a government of Soviets was now in charge.

The Bolsheviks could hardly believe how easy it had been. They ignored proposals that they now reconstruct a broad socialist coalition: they had made the revolution, and, as the "vanguard of the proletariat," they would lead it. When the Mensheviks, in protest against this high-handed action, walked out of the Congress of Soviets, Trotsky thundered after them, "Go back where you belong! To the garbage can of history; you have played your role!"

Save for a few concessions to the Left SR's, who were sympathetic to the Bolshevik insurrection, the Bolsheviks were now the sole governmental force, at least in Petrograd. Seizing power, however, was one matter; retaining it was another. It was to take several years of civil war and carnage before the regime was firmly established. But in November 1917, the first avowedly Marxist revolutionary regime in the world had come into being, and world affairs would never be the same after this event.

The news of the Bolshevik Revolution came as a tonic for virtually all socialists who still thought of themselves as revolutionaries. Even Rosa Luxemburg, who remained critical of Lenin's elitism, declared that Lenin and Trotsky had rescued the reputation of Marxism. The initial impression throughout the socialist world was that a great blow had been struck for the proletariat and that the Bolshevik victory was their victory as well.

The feeling of solidarity with the Bolsheviks was particularly strong amongst the leaders of the Zimmerwald movement, then headquartered in Stockholm. Led by the Russian-Italian exile, Angelica Balabanoff, the Zimmerwald movement had been undergoing progressive radicalization as a result of the failure of its peace manifestoes. In September 1917, the movement held its third conference, this time in Stockholm. At that time the Overseas Bureau of the Bolshevik Party, established during Lenin's brief stopover in Stockholm, was working diligently to diminish the stature of the Zimmerwald movement while simultaneously trying to infiltrate the Zimmerwald leadership. There had been a brief conflict when Karl Radek, pursuing these twin goals, had deliberately leaked a secret manifesto of the Zimmerwald movement to the Swedish press, but the anger at Radek had been swept away by the Bolshevik triumph. In November, with the news of Bolshevik victory, Balabanoff endorsed Lenin's triumph as a boon to the Zimmerwald cause and regarded all earlier disputes as moot. She even prepared to go to Russia herself, in the name of Zimmerwald. Balabanoff, of course, had no authority or mandate to throw the prestige of the antiwar socialist movement behind the Bolsheviks. However, in the euphoria of the moment few in the Zimmerwald movement challenged her efforts. For all practical purposes the Zimmerwald movement now ceased to exist.

Ironically, Lenin had long since written off the Zimmerwald movement as being too willing to compromise with moderates and insufficiently committed to revolutionary activism. In fact, he had even written to Radek to suggest that the latter sabotage the Zimmerwald movement lest it impede the radicals in international socialism. However, he quickly accepted Balabanoff's support and elevated her to the post of personal confidant. Still, he ignored the Zimmerwald movement itself and, in general, claimed that with the Bolshevik Revolution—the fight against the "imperialist war"—had now moved to Russia. Indeed, since one of the first acts of the new Bolshevik regime was a "Decree on Peace"—a call for an immediate peace without annexations or idemnities—Lenin saw no reason for the continued existence of Zimmerwald.

For other socialists, the victory of the Bolsheviks presented new issues. Perhaps the overall enthusiasm was greatest in Germany, where socialists both on the Left and Right were pleased by the Bolshevik victory. The Left hailed the Bolshevik triumph as the harbinger of an international revolution, whereas the Right, many of whom had become good patriotic Germans and in some cases members of the German government, reasoned that a closing of the Russian front would enable Germany to devote all of its energies to a new drive in the West and to the victorious conclusion of the long war.

Others had no such facile rationalizations. In France and England, socialists loyal to their respective countries were apprehensive about the meaning of the revolution for the same reasons that German socialists might support it. Though there had been a continuing radicalization of the French socialist organization, French socialists were not indifferent to the consequences for France of a closed Russian front; for similar reasons British socialists also equivocated in their support of the Bolshevik Revolution.

It is important to note that overthrowing the provisional government in Petrograd was not the same as securing unchallenged control throughout the Russian Empire. It took several more days of fighting before Bolshevik control in Moscow was secured; in the other cities of the Empire, to say nothing of the rural areas, acceptance of Bolshevik authority was widely challenged. Although little support for the deposed Provisional Government was evident, the Bolsheviks were by no means acclaimed as the automatic successors.

## THE BOLSHEVIK REGIME'S FIRST ACTS

From the day of their revolution, the Bolsheviks faced multiple tactical and ideological problems. One of the former was faced immediately: the promised Constituent Assembly. Surprisingly, the Bolsheviks allowed the elections to take place on the scheduled date, November 25, 1917, well aware that they were unlikely to win. The Social Revolutionaries, capitalizing on their identity with the peasant cause, won a clear majority, and when the Assembly met under SR domination, they declared that the Assembly, and not the Bolshevik regime, was the legitimate source of authority in Russia. After a day of speechmaking, Lenin simply ordered the Assembly dissolved, thus ending any legal threat to the continuation of the Bolshevik regime.

Dissolution of the Constituent Assembly was the easiest of Lenin's tasks. The dispatch with which it was accomplished, without any serious challenge, indicated how shallow were the roots of constitutional procedures in Russia. More basic problems than legitimacy confronted the new regime, and its success in resolving these problems would determine not only its fate but the future of revolutionary socialism.

The seizure of power in Russia by a Marxist organization, in the name of the proletariat, portended the launching of the international revolt against capitalism. The Bolshevik action could not, in theory, be confined to the Russian Empire; Trotsky's theory of permanent revolution had specifically claimed that such isolation would lead to the success of counterrevolution and an overthrow of the Bolshevik regime. Throughout 1917, Lenin, using more indirect language, constantly referred to the common struggle of the European and Russian proletariat, suggesting that the victory of the latter relied on the common struggle with the former.

The realities of the winter of 1917 and 1918, however, offered formidable obstacles to a launching of the international proletarian revolution. First of all, there was the very tenuous power base enjoyed by the Bolsheviks. Overshadowing that was the commitment by the Bolsheviks to get out of the war. From the beginning, the Bolsheviks had denounced the war as benefiting only capitalists at the cost of worker and peasant casualties. However, the political arithmetic of disengaging from the war provided Lenin with some thorny problems.

Russia's immediate neighbor to the west was Imperial Germany, the country whose proletariat had to rise up if the Bolshevik Revolution was to have any international validity. Yet if Lenin withdrew Russia from the war, it appeared that the major beneficiary would be the German government, which would then be free to launch a final offensive against France. Some Bolsheviks had once joked bitterly that "in Germany it was impossible to have a revolution because the government would not allow it." Since the German proletariat had not hitherto revolted, it was plain they would be even less inclined to rise against a German regime that ended the war in victory. A Bolshevik withdrawal from the war might, thus, render impossible a German revolution.

The winter of 1917 and 1918 was the first test of what would become a continuing dilemma for the Bolshevik regime: how to satisfy the national and international interests of Bolshevik Russia. In this first year of revolution national interests won out, as they would continue to do for the next sixty years. In March 1918, after first stalling the Germans, Lenin agreed to the humiliating Treaty of Brest Litovsk, in which he surrendered huge portions of the Russian Empire to Germany so he might be able to concentrate on retaining power. This decision meant the deferral—some were to say abandonment—of his commitment to world revolution.

Lenin did not take this step without considerable misgivings. In his own Bolshevik Party one faction, the so-called Left-Communists, openly accused him of selling out the world revolution to placate the Russian peasants. He himself lamely apologized for the treaty as a temporary step to gain "a breathing space." The treaty was a bitter pill to swallow, not only for the Bolsheviks but for their sympathizers abroad as well. The charge that it represented a capitulation to Russian national interests was a serious one. Lenin's policy could only be justified if the temporary tactical advantage it gained could ultimately be used to launch the world revolution.

The very survival of Lenin's new regime was challenged by the outbreak of a major anti-Bolshevik uprising in the spring of 1918. A full-scale civil war ensued, and the anti-Bolshevik forces, known as the White Armies, almost toppled the Bolsheviks, with considerable approval, and some aid, from the Western powers. In this situation, desperate to survive, Lenin had nothing to offer revolutionaries elsewhere except the "inspiration" of the perseverance of the Bolshevik Revolution.

## GERMANY'S ABORTIVE SOCIALIST UPRISING

Not until 1920 did it really become clear that the Bolsheviks would survive, but even during the darkest days of the civil war Lenin kept up a steady interest in the international scene, paying at least lip service to the commitment to world revolution. Changing the name of the Bolshevik Party to the Communist Party, he insisted that revolutionaries abroad also call themselves Communists, since the old name of Social Democrats, or Socialists, had been tarnished by those who had accepted their countries' war efforts in the critical days of 1914.

When the German western offensive collapsed in the fall of 1918, the impending defeat of Germany implied new opportunities for revolutionary development. On October 30, 1918, the German naval garrison at Kiel mutinied against last-minute heroics by the admiralty, and within a very few days the German Emperor fled and the war effort collapsed. An armistice was signed on November 11 which left Berlin in the hands of an amorphous governmental authority.

After considerable shuffling of personnel, a temporary government led by the old right-wing socialist Friedrich Ebert emerged, claiming authority until some form of constitutional government could be devised. Perhaps grasping at straws, the Bolsheviks overestimated the revolutionary potential of the situation. They saw Ebert as a German Kerensky and inferred numerous other parallels between Russia in November 1917 and Germany in November 1918. The abdication of the monarch, the creation of workers and soldier/sailor soviets, and the return from jail of revolutionary leaders such as Rosa Luxemburg and Karl Liebknecht reinforced the Bolshevik contention that the Russian scenario was being repeated in Germany. What they failed to appreciate was that the German Army had not disintegrated, nor had the police or bureaucracy. These factors were to be decisive in precluding a successful German revolution.

One way in which the German situation differed was in the organization of the German revolutionaries, which could not accurately be compared with that of the Bolsheviks. Although Rosa Luxemburg was as firm as ever in her commitment to proletarian revolution, she did not want for Germany the same kind of revolutionary regime that Lenin had created in Russia. Writing rather bitterly on the events of the times, she applauded the Bolshevik Revolution itself but denounced the dictatorship of the Bolshevik Party that Lenin had imposed on Russia. As she saw it, this was in practice the elitism she had denounced in theory some fifteen years earlier. True, Marx and Engels had spoken of "a dictatorship of the proletariat" as a transition between capitalism and socialism, but she argued that Lenin had made the Bolshevik Party a substitute for the proletariat. She reiterated her view that a "dictatorship of the proletariat" must be a "dictatorship of the masses," not an elite proxy; she rejected what she considered a Leninist conceptualization of the German revolution.

At the close of 1918, when the various German radicals—the

Luxemburg-inspired "Spartacists," the Bremen Left-Radicals, and the Berlin Shop Stewards[3]—gathered in Berlin to found the new German Communist Party (KPD), Luxemburg warned that the German revolution was not immediately at hand. Should the KPD go out into the streets to do battle that winter, she believed, Lenin's ego might well be served but not the German workers. Not only was she alarmed at the prospects of an elitist-vanguard coup, she was further disturbed by word from Moscow that Lenin had called for the founding congress of a new "Communist International," dedicated to revolution, to meet in Moscow in a few weeks. Recognizing that under these circumstances the "International" would be excessively subject to Lenin's control, she urged her German comrades not to go running hastily to Moscow, admonishing that such a new organization should be formed only under truly international conditions. In short, while Luxemburg supported the development of international revolutionary consciousness, she refused to accept Lenin's call for a new international and did not support an immediate insurrection in Berlin.

Even Karl Radek, who had sneaked into Berlin as Lenin's emissary, recognized the correctness of Luxemburg's analysis. Well aware that a truly revolutionary opportunity did not exist, he joined Luxemburg in speaking against any KPD revolutionary action for the moment, although he resorted to Aesopian language in doing so, noting that the German situation resembled the Russian one of April, 1917.

Events, however, quickly outran both Luxemburg and Radek. In the bitterness of the aftermath of the war, there were constant altercations between German radicals and police forces, and, in January 1919, the radicals, overconfident about the revolutionary potential of the situation, launched the ill-fated Spartacist uprising in Berlin. That the insurrection never had a chance Luxemburg knew, but she allowed her commitment to the revolutionary proletariat to overrule her better judgment. Although she had joined the uprising with

---

[3] The Shop Stewards were not a union group, as their name suggests, but a small organization of radicals; the Bremen group, led by Johannes Knief, had ties to Radek and others of the Zimmerwald Left. The term Spartacus, used by Leibknecht as a psuedonym during the war, derived from the slave revolt against Rome in 73 B.C. and led by a gladiator of that name.

great misgivings, upon being captured both she and Karl Liebknecht were summarily executed. The uprising itself was suppressed and the German revolution came to an abrupt halt. Radek, who had none of Luxemburg's sense of commitment, had never joined the uprising and managed to hide for several weeks. He was then captured, imprisoned, and eventually returned to Russia in 1920.

In the south of Germany, Bavarian revolutionary prospects were also aborted. There a "socialist republic," with support not only from Munich workers but from disaffected Bavarian peasants, was established at the end of the war. However, in February 1919 its leader Kurt Eisner was assassinated, and by spring the Soviet Republic of Bavaria came to a bloody end.

Lenin was, of course, painfully aware of his inability to help either the Berlin Spartacists or the Bavarian separatists. The assassination of Rosa Luxemburg came as a particular trauma. In the Second International she had personified the commitment to revolutionary socialism as no one, not even Lenin, could. Although she had declined to support his revolutionary tactics, he was genuinely grieved by her death and the subsequent curtailment of revolutionary opportunity in Germany.

On the other hand, Luxemburg's death and the German debacle did provide Lenin with an opportunity to assert his leadership over international communism by removing the one person who could, and probably would, challenge him on this score. Even with the Russian civil war raging on several fronts, Lenin was determined to convene as quickly as possible the founding congress of a new Communist international. The Second International had effectively become moribund with the outbreak of war in 1914, but, as talk began to develop amongst socialists after the war about reviving the Second International, Lenin felt an even more urgent need to call his international into being.

In March 1919 a motley crew of forty-three "delegates" assembled in Petrograd and then, because of the proximity to the city of anti-Bolshevik forces, moved to Moscow. Of this assemblage, thirty-eight were for one reason or another already resident in Soviet Russia. Only five had actually traveled to Russia to hear the Bolsheviks proclaim the existence of the Third, or Communist, International (later more commonly known by the acronym *Comintern*). Luxemburg's worst fears were realized; Lenin had exploited the situation to create a Bolshevik-dominated organization. Hugo Eberlein, a German Communist, came to Russia bearing Rosa Luxemburg's posthumous veto, but on the crucial founding vote he was cowed into abstention. To wrap up some semblance of legality, the conference declared that the Zimmerwald Movement had terminated its mission and that Balabanoff would serve as secretary of the Comintern's Executive Committee, thus providing a final transition between Zimmerwald and the new International.

## LENIN POSTPONES "WORLD REVOLUTION"

The First Congress of the Communist International did little more than proclaim the new international's existence. The prospects for revolution were not as rosy as the rhetoric sounded. The Bolshevik regime was engaged in a life-and-death struggle whose outcome in mid-1919 seemed highly problematical. The Spartacists were nothing but a bitter memory; so too was the short-lived Bavarian Soviet Republic. A new hope emerged in Budapest where, in reaction to popular discontent with the borders assigned the new Hungarian state, the Communist leader Bela Kun in April 1919 formed a coalition government and proclaimed a Republic of Soviets. Kun was, however, pursuing an illusion. The support for his regime emanated not from anticapitalist sentiments but from nationalism. By the summer of that same year it was clear that he was no more able to prevent the shrinkage of Hungary's borders than his predecessors had been. The march of a Rumanian army into Budapest was the last straw, and Kun's "Republic of Soviets" fell.

As with Germany, Lenin had to watch the Hungarian developments from the sidelines. No common border between Hungary and Russia then existed which might have facilitated a Soviet rescue of the Kun regime. In any case, considering the dire position at that moment of the Bolsheviks in their own civil war, it would have been unlikely that Lenin could have spared troops for Hungary even if the common border existed.

The final crisis of international revolutionary commitment came in the showdown with Soviet Russia's new western neighbor, the Republic of Poland. One immediate result of the collapse of the German Empire and the concomitant disintegration of the Austrian Empire had been the resurrection of the Polish state in Eastern Europe.

The borders of the new Poland, particularly its Russian border, were vague. Since they lacked any clearly defined ethnic, natural, or historic basis, they tended to reflect the lines occupied by the respective armies. Since February 1919 there had been constant friction on the Russian-Polish frontiers, and with the Russians mired in civil war Polish troops usually got the better of the encounters. Although the Poles had no love for the Bolsheviks, they were also suspicious of the anti-Bolshevik forces, who they feared would seek to reestablish the Tsarist Empire, which formerly had included a substantial portion of the new Poland. Throughout 1919 Lenin had been successful in exploiting this fear and precluding any alliance between the Poles and the White Armies, an alliance that could have conceivably toppled the Bolsheviks in 1919.

By early 1920, however, when for the first time a Bolshevik victory seemed likely, Bolshevik relations with the Poles deteriorated as fears of a Tsarist revival ebbed. The Poles now began to maneuver for a Polish hegemony in East Europe, and toward this end they launched in April 1920 an invasion to "liberate" the Ukraine from Russian rule. The result was that what had been border skirmishes now developed into full-scale war between Poland and Soviet Russia.

Lenin's initial problem was military—becoming quite serious when the Polish army seized Kiev—but that was alleviated in June by a successful counteroffensive in the north by the Red Army. Political matters were of greater consequence, however. Lenin had to consider whether the Red Army's mission was to defend Russian soil, or, given the prospects of the moment, to lead the world revolution westward. Britain and France made it clear that they would not tolerate an "On to Warsaw" drive, but should the Soviet regime be bound by threats of capitalist powers?

Buffeted by conflicting advice from Polish Communists, fellow Bolsheviks, and his military chiefs, Lenin wavered on the issue. Seizing upon Lenin's hesitation, the leaders of the Red Army, headed by the then twenty-seven-year-old General Mikhail Tukhachevsky, took it upon themselves to proclaim the world revolution reborn. On his own authority Tukhachevsky announced a "revolution from without," in which the Red Army would "liberate" the proletariat of Poland.

As the Red Army's counteroffensive drove westward, Lenin alternated between a policy of negotiating with France and England over a Soviet-Polish armistice and waiting to see just how much the Red Army could accomplish. British and French threats notwithstanding, Tukhachevsky led his armies toward Warsaw, and there, in mid-August 1920, he fought the battle that was to decide the extent of Lenin's commitment to the pursuit of world revolution. Tukhachevsky, who had overextended his army's resources in the drive on Warsaw and greatly underestimated the determination of the city to resist, lost the battle for Warsaw, and his forces fell back into retreat across eastern Poland. A few weeks later they were forced to accept an armistice, thus ending the brief existence of the "revolution from without."

The Warsaw defeat proved to Lenin, who had never fully committed himself to the wedding of military and revolutionary action, that the Europe of 1920 was not ready for proletarian revolution. Speaking to a workers' group in Moscow in October of that year, he made it clear that he now considered the task of the regime to be to concentrate on its own survival and to defer revolution for some later date.

## THE NEP AND THE BEGINNINGS
## OF SOVIET ACCOMMODATION

If Lenin needed any reassurance that his fears were well founded, it came quickly. Early in 1921 the garrison at Kronstadt, the naval base that guarded the approaches to Petrograd, mutinied. The mutiny was more than a military action; it was an ideological challenge to the legitimacy of Lenin's Communist regime. The sailors of Kronstadt, who had been involved in the original overthrow of the provisional government, enjoyed great prestige as revolutionaries, and they now demanded the creation of a government of soviets based on democratic procedures. This was seen as a direct threat to Bolshevik control; as such it was suppressed by a full-scale military operation led by Tukhachevsky, who had only recently returned from Poland. The fortress of Kronstadt was stormed and heavy casualties inflicted. For years after, the bitter irony of the Red Army storming a bastion of revolution haunted Lenin and his supporters.

The crisis was further exacerbated by the rising tide of peasant riots in the countryside. Throughout the civil war the peasants had frequently shown hostility towards the White Armies, which they feared would restore the estates to the landlords. They were now becoming equally hostile to the Bolsheviks, who were requisitioning grain in spite of their inability to offer suitable compensation, and during the winter of 1920 and 1921 several serious peasant rebellions against Bolshevik control erupted.

In 1921, faced with the deteriorating situation at home and the lack of immediate revolutionary prospects in Europe, Lenin sounded an ideological retreat. Rationalizing it as "one step backwards in order later to take two steps forward," Lenin proclaimed a New Economic Policy (NEP). The government now replaced outright grain requisition with a "tax in kind" which left peasants free to sell in the open market all grain in excess of their "tax." In this way the peasants were not only to be pacified but, so expected Lenin, to be positively induced to maximize production. Such a policy was hardly consistent with Marxism and obviously reflected the extent of the food shortage. The NEP also permitted limited private enterprise and, where needed, concessions to foreign capitalists.

The strategic retreat represented by the NEP made good economic sense, and indeed during the 1920s the Soviet economy registered a marked improvement. There was no doubt, however, that the NEP did violence to socialist ideology, but Lenin used this time to reinforce further the Boshevik Party's monopoly on power, hounding Mensheviks and SR's, jailing some and exiling others. Within the Bolshevik ranks some remained unconvinced of the wisdom of Lenin's policy; they felt that, in the interests of pacifying the peasantry, Lenin had compromised the position of the proletariat, not only of Soviet Russia but of the world.

Furthermore, Lenin did not confine his policy of retrenchment to internal affairs. Now that the civil war was over and the drive on Poland had failed, it seemed prudent to end the Soviet regime's isolation from the rest of the world. Under the skilled leadership of Georgi Chicherin (1872–1936), the Bolsheviks cultivated "normal" relations with the West, and by 1924 Chicherin had succeeded in obtaining diplomatic, and in many cases economic, ties with every major European power. While the NEP and the new foreign policy did much to contribute to the stability of the Soviet regime, the inevitable consequence was a downgrading of its commitment to revolution. Revolutionaries everywhere were forced to abandon their hopes that the Bolshevik Revolution would be the starting point for the international revolution. In 1922 Lenin suffered the first of the debilitating strokes that were to gradually remove him from the political arena, and in January 1924 he died. He was properly honored as the man who had brought the revolution to Russia. He had done so, however, only by the Machiavellian decision to put aside the world revolution so that the Russian Revolution might survive.

# SELECTED READINGS

E. H. CARR, *The Bolshevik Revolution, 1917–1923*, 3 vols. (New York: Penguin, 1976).
Carr has been criticized as pro-Lenin, insufficiently appreciative of Trotsky, and so on, but he offers by far the most-detailed analysis of the establishment of the Bolshevik regime.

STEPHEN F. COHEN, *Bukharin and the Bolshevik Revolution* (New York: Knopf, 1973).
This is a fine political biography which not only traces Bukharin's career but is extraordinarily perceptive in its analysis of revolutionary Russia and the kind of society people such as Bukharin were trying to build.

ROBERT V. DANIELS, *Red October: The Bolshevik Revolution of 1917* (New York: Scribner's, 1967).
Daniels concentrates on the momentous year 1917 and reconstructs the events that made possible a Bolshevik victory.

ISAAC DEUTSCHER, *The Prophet Armed: Trotsky, 1879–1921* (New York: Oxford University Press, 1954).
This is the first volume of a highly sympathetic three-volume biography of Trotsky. Probably the best of the three, it offers an insightful look at the young Trotsky and his development into a revolutionary leader.

IRVING HOWE, *Leon Trotsky* (New York: Penguin, 1978).
A short but brilliant essay on Trotsky and revolutionary responsibility.

V. I. LENIN, *State and Revolution* (New York: International Publishers, 1974).
Lenin wrote this work against the background of the 1917 revolution, offering a tactic to cope with the scenario of that year.

WARREN LERNER, *Karl Radek* (Stanford: Stanford University Press, 1970).
Radek's adoption of the Bolshevik cause illuminates the desperation of European radicals for a cause and a base.

LEONARD SCHAPIRO, *The Origin of the Communist Autocracy, 1917–1922* (Cambridge: Harvard University Press, 1955).
Schapiro reconstructs the steps used to eliminate all forms of political activity, even of other socialists, in Lenin's Russia.

LEON TROTSKY, *The Russian Revolution*, 3 vols. (Ann Arbor: University of Michigan Press, 1959).

Trotsky has all the prejudices of a victorious participant but writes exciting history.

ADAM ULAM, *The Bolsheviks* (New York: Macmillan, 1965).

In some ways, Ulam's book is a thinly disguised biography of Lenin, despite its misleading title. Ulam skillfully develops the march of Bolshevism, always headed by Lenin, to power in 1917 and its successful maintenance of that power in the years immediately following the revolution.

# 7

# International Communism and Socialism between World Wars

When Lenin led the Bolshevik Party to power in 1917, he was undoubtedly sincere in his claim that he was igniting an international proletarian revolution. In his own words to the founding congress of the Communist International, Lenin emphasized the necessity "of subordinating the interests of the movement in each country [Russia?] to the common interest of the international revolution." Yet, as we have seen, the realities of political survival forced him repeatedly to compromise his commitment to international revolution and then to postpone it entirely in 1921 for an indefinite period of time. Only in the march on Warsaw had Lenin taken any real risks for the world revolution, and even then he had seemed all to easily reconciled to abandonment of the venture.

## THE SECOND COMMUNIST INTERNATIONAL

In the summer of 1920 Lenin summoned the Communists of the world, as well as those who were not Communists but considered themselves revolutionaries, to the Second Congress of the Communist International. The invitation to the Congress was worded broadly enough to include almost anyone who could be described as part of the revolutionary movement. This time socialists, labor leaders, pacifists, all sorts of people disaffected with a system that had caused millions of casualties in a meaningless war came to Moscow seeking a movement that would provide an antidote to the ills of society. In contrast to the founding congress of 1919, access to Soviet Russia was now much easier, and there was time enough to make necessary travel arrangements. Unlike the narrow group who had attended the first congress, the 1920 Comintern Congress received delegates from thirty-seven countries, many of them, however, people whom Lenin would have preferred to be absent.

The agenda of the Congress was long and diversified, but the most important item by far was the introduction of a new set of criteria for admission to Comintern membership. In what seemed to be an expanded version of the vanguard approach first advanced by Lenin in 1902, the Comintern now offered a set of "Twenty-One Conditions" to be met by all prospective members. The terms were shocking to many foreign delegations.

Some of the Twenty-One Conditions were concerned with minor organizational points, but overall their requirements were severe: the unquestioning obedience of members to all Comintern directives; the establishment of secret organizational apparatus in all countries whether the Communist Party there was legal or not; purges of dissident members; and other strict measures which seemed both undesirable and unnecessary to delegates from democratic countries. In other words, the price of admission to the Comintern (and by extension to any part of the Communist movement) had become total obedience to Lenin and subservience to Moscow's demands and Moscow's needs. That many could not or would not accept such a price did not bother Lenin in the least; he did not want such people in the international Communist movement.

Over the next several months various Western revolutionary groups met to consider the Twenty-One Conditions, and in each case the pattern was distressingly similar: a confrontation between those who wished to tailor objectives and strategies to the needs of their own movements and those who placed Moscow's needs above all, claiming that support of the one communist regime in the world took primacy over everything, even the interests of one's own national revolutionary movement.

In the larger nations of Western Europe, the Twenty-One Conditions and the rigid discipline they implied created a major division in the ranks of revolutionary socialists. In Germany, for example, there had developed out of the antiwar faction of socialists a large separate socialist party known as the Independent Socialist Party of Germany (USPD). As far back as 1916, these socialists had broken with the old SPD on the issue of socialist acceptance of the war. Although they generally applauded the 1917 Bolshevik Revolution, the Independent Socialists had great difficulty in defining their own relationship to the German Communist Party (KPD) created at the end of 1918 or to the Communist International. Keeping their own separate identity, and steering a path between the now distinctly nonrevolutionary SPD and the presumably revolution-oriented KPD, by 1920 the USPD had succeeded in recruiting almost a million members. Lenin recognized the importance of this group and, despite some initial misgivings about the group's revolutionary commitment, had invited the USPD to send a delegation to the 1920 Comintern Congress.

At this Congress the indecision of the USPD leadership became particularly marked when faced with Lenin's Twenty-One Conditions. A divided USPD leadership carried the demands back to Germany for presentation to the membership. For almost a year the USPD leaders wrangled with each other and with the Comintern, until finally, at a special USPD congress in October 1921, the Conditions were accepted. A substantial number of delegates at this congress demurred. Those who accepted the Conditions joined the KPD—which was one of the document's requirements—while the remainder drifted back to the SPD, or, totally disillusioned, left the socialist movement. Lenin had achieved his goal of eliminating potential dissidents and retaining only those willing to accept Moscow's primacy.

With some variations, the German experience was repeated in France and Italy where revolutionary socialists had to choose between Moscow and their own national loyalties. One Italian leader, Giacinto Serrati, attempted to maintain Comintern membership without strict adherence to the Conditions. Lenin, who would have none of this, demanded that Italian Communists expel Serrati and his followers. Asked what he would do if Serrati then conceded on the Twenty-One Conditions, Lenin is said to have replied: "We will then write a Twenty-Second Condition!"

## THE EARLY COMINTERN

With the imposition of the Twenty-One Conditions, all pretense at an international organization composed of revolutionaries striving as equals to generate an international revolution became difficult to sustain. In its heyday, that is, the first six years after the Bolshevik Revolution, the Comintern met no more frequently than once a year; it's day-to-day authority it delegated to an Executive Committee of the Communist International (ECCI) and several spinoff groups.[1]

The ECCI always included a substantial number of foreign Communists, but practically speaking almost all of these were permanent residents of Moscow and had no real mandate from the Communist parties of their country of origin. Thus Karl Radek, one of the most prominent members of the ECCI from 1920 to 1924, was sometimes counted as a representative from Poland; likewise, Otto Kuusinen was a "Finnish" delegate, Bela Kun, a "Hungarian" delegate, and so on. Although none was in a position to return "home," the presence of these "foreign" delegates on the ECCI helped maintain the fiction that the Comintern leadership was international. For all practical purposes, however, the dictates of the ECCI were the dictates of Moscow, and few people were deceived into believing otherwise.

After 1920 the question of whether Lenin had ever seriously intended the Comintern to serve as an instrument of revolution, even a Soviet-dominated instrument, seemed more doubtful than ever. Lenin never trusted the Comintern to discuss policy, much less make it. The 1920 Congress had taken place against the background of the Red Army's march on Warsaw, but the Comintern, although naturally cheering the progress of the Red Army, was not even allowed to discuss openly the options and policies that might follow a Red Army victory. If the export of the revolution was not suitable for Comintern discussion, what then was?

After 1920 Lenin's immediate aim was the rebuilding of the Soviet economy. The success of the New Economic Policy depended

---

[1] The most important was the "Little Bureau," a small group of as few as five Communists who were the most influential Comintern leaders. However, the decisions of the "Little Bureau" were usually announced as ECCI decisions.

upon a period of respite from external confrontations that would allow full concentration on this economic revitalization. The development of a revolutionary situation which might force Lenin's regime to act beyond its capacity was to be avoided at all costs. Thus the ECCI began to develop an ideology which stressed that capitalism's crisis had temporarily abated and that what was needed in the immediate future was a period of moderation during which the workers were to be prosletyzed for the ultimate—not the immediate—victory over capitalism. At least temporarily, the Comintern was converted into an instrument of retrenchment, its role to avert a revolutionary confrontation rather than to generate one. The Comintern now served as a lightning rod to catch revolutionary rhetoric and render it harmless.

In early 1921 the first major harbinger of this new policy was a so-called "Open Letter" which appeared in the pages of the German Communist press. It suggested that all worker groups, Communist, socialist, or even nonsocialist, join in a common effort against capitalism. Such a tactic of cooperation belied the Leninist idea of vanguard organization and suggested a commitment to labor-union activities rather than toward revolutionary activism. It was not publicly known at the time, but the writing of the Open Letter had been supervised by Radek, then the ECCI's "expert" on German affairs, and was intended as a trial balloon to see how such an approach might be received.

While the ECCI was engaged in developing a strategy of cooperation with noncommunist forces, there still occurred an occasional foray into revolutionary activity which cast doubt on how consistent the ECCI could be in its policy of restraint. In March 1921 German Communists, assisted by Bela Kun, an ECCI member, tried to escalate a miners' strike into a political challenge. The ensuing violence, which resulted in almost 150 deaths, discredited the KPD. The Comintern was quick to disown the "March Action" as completely independent of Comintern directives or strategy. When the Third International Congress of the Comintern met a few months later, the ECCI openly denounced "left-wing extremism," blamed the KPD for impatience, and ignored the role of Bela Kun.

Putting the March Action behind, the ECCI now began to speak in the language of the Open Letter, setting forth a new strategy which it shortly proclaimed as obligatory for all Communists. This new strategy, known as "the united front," called for temporary collaboration with non-Communist worker organizations. Eventually there emerged two varieties of this tactic: a "united front from above" and a "united front from below." The former stressed cooperation with labor leaders for the sake of the workers; its only major activity was the convening in Berlin in 1922 of a meeting of all varieties of socialist leaders: the Comintern, the Second International, the Mensheviks, and others. Except for this one meeting, which produced more charges and countercharges than anything else, the "united front from above" did not fare very well.

On the other hand, the "united front from below" was a different matter. It aimed at winning over the rank-and-file membership of non-Communist organizations. Workers were to be persuaded that because their non-Communist leadership did not have their best interests at heart they would do well to look toward Communist leadership. The "united front from below" had as its ostensible goal the separation of workers from their leaders, but it did not offer the revolutionary alternative that it might have a few years earlier.

Absent from both varieties of the united front was any program for a vanguard leadership to prepare for future insurrection. The united front seemed only intended as a means to defuse rebellions and build strength for the future.

The adoption of the "united front" was paralleled by a new course for Soviet foreign policy. Now that Lenin had recognized that extension of the revolution was not immediately at hand, he began openly seeking some form of diplomatic and commercial relations with the Western capitalist world. This quest received an enormous boost in May 1922 when Soviet Russia signed the Treaty of Rapallo with Germany. This treaty, which reflected the ostracism both countries were suffering in the post-World War I world, provided the Soviet regime not only with diplomatic recognition but with important economic and military considerations. For this reason it now became incumbent upon Lenin not only to keep tight reins on the KPD but on the ECCI as well, in order to avoid any future March Actions.

Within the next two years most other European powers followed Germany's lead and reluctantly extended diplomatic recognition to the Bolshevik regime. Only the United States refused to follow the European example and withheld diplomatic recognition until 1933.

The "respectability" which the Soviet Union was now gaining further reduced the chances that Lenin would allow the Comintern to generate revolutionary activity on its own. Even after 1922, when Lenin's failing health effectively removed him from the decision-making process of both the Soviet regime and the Comintern, his comrades regarded his policies as binding and hesitated to launch any course of action not in accord with his priorities.

The Comintern's open commitment to united front tactics and its unspoken agreement not to interfere with Soviet foreign policy hampered its ability to cope with several revolutionary possibilities that developed in the 1920s. For instance, it chose to ignore the 1926 overthrow of the parliamentary republic in Poland by Marshal Pilsudski, as well as Gandhi's organization of a resistance movement to British control of India, both situations which Comintern activity might have been expected to exploit for revolutionary purposes had it remained true to its original charge of 1919. In 1923, however, the German situation took a dramatic turn which forced the Comintern to take note and once again consider revolutionary tactics.

## THE COMINTERN'S ATTEMPT
## TO INCITE REVOLUTION

The original impetus for the Treaty of Rapallo had come from the high-handed way Germany was being treated by the victorious powers, especially France, after World War I. The negotiator for Germany at Rapallo had been Walter Rathenau, a wealthy industrialist and presumably the last person to strike a bargain with Communists. Mutual needs of Germany and Russia had simply overridden the obviously disparate ideologies of the two regimes. Then, early in 1923, a new crisis—for both Germany and the Comintern—emerged. The French Army, claiming that Germany was derelict in payments of wartime reparations, occupied the Ruhr River valley, the center of German industry.

In the industrial cities of the Ruhr valley, German workers refused to work for foreign occupation armies, and the German government backed their patriotic endeavor by advancing the striking workers' wages anyway. To provide this money the government resorted to the printing press, thereby escalating to unbelievable heights what had already been a serious problem of inflation. Paper money soon became worthless—it took four *billion* marks to buy a dollar!—and the economy of the country fell apart. Many German Communists believed the crisis to be the collapse of German capitalism and the signal for proletarian revolution.

Soviet leaders, anxious not to ruin the new rapprochement with Germany, were reluctant to accept the challenge of the situation. Some, such as the influential ECCI member Radek, the only Soviet leader who had personally witnessed the Spartacist catastrophe of 1919, warned against any revolutionary adventures and secretly visited Germany several times to advise the KPD to be cautious. However, as the German crisis worsened through the summer of 1923, Comintern leaders became concerned that if they failed to act they would permanently forfeit the leadership of a German revolution. A new revolutionary group, the anti-Communist Nazis, now made its first appearance, causing alarm within the Comintern because of their success at rallying crowds with patriotic and vindictive appeals. The Nazis too were demanding a German revolution; their simplistic jingoism, which included fiery speeches by the then youthful Adolf Hitler, appealed to many of the same people who might have been attracted to the Communist cause. Revolutionary fervor appeared to be running high, and the ECCI was painfully aware that it was failing to utilize it.

The persistence of the economic crisis, the apparent militancy of the workers, the strident advance of the Nazis into the public eye, and the Communists' own reading of the revolutionary potential of the German situation gradually convinced most of the Comintern leaders that some strategy other than the "united front" was called for. Haphazardly, erratically, and above all belatedly, the Comintern leaders finally plotted a German revolution. They attempted to make common cause with the "honest patriotic masses" who were attracted to the Nazis, and they carried off a few joint Communist-Nazi rallies in the summer of 1923—although Hitler would have none of it—but the repercussions of this "National Bolshevism" strategy hurt the

Communists more than it helped. Some workers simply could not understand the common bonds between the supposedly idealistic Communists and the frankly bellicose and bullying Nazis. At rallies called to celebrate a common goal, Nazi and Communist followers openly brawled despite their leaders' calls for a common effort.

In desperation the ECCI finally consented to a strategy which involved Communists attempting to seize power in the regional governments of two German states, Saxony and Thuringia. The strategy, never well formulated, was canceled at the last moment, but due to poor communications not all of the KPD leadership learned of this. In the city of Hamburg, a KPD-led insurrection was easily suppressed by local police, and the German government, to whom the army had remained loyal, aborted the attempt to take power in Saxony and Thuringia. A revamped national government in Berlin then was able to induce French troops to withdraw from the Ruhr valley. It proceeded to initiate economic reforms that restored a stable currency and actually began several years of reasonable prosperity. The big loser in the 1923 situation was the Comintern, which had so grossly mismanaged events that it lost credibility with a large number of German Communists, not to mention the German workers.

In 1923 the Comintern experienced another less-important setback in the small East European country of Bulgaria. There, ever true to Comintern policy, the Communists had been dormant when a military-led coup had overthrown the agrarian leader who dominated the government. It wasn't until *after* the coup had taken place that the ECCI instructed Bulgarian Communists to form a "united front" with the deposed agrarian leaders and to launch a new uprising. By this time the moment had passed, and the insurgents, isolated from outside help, suffered not only political defeat but hundreds of casualties as well.

Lenin never had to confront the consequences of the Comintern's inept policies of 1923. Much of the last few months of his life spent in a semicoma, he finally died in January 1924. The Comintern leaders, however, could not so easily escape the consequences. In the political postmortems that followed, several prominent Communists, most notably Radek, were blamed for their poor advice in 1923 and removed from the Comintern leadership.

## POST-1923: THE "BOLSHEVIZATION"
## OF INTERNATIONAL COMMUNISM


At its 1924 Congress, the Comintern—which met after Lenin's death and hence was free of any directives from him—announced that the time had come for a major reorganization: henceforth, all Communist parties were to be restructured along the rigid lines of the Soviet Communist Party. This policy, known as "Bolshevization," was accompanied by "purges" to expel difficult members, for the discipline of the Comintern was to be carried out more strictly than before. The annual meetings, which had hitherto provided at least some forum for dissenting views, now lapsed into irregular convocations; in fact, the next Congress was not convened until 1928, and no others were to follow until 1935. Under such circumstances the ECCI and its smaller executive bodies became in effect the Comintern itself. In the mid-1920s, while Joseph Stalin gradually emerged as the new Soviet leader, the Comintern passed more and more into the exclusive control not only of the Russian Communist Party but of leaders whose political careers had been largely developed in Russia and who had little first-hand contact with the realities of the outside world.[2]

Then, in the late 1920s, the Comintern—hampered by a leadership that had little appreciation for the unique features of other societies and limited by a fixation on what was good for Moscow—committed its greatest blunder of all: its policy on China.

In the founding of the Comintern there had been no provision for any Chinese Communist activities—nor were there really any Chinese Communists for whom such provisions could have been justified—and, when the first Chinese delegates arrived at a Comintern Congress in 1922, they were treated rudely and not taken very seriously. The Communist Party of China, such as it was, had only been formally organized in July 1921, and even then it included only a small group of intellectuals who gathered under the "protection" of the European quarter of Shanghai. As such they were considered to have almost no direct mandate from the Chinese workers and were

---

[2] Stalin's rise to power is discussed in more detail in chapter 8.

treated by the Comintern leadership in the most condescending manner.

In Lenin's time the Chinese situation had been truly chaotic; regional leaders or warlords contested for hegemony, and there was no true central government in control. Foreign domination of the coastal cities had further complicated the Chinese situation. Moscow dealt with one or another regional leader, aware that political allegiances amongst them were uncertain and that in no way were any of them, in any sense of the word, communists.

In the search for a Soviet ally in China, some of the Comintern leaders—especially the Indonesian Communist leader Maring (also known as Hendricus Sneevliet), who had traveled extensively in the area —were much impressed by the revolutionary organization known as the *Kuomintang*, headed by Dr. Sun Yat-sen (1866–1925). The Kuomintang was not a Marxist group, much less a communist one, but many of its leaders had been impressed by the publication in 1920 of a Chinese translation of the *Communist Manifesto* and now began to talk in terms of historical materialism. For this reason the embryonic Chinese Communist Party began to consider seriously whether it might be able to make common cause with the Kuomintang.

As long as Sun Yat-sen lived, however, the Kuomintang was dominated by him, and he had his own political theory of socialism, a socialism that was far more Chinese than it was Marxist. Sun summed up his theory in the simplistic "Three People's Principles": nationalism, democracy, and livelihood. This was a personal theory of socialism, which he considered more appropriate to the Chinese situation than the dictatorship of the proletariat. Sun's independence and his insistence on keeping absolute control over the tightly knit Kuomintang discouraged any serious courtship by Lenin, who could not visualize any circumstances under which Sun would accept the Twenty-One Conditions.

Others, however, were more impressed by the Kuomintang's long-range potential as a compensation for the Chinese Communist Party's weakness, and in 1923, with Lenin seriously ill and unable to exercise the sweeping control of such matters that he once had, an arrangement was negotiated whereby the Kuomintang would become a "sympathizing member" of the Comintern and thus not subject to the Twenty-One Conditions. In return, the fledgling Chinese

Communist Party was ordered by the ECCI to join forces with the Kuomintang in the common struggle against foreign capitalist imperialism. By attaching the Chinese Communist Party to the Kuomintang, they believed they were implementing the united-front policy and thereby preempting any premature action. Soviet military and political advisors were sent to the Kuomintang to further guard Moscow's interests as well as to offer expertise.

The Comintern had, however, grossly underestimated the volatility of the Chinese situation. In March 1925 Sun Yat-sen died and was duly honored by the Comintern as a great revolutionary leader. His successor, Chiang Kai-shek (1887–1975), had visited Moscow in 1924 and was known to many Comintern leaders; he was expected to continue Sun's policies of cooperation with the Chinese Communists. Two months after Sun's death, however, there were demonstrations in Shanghai which led to the killing of twelve participants by British police. A wave of xenophobia swept the country, and Chiang used his Communist allies to take advantage of the situation. In early 1926, determined to expand his base of power, Chiang launched a northern march which was an enormous success, overthrowing the rival government in Beijing (Peking). As he increased his power he had less and less need of Communist support, however, and he began to divest himself of it. The Comintern, failing to perceive how far away from the alliance Chiang was now moving, hailed him as a new Chinese national hero and insisted that the Chinese Communists continue to support him. Only in April 1927, when Chiang marched into Shanghai and arrested Communist leaders, was the truth apparent. When Shanghai Communists attempted to protest the turn of events, Chiang repressed their protests with incredible cruelty, inflicting countless casualties on them and their supporters. Finally the Comintern reluctantly admitted that they had been backing an enemy.

The Comintern denounced Chiang for having "sold out," but it continued to insist that its basic strategy had been correct. Throughout 1927 various contradictory Comintern directives continually placed the Chinese Communists at peril, ordering alliances and uprisings that belied reality and simply increased Communist casualties. In retrospect, it is debatable whether a Chinese Communist revolution had any prospects of success in 1927, regardless of what tactics were pursued; if in fact there were any prospects, the bizarre, self-serving strategy of the Comintern served to preclude them. To make matters worse, at its 1928 Congress the Comintern congratulated itself on the "correctness" of its China policy and issued more directives to the pathetic remnants of Chinese communism, urging upon them the impossible strategy of rallying the "revolutionary workers." The predictable failure of this strategy led to more Communist defeats, which the Comintern repeatedly blamed on the dwindling number of faithful Communists in China, accusing them of being unable to understand and implement the "correct" Comintern strategy.

In the final analysis, only those Chinese Communists perceptive enough to admit the imbecility of Comintern strategy—and the importance of ignoring it—had any future in the Chinese Communist movement. The so-called "revolutionary workers" had been sufficiently cowed by the Shanghai massacre of 1927 so that, despite any number of Comintern directives, they were not about to launch a new revolution. If there was a disaffected class that could be recruited to the revolutionary cause, it was the Chinese peasant who had little to lose by a reordering of society. One of the first to perceive this was the school teacher–turned–revolutionary Mao Zedong (1893–1976), who refused to be trapped by the Comintern's suicidal tactics.[3] Recognizing the folly of ignoring the peasants, as well as the reality of Chiang's military prowess, Mao led a guerilla group in a retreat to the interior of China, where, away from the Kuomintang-dominated cities, they intended to rebuild the Chinese Communist movement. In the 1930s they did just this, largely by ignoring the Comintern and emphasizing the realities of their own situation.

The Comintern continued its existence throughout the 1930s and even held one final Congress in 1935. Its organizational apparatus still issued directives to foreign Communists, and in all too many cases it still could claim the loyalty of those who felt that the dangers of the world required continued fidelity to the Soviet cause. Yet the repeated purges, the self-justifying shift of blame for Comintern mistakes to others, and the emergence of a bureaucratic leadership unable to appreciate the broader dimensions of the problems of Communist

[3] Mao was for some fifty years referred to in Western literature as Mao Tse-tung. However, in 1979 the so-called *pinyin* version of Chinese names was formally adopted for English-language usage, hence the revised spellings in this volume.

revolution had so changed the organization that it was unrecognizable to many of its original adherents. When it was finally dissolved by Moscow in 1943, it was largely unmourned, even by revolutionaries.

## INTERNATIONAL SOCIALISM
## BETWEEN WORLD WARS

If it had accomplished nothing else, the Comintern had succeeded in separating revolutionary socialists, who were now called communists, from other socialists. After 1919, the term *socialist* used in a political sense came to mean a social democrat; there now was a clear distinction, at least in terms of political loyalties, between a socialist and a communist. The Comintern spoke of the socialists with disparagement because they considered them to have capitulated to the capitalist hegemony and to have rejected the communist commitment to revolution. Nevertheless, social democrats, or socialists as they were more commonly called, continued to claim political allegiance from European workers, in most cases more successfully than the communists.

The socialists had unquestionably abandoned their role as leaders of the revolutionary movement when they had acquiesced in the decision to go to war in 1914. For some socialists this had been an opportunity to legitimately enter the body politic, and once there they never wished to leave; others had been unhappy with involvement in the war and, as the war continued year after year, they had drifted into various forms of opposition. Eduard Bernstein, the father of evolutionary socialism, nevertheless joined the antiwar movement in Germany. In one case, the Austrian socialist Fritz Adler was so aghast at the carnage of the seemingly endless war—and to some extent the socialist complicity—that in a fit of desperation he assassinated the Austrian minister of war. Such an action, suggestive of anarchist rather than Marxist tactics, was disavowed by all socialists, but they were moved nonetheless by the extremes to which the hitherto pacific Adler had been driven by the war. It spurred many into asserting that socialists must act if socialism was to have any meaning for European workers. A broad coalition of socialists, including many moderates, called for an international meeting in neutral Sweden in the summer of 1917 to deal with the wartime dilemma. However, the Western powers refused to issue passports to the various socialists, and the one attempt to revive even a shadow of the Second International during World War I collapsed.

When the war finally ended in November 1918, the socialists were uncertain as to whether and how they should assert themselves. The situation was particularly acute in Germany, where the flight of the emperor to Holland had left behind a political vacuum. The more radical socialists, inspired by Lenin's triumph in Russia, were claiming that they could fill this vacuum. In this crisis the moderate socialists, led by Friedrich Ebert (1871–1925), perceived an opportunity not only to head off a Soviet-type regime but also to lead Germany in the social-democratic tradition.

Ebert had never been a revolutionary; prior to World War I his major activity had been to keep the SPD solvent and respectable. In this endeavor he had succeeded—some would say all too well, since solvency seemed to have replaced social change as a goal in some sectors of the SPD. Ebert now was gambling that in the reconstruction of a democratic Germany the socialists could, through the democratic process, gradually bring a socialist way of life to Germany that would be an antidote to the Soviet experience and to the challenge posed by the Comintern. Toward this end he secretly made an agreement with a major military leader to help suppress any Communist takeover if, in return, the military would accept socialist leadership of a provisional government. When the January 1919 Spartacist uprising was suppressed and Rosa Luxemburg and Karl Liebknecht were murdered, Ebert's party had to assume some of the responsibility since the action was taken in the name of a socialist-led government.

In 1919, in the city of Weimar, a new democratic constitution was drawn up for Germany, one which promised to allow the kind of democratic road to socialism Ebert envisioned. The resultant republic, known as the Weimar Republic after the birthplace of its constitution, did indeed offer hope for the development of socialism. Ebert became its first president, a position he retained until his death in 1925. Although the SPD was never able to elect a majority to the parliament, it often achieved a plurality of votes in elections and was often the parliament's largest party. Though the SPD fought for various labor

laws with some success, it never attempted any truly socialist legislation such as the nationalization of industry. When the economic
crisis of the Great Depression hit Germany in 1929, they continued to
fight for a democratic republic, a fight that was lost when Adolf Hitler
and the Nazis came to power in 1933.

The Second International had much more difficulty finding a
rationale for its continued existence after World War I. Immediately
after the war there were attempts to revive the International, and initially there seemed to be some chance that the organization would
recoup its old status. It began to meet regularly, and in 1923, with the
addition of some other socialist groups, reconstituted itself as the
Labor International, a title that diminished its historic ties to Marx
and emphasized its dependence on trade union leaders.

The Labor International never developed into the serious socialist organization that its predecessor, the Second International,
had been. It served mainly as a platform for the views of democratic
socialists, with no attempt to formulate an official program or strategy, and survived only as a weak organization, until World War II
made its continuation impossible.

## THE RISE OF FASCISM

If any movement seemed to offer radicals a viable alternative to the
Communists, it was fascism. The term *fascism* is correctly applied
only to the movement introduced in Italy in the 1920s, but practically
speaking it became a generic term used to describe a wide variety of
authoritarian, antisocialist movements, most notably in Italy, Germany, and Spain. Fascism had its birth in Italy. There, the aftermath
of World War I had left an insecure and economically depressed country in chaos. Disaffected workers not only organized strikes but occupied the factories as well. The Italian socialists, badly split among
various factions, were unable to make the most of their strong electoral showings and seemed helpless to prevent the deterioration of
labor relations and the economy as a whole.

The socialists' inability to cope with the situation was but one contributing factor to the national acceptance of a strong-man government, formed by the erstwhile socialist Benito Mussolini (1883–1945) in October 1922. Back in the days of the Second International, Mussolini had been not only a member of the Italian socialist movement but had usually been identified with its radical segment. However, shortly before World War I he had broken with Marxism over the issue of nationalism and become an ardent patriot. After the war he had organized a group of disaffected veterans into a "fighting force." Well versed in history, Mussolini had tried to evoke the glories of ancient Rome, calling his group fascists after the *fasces*, or bundles of sticks, once carried as symbols of imperial Roman power.

The fascists, who declared themselves to be guardians of law and order, harassed Communists and socialists alike. Mussolini was able to induce the king to name him prime minister, and from this post he used the force of the state to terminate all political activity. He then proceeded to reconstruct Italy as a repressive authoritarian state. The murder of the socialist leader Matteoti for his criticism of fascist excesses made it perfectly clear that Mussolini had foresworn any legacy of the Second International.

Mussolini had indeed abandoned Marxism, but he remained interested in socioeconomic theory. The fascist system he set up in Italy organized the country into twenty-two major components called "corporations." Some observers considered this arrangement a revival of syndicalism, and syndicalism's old mentor George Sorel even applauded Mussolini for his initial actions; Sorel did not, however, live long enough to view the brutality that became part of the fascist state. Through the new corporate structure the fascists presumably governed wages, prices, productivity, and, most importantly, policy. The system appeared to have possibilities, and, considering the chaotic society which Mussolini had taken over in 1922, many regarded it as an answer to both capitalism and communism, overlooking the fact that it meant the end of democracy in Italy.

A decade later, when Hitler led his Nazi party to power in Germany, the success of Mussolini's fascism was much on his mind. Nazism had a great deal in common with fascism, especially its get-even mentality and its chauvinism, but it also had many important differences, not the least being Hitler's stress on racial doctrines and his fanatic anti-Semitism. Unlike Mussolini, Hitler was poorly versed in socio-economic theories and had at best a minimal understanding of economics in any sense. He did have a flair for exploiting economic resentments, however, and in the hard times of the early 1930s these resentments abounded. Much of his rhetoric was laced with parasocialist ideas—such as the nationalization of department stores—but the stress was on ethnic enemies, who were presumed to be the cause of economic hardship, rather than the class enemies depicted by Marxists. As the German economy deteriorated in the Great Depression, starting in 1929, the Nazis began to acquire increasing electoral strength from a desperate population, some of whom obviously believed in Hitler's ideas that Jews, Bolsheviks, and other outsiders were at the root of Germany's problems. So pervasive was his appeal to a large sector of the voters that on January 30, 1933, the president was compelled to appoint him chancellor of Germany. In this post, Hitler then proceeded—as had Mussolini before him—to reconstruct the entire fabric of society.

His most immediate targets were the Communists and socialists. The former were blamed for burning the parliament building and outlawed in the name of public safety; the latter were rendered impotent by Hitler's abolition of parliament in 1934. Both Communists and socialists soon found themselves to be police targets and were forced to emigrate or to face indefinite imprisonment and eventually worse fates. Both the KPD and the SPD disappeared from German politics; only the Nazis remained.

For the next dozen years the Nazis remained in power, terrorizing not only Germany but most of the European continent as well. The Nazi trauma is well known and does not need recounting here. What is often ignored, however, is the threat posed by the Nazis not only to democracy but to the socialist and communist movements as well. While much has been written on the failure of democracies to perceive the threat of Nazism, and justly so, it ought to be noted that the Comintern was no more perceptive than the West and gave the Nazi problem a low priority, invoking until 1933 more calumnies against the socialists than the Nazis.

## THE POPULAR FRONT

The popular acceptance of such a brutish movement as Nazism in a country such as Germany still seems almost impossible. Perhaps only the desperation of the times even begins to serve as an explanation for this enigma. Socialists and Communists recognized and were concerned by the appeal that national revival, as exploited by the Nazis, had for unemployed workers and others living on the margin of the economy. The fact that to varying degrees a number of Central European leaders sought to emulate Hitler or Mussolini in establishing mini-fascist dictatorships—in which Communists and socialists were usually persecuted—was further cause for alarm. Even in the older democracies of the West fascist movements enjoyed some popularity; in 1934 one came perilously close to overthrowing the French Republic.

The growing threat of militant anti-socialist and anti-Communist movements finally convinced the Comintern that their own anti-socialist program was ill advised. Both socialists and Communists began to soften the mutual attacks and false charges they had been directing against each other. The Comintern dropped the term "social fascists" which they had been using for years to discredit the socialists; instead they began to speak in terms of a new cooperation. The venerable Comintern was even assembled, in 1935, for an International Congress. The major task, for what was to be the Comintern's last meeting, was the adoption of a formula for cooperation between Communists and socialists against the fascist menace. Called the "popular front," it was addressed primarily to France as an extension of the newly negotiated Franco-Soviet alliance.

The "popular front" was an alliance of Communists with other anti-fascist elements against the workers' most immediate danger, fascism. As had been the case with the Treaty of Brest Litovsk, the New Economic Policy, and other compromises with revolutionary commitments, the popular front was presumed to be a tactic of the moment, an outgrowth of the cooperative activity that had already begun in France.

In the spring of 1936 the French socialists, led by Leon Blum (1872–1950), a disciple of Jean Jaurès, won a plurality but not a majority in parliamentary elections. Blum then put together an unusual governmental coalition composed of his own socialist group, the French Communists—under instructions from the Comintern to cooperate in antifascist, popular-front groupings—and the Radical Socialists—who were, despite their name, neither socialist nor radical. Blum had formed a government designed to give France a progressive, antifascist regime; the Communists did not actually join the cabinet but helped to provide the parliamentary majority Blum needed for his program.

The Blum popular-front government, which remained in office for almost a year, marked the high-water mark of socialist-Communist cooperation. A good deal of labor legislation was passed but the deteriorating international situation weakened the government's claim that the time was ripe for such domestic changes. Further, the Communists and socialists split on the issue of the Spanish Civil War, which was then in progress, with the Communists urging direct French aid while Blum chose the more careful path of nonintervention.[4] The Radical Socialists further inhibited any plans Blum had for introducing basic changes in French economic life. Under such conditions the popular front could not long survive. When the government coalition broke down in 1937, so did meaningful cooperation between socialists and Communists, along with the illusion that they could bridge their differences in order to protect the French workers.

The 1930s were grim years for Western society. Problems like unemployment and economic stagnation whittled away at the belief in basic Western values such as democracy. The growth of totalitarian regimes, and their seeming success in coping with these problems, made many wonder if the inevitable price of democracy was economic depression. True, the prosperity of the fascist regimes was illusory, but few perceived this immediately. In the desperation of the times, many embraced the violence inherent in the fascist doctrines as a positive and necessary feature. Those who still hoped for a socialist resolution of Europe's problems were few. For some who remained socialist believers, only the Soviet Union offered any promise for the future.[5]

---

[4] See chapter 8 for a detailed look at the Spanish Civil War.

[5] The Soviet Union took its modern name in 1923, when it adopted a federal constitution.

# SELECTED READINGS

WERNER ANGRESS, *Stillborn Revolution* (Princeton: Princeton University Press, 1963).
This is a fine "case study" of the failure of Communist revolutionary attempts in Germany, 1921–1923.

FRANZ BORKENAU, *World Communism* (Ann Arbor: University of Michigan Press, 1963).
Borkenau's work is a history of the Comintern to 1938 as seen by an insider. Borkenau does have his own heroes and villains, but he is well informed and offers insights that are unavailable elsewhere.

JOEL COLTON, *Leon Blum: Humanist in Politics* (New York: Knopf, 1967).
A careful study of one of the major socialist figures of the interwar period, highlighting the dilemma of a democratic socialist caught between self-serving Communist allies and the growing menace of fascism.

NATHANAEL GREENE, ed., *European Socialism Since World War I* (Chicago: Quadrangle Books, 1971).
These essays chronicle the problems of non-Communist socialism in Europe.

HELMUT GRUBER, *International Communism in the Era of Lenin* (New York: Fawcett Books, 1967).
The Third International and its Zimmerwald forrunner are viewed through relevant documents.

——, *Soviet Russia Masters the Comintern* (New York: Anchor Books, 1974).
This volume completes the documentary history of the Third International.

GUNTHER NOLLAU, *International Communism and World Revolution* (New York: Praeger, 1961).
Nollau lacks the insider's information Borkenau has, but he offers a broader view of the history of the Communist movement, particularly in Europe, since the Bolshevik Revolution.

BENJAMIN SCHWARTZ, *Chinese Communism and the Rise of Mao* (Cambridge: Harvard University Press, 1951).
Schwartz documents Mao's development of a Chinese Communist movement, stressing Chinese rather than Soviet factors.

EDGAR SNOW, *Red Star over China* (New York: Random House, 1938).

A classic study of the early career of Mao and his movement, based in part on the author's interviews with Mao in the 1930s.

ADOLF STURMTHAL, *The Tragedy of European Labor, 1918–1939* (London: Gollancz, 1944).

As the title suggests, this book chronicles the inability of the European labor movement to cope with the dual challenges of communism and fascism.

# 8

# Stalinism Triumphant in the Soviet Union and in World Communism

# THE RISE OF STALIN AND THE REPUDIATION OF TROTSKY

At the time of the 1917 Bolshevik Revolution and for several years after, Joseph Stalin seemed one of the least likely people to emerge as the most powerful man in Soviet and world communism. Stalin had been an active Marxist revolutionary since the beginning of the twentieth century but not in the kind of role that one usually envisaged for Marxist leaders. His knowledge of Marxism was eclectic—some of his detractors claimed that he had never even read *Capital*—and his experience in the international Marxist movement prior to 1917 had been at best peripheral. He knew no Western languages, had spent only a very short period of time in the West, and was not at all involved in the Second International. Furthermore, he was not a Russian but a native of the ancient mountain kingdom of Georgia; to his dying day he spoke Russian with a decided accent.

That he was clever, well organized, and efficient was never in doubt. That he possessed qualities of national and international leadership, particularly in a movement where command of political ideology was so important, seemed unlikely, however. Even friendly comrades spoke of his being on thin ground in discussions of Marxism. Prior to 1917 his only important contribution to political ideology had been his booklet *Marxism and the National Question,* and even then it was rumored that Nikolai Bukharin had actually done most of the writing.

In the hectic year 1917 Stalin had been one of the first Bolsheviks won over to Lenin's strategy, an allegiance Lenin no doubt appreciated. When the Bolsheviks took power in November 1917, Stalin was rewarded with the governmental post of People's Commissar of Nationalities and eventually with the more important post of General Secretary of the Communist Party.[1] Few foresaw how effectively he would use the second post to develop his own power base. Lenin, on his deathbed, had belatedly dictated a warning to the Party leadership that Stalin was accruing excessive power through this post, but most of the Communist leadership of that time disregarded what was considered a dying man's blurred political vision.

It was a surprise to most observers that Stalin emerged as the major speaker at Lenin's funeral. Considering Trotsky's undeniable oratorical gifts one would have expected him to deliver Lenin's eulogy, but, for reasons that can only be attributed to Trotsky's lack of political acumen, Trotsky was far away on a duck hunt in the Caucasian Mountains and missed the funeral altogether.

In Lenin's last year the clear outlines of a party struggle for his position had already emerged. Just whom Lenin would have preferred to see as his successor is uncertain since he failed to nominate anyone. He made it amply clear, however, particularly in a "political testament" dictated to his secretary in his last year, that he wanted Stalin out of the top echelons of Bolshevik leadership, perceiving him as ruthless and self-serving. He equivocated on his support for Trotsky, but it was not hard to extrapolate from his remarks that if the choice were to be between Stalin and Trotsky, he much preferred the latter.

Trotsky, who considered himself the leading Marxist theorist in the world—modesty was never one of his virtues—was a clearcut contender for the post. His prominence and talent were obvious but so were his political liabilities. He had offended far too many party members by his abrasive personality and his obvious intolerance of those he did not consider to be his peers. Grigori Zinoviev (1883–1936), chairman of the Comintern's ECCI, offered himself as the leader of the anti-Trotsky movement, calling attention to the fact that

---

[1] Stalin did not receive the full title until April 1922, but he was, after March 1919, head of the Orgburo (Organizational Bureau), which controlled party personnel.

Zinoviev himself had been Lenin's closest comrade since 1907 and that Trotsky had not even become a Bolshevik until 1917. Actually Zinoviev was even less liked and certainly less admired than Trotsky, but he served as a convenient vehicle for the forces that were determined to abort Trotsky's drive for the leadership position. In the acrimonious debates that ensued, Stalin remained in the background, letting Trotsky and Zinoviev discredit each other.

When Lenin died, the leadership of the Bolshevik Party passed to a triumvirate of Zinoviev, his close friend Lev Kamenev (1883–1936), and Stalin. The common bond among the three was their anti-Trotsky commitment. Characteristically, however, Stalin retained a low profile while he marshaled his strength in the middle echelons of the Party apparatus, in which, since 1917, he had been advancing his own supporters through the ranks. Toward this end Stalin instituted a new recruiting plan for the Bolshevik Party, which in keeping with Lenin's vanguard approach had always restricted membership, numbering less than 400,000 at the time of Lenin's death. Now, within a few weeks, 250,000 new members were inducted; it was obvious that they had been chosen on the basis of their identification with Stalin.

The intraparty struggle had the overt appearance of an equal battle. The supporters of Trotsky could take comfort in his position as commissar of war, from which post he commanded the armed forces; the triumvirate, thanks to Stalin, had indisputable control of the party mechanism. The security forces, including the dreaded secret police, remained under the control of Feliks Dzerzhinsky (1877–1926) who out of dedication to his position refused to become embroiled in the succession struggle, although he was in most matters more sympathetic to the triumvirate than to Trotsky.

The appearance belied the reality, however. Trotsky, despite his success in guiding the Red Army through the Russian civil war, was not a military man and he enjoyed few strong loyalties among the Red Army leaders. Although he was still a member of the Politburo, the executive body of the Central Committee of the Party, he commanded nothing comparable to Stalin's well-organized cadre. Stalin dominated the entire structure of the Party, a fact Trotsky failed to take seriously until it was too late. Trotsky foolishly spent too much time building ideological "houses of cards," while neglecting necessary political work which he considered demeaning to someone of his stature and intellect.

In January 1925 Stalin exercised his new political power by inducing the Central Committee to request Trotsky's resignation from the War Commissariat. Trotsky, still trusting his mastery of Marxist theory to win out in the end, complied and gave up the one potential base of power he had. Then Stalin forced a break with his erstwhile collaborators, Zinoviev and Kamenev, who now joined Trotsky in a "united opposition" to Stalin's apparent takeover of the Bolshevik Party. Stalin defended himself simply by reiterating the charges Trotsky and Zinoviev had been hurling at each other only a short time earlier; at the same time he continued to tighten his own control of all key positions in both the government and Party.

The thoroughness with which Stalin maneuvered his opponents out of all positions of influence, discredited them, and broke their political power is almost a masterpiece of political strategy. His patience and willingness to wait for the proper moment complemented that thoroughness.

For example, when Trotsky was ousted as Commissar of War, Stalin was careful not to assign the post to someone too closely identified with him. Instead, the Central Asian Bolshevik, General Mikhail Frunze (1885-1925) was selected to succeed Trotsky. Seven months later Stalin felt emboldened enough to make the change and he summoned Frunze to tell him that the Central Committee had discussed his health (he had a gastroenterological problem) and decided that corrective surgery was in order. Frunze did not really want the surgery but, obedient to party discipline, underwent an operation which proved fatal. He was given a hero's funeral and replaced by Klimenty Voroshilov (1881–1969), a close associate of Stalin. Even Dzerzhinsky, who had been reasonably cooperative with Stalin, was not considered reliable enough. In 1926 Dzerzhinsky suffered a fatal heart attack at a Party meeting, an attack some say was induced by overwork, possibly loaded onto him by Stalin. Whatever the truth of the matter, Dzerzhinsky's post was filled by a Stalin subordinate and over the next decade by a succession of Stalin appointees.

By 1927 Stalin felt strong enough to move against the "united opposition." Anxious, however, to make certain of total victory, he sought the aid of the so-called "Right" faction led by Nikolai Bukharin (1888–1938). Stalin led Bukharin to believe that by routing the "united opposition" they would save Lenin's New Economic Policy, which Bukharin regarded as critical to the Soviet economy of the 1920s. Bukharin had become a champion of peasant prosperity through NEP's policies. Trotsky had urged heavy taxation of "prosperous" peasants (known as Kulaks) to help the urban workers. As such, Bukharin was all too easily recruited to Stalin's cause.

At the Party Congress of December 1927 Stalin and his allies combined to eliminate Trotsky and other members of the opposition from the Bolshevik Party. Even in his moment of triumph, however, Stalin used a tactic of patience and caution. Instead of treating the defeated oppositionists as criminals, he contented himself with scattering them in places of exile across the vast expanses of Soviet Central Asia and Siberia. Trotsky himself was sent to the small city of Alma Ata near the Chinese border. The exiles were decently quartered and allowed to work on political tracts and correspond with each other. On the other hand, they could neither gather together nor return to European Russia unless they recanted their support of Trotsky.

One by one, throughout 1928 and 1929, most of these people reasoned that loyalty to Trotsky's lost cause was not worth wasting away in remote exile, and they petitioned Stalin for a return to Moscow, promising loyalty to Stalin, his leadership, and his program. Stalin had achieved his objective: Trotsky, denouncing his former supporters as traitors and turncoats, was nevertheless almost totally isolated. Had Stalin chosen to have Trotsky executed in 1927, he might have endowed him with a martyr image that would have presented a serious challenge. Instead, Stalin had patiently awaited the effects of time and exile, a strategy which was completely effective in breaking the solidarity of the opposition. Stalin then ordered Trotsky expelled from the Soviet Union. Since few countries wanted Trotsky as a resident, for years he wandered from place to place. In 1937 he was invited to Mexico where he lived until his mysterious assassination in 1940.

## "SOCIALISM IN ONE COUNTRY"

With the expulsion of Trotsky, Stalin's triumph was assured. The adulation that began with the public celebration of his fiftieth birthday in December 1929 signalled the beginning of a personality cult that was to envelop Stalin for the next generation. Stalin, who had never claimed to be a Marxist theorist in Lenin's day, now even bested Trotsky in this area by enunciating, developing, and implementing a whole new approach to Marxism.

When the intraparty struggle had begun in 1923, there had been little to suggest that Stalin had any contributions to make to Marxist theory; in fact, he was not considered an authoritative voice on the exposition of conventional Marxist ideology. Yet in 1924, only a few months after the death of Lenin, he stunned the party theoreticians by advancing his own theory of "socialism in one country," a theory which claimed that since world revolution was not imminent, the Soviet regime should construct its own road to socialism. Utilizing the semidivine status to which Lenin had been elevated after death, Stalin claimed that "socialism in one country" was the logical extension of Lenin's policies. Fortunately for Stalin, Lenin had written enough that was ambiguous over the years to make such an interpretation possible.

To Trotsky, and indeed to most Marxist revolutionaries, the connection between the Russian Revolution and world revolution was inseparable. In fact, the Bolshevik rationalization in 1917 had argued that a revolution in Russia made sense only in the context of a world revolution. Trotsky had been openly unhappy with the Treaty of Brest Litovsk, the New Economic Policy, and other compromises which seemed to defer any attempt at widening the Russian Revolution into global revolution. Stalin's apparent defection from the cause of world revolution—as implied in his theory of "socialism in one country"—had been one of the major reasons that Zinoviev and Kamenev had broken with him in 1925. Yet Stalin's argument, despite the simplicity of its rationale, had great cogency both for the rank-and-file party member and, in the long run, even for the serious Marxist.

What was particularly sinister about "socialism in one

country" was its implications of nativism. It seemed as if Stalin wanted to purify Soviet communism by removing non-Russian elements. "Socialism in one country" emerged as the antithesis of Trotsky's theory of "permanent revolution." Stalinists charged that Trotsky was ready to sacrifice the fledgling Soviet regime for the gamble on an international revolution, implying that Trotsky was not patriotic, held Russia in contempt, and believed only in a Western revolution even though anyone could see that the West was not facing imminent revolution in the 1920s. When referring to Trotsky and other members of the opposition, it became commonplace for the Soviet press to use their original names rather than the revolutionary aliases by which they had become known to the world.[2] It so happened that many of the opposition were of Jewish descent, a fact that became obvious when their original names were published: Trotsky (Bronstein); Radek (Sobelsohn); Kamenev (Rosenfeld), and so on. The implication was clear: these people were not Russians but Jews whose loyalties were elsewhere. The charge was never made openly, but the message was there. Stalin, who ironically was not an ethnic Russian himself, was appealing to the old anti-Semitism of Russia, to the new party cadre who had never been involved in international socialism, and to the deeply rooted suspicion of all things alien that had always been part of the Russian scene. It was probably an unnecessary weapon, but it added to Stalin's support and laid the groundwork for the gradual diminution of Jewish personnel in the ranks of Soviet leadership.

Trotsky and his followers had hardly been defeated before Stalin revealed his plans for implementing "socialism in one country." His intention was to bring about an economic revolution in Russia of staggering dimensions through a policy known as the Five-Year Plan, an economic program which called for a total national commitment to industrialization. In fact, Trotsky himself had urged an emphasis on industrialization, and Stalin's plan came as a shock to Bukharin and others whose support of Stalin was partly based on saving the NEP and the opportunities for the Russian peasant.

---

[2]Because of the harassment of tsarist police most revolutionaries had adopted aliases. Thus Lenin's original name had been Ulianov; Stalin's, Dzhugashvili; Trotsky's, Bronstein; etc.

Basically the plan called for tripling industrial productivity and raising agricultural productivity by at least 150 percent, primarily to secure the trade credits necessary for the import of heavy machinery. It was an extraordinarily ambitious plan and had few chances of success. It assumed absolutely optimum conditions for the five-year period and total commitment by the population to its success.

The big loser in this new revolution was the Russian peasant. The plan called for 20 percent of the peasantry to be resettled in large collective farms which would be presumably more efficient and more productive than individual units. Actually about half of the peasantry was at one time or another herded into collectives, but the results were far from Stalin's hopes. Unable to resist collectivization any other way, Russian peasants slaughtered and ate their livestock rather than deliver them to a collective. Livestock herds were halved during the first five-year plan, resulting not only in diminished meat supplies but—in an agrarian economy short on tractors—diminished power supplies as well for pulling farm machinery. Food production not only failed to increase, it plummetted.

The industrial scene was also marked by chaos, although the agricultural disaster took precedence over everything. Despite the lowered productivity, grain was still exported to pay for machinery. The horrifying result was that by 1932 Russia was suffering a famine of unprecedented dimensions. The exact number of casualties will never be known, but millions of people died as a result of the First Five-Year Plan. This was hardly an auspicious beginning for Stalin's "Second Revolution." One of the casualties was Stalin's own wife, who apparently committed suicide in protest over the human cost of the plan to the nation.

The dilemma was particularly acute for those Bolsheviks who had supported Stalin on the premise that his program put Russian interests first. Although the First Five-Year Plan was officially proclaimed a success, Bolshevik Party leaders knew better. One wing of the party, led by Stalin's protege Sergei Kirov (1886–1934), was in favor of retreat and retrenchment; others, who apparently had Stalin's ear, were persuaded that only resolute commitment to industrialization was acceptable, whatever the cost to the nation. The latter faction prevailed, and the Second Five-Year Plan which was meant to "eliminate all capitalist elements" in the economy, went into effect.

For some the adoption of the Second Five-Year Plan seemed a callous and even traumatic step considering the consequences of the first plan. The major shock of the new plan, however, was not its economic goals but its political consequences, which were to become its most startling and indeed horrifying features.

The beginnings of crisis came in December 1934 when Kirov was assassinated in his office under highly suspicious circumstances. Kirov's death set in motion a chain of events which for the next four years was marked by a number of spectacular trials against old Bolsheviks, long prominent in the revolutionary movement. Starting with Zinoviev and Kamenev, the trials continued for three years, involving many well-known Bolsheviks including Radek, Bukharin, and scores of others. In most cases, the defendants confessed to all sorts of crimes against the Five-Year Plan, against state security, and in many cases to collaboration with the exiled Trotsky through intermediaries abroad. More often than not, the defendants were sentenced to death. This situation, in which the Soviet government appeared to be cannibalizing the former leaders of the Comintern and of its own regime as well, was a sobering one indeed.

The public trials were but the tip of the iceberg. Throughout the country people were arrested—sometimes tried, sometimes not. Millions of people disappeared in this period that has come to be known simply as "the purges." To this day historians have sought a plausible rationale for this national trauma of incredible proportions. Perhaps only in the works of Alexander Solzhenitsyn (1918–), the exiled Soviet writer, has it become even remotely possible to grasp the dimensions of what life was like under such circumstances.

Even Stalin's worst enemies had never expected him to engage in such a blood bath. He had always been known as a strict disciplinarian, but not as a terrorist. In the late 1920s he had not tried to have Trotsky executed, and in the 1930s few of the defendants had any real political power, certainly not of the sort Trotsky had wielded in the previous decade. Zinoviev, Bukharin, Kamenev, Radek, and the others had lost whatever political influence they once had in the intraparty struggles of the 1920s. What purpose was served by purging them? Moreover, along with Stalin's political enemies went many of Stalin's original supporters: Kirov, Kuibyshev, Ordzhonikidze (who, while not purged, died during these years under circumstances that retrospectively suggest foul play), and many more. Were these latter erstwhile supporters of Stalin the real target, because they had desired to pull back after the failure of the First Five-Year Plan? The answers are unlikely ever to be known. What is known is that the purges, whatever their rationale, terrorized the entire nation and probably precluded any effective opposition to the Stalin regime from organizing within the country.

Most remarkable of all during this period was the acquiescence of Western Communists to the events in Moscow and the willingness of many people who were not Communists to believe the incredible confessions that were frequently wrested out of the accused. Terrified by what they considered the primary menace—fascism—some Western intellectuals even denounced their own colleagues who dared to point out the evidence of their own senses: that in a perverted defense of socialism in one country, Stalin was murdering millions of people.

Stalin was not about to allow Western Communists to discuss Soviet affairs or to call the Soviet Union to account for its actions. In fact, the purges were extended to foreign Communists; many of them were summoned to Moscow and then never seen again. Furthermore, foreign Communists were cautioned not to start any adventures of their own in this period but to follow the tactic of the popular front and other strategies of a cautionary nature. Because of the decimation of their leadership by the Soviet purges, some foreign Communist parties were unable to function in their respective countries; in Poland the Communist Party was dissolved at the Comintern's behest.

From his exile Trotsky accused Stalin not only of murder but of ending the Soviet commitment to world revolution. On the latter charge even some of Stalin's supporters seemed to agree, albeit for different reasons. Trotsky's charges carried enough credibility to compel Stalin to make one final statement on the inexorable connection between the policy of "socialism in one country" and the eventual world revolution. In a so-called "Letter to Comrade Ivanov" written in 1938 and widely publicized, Stalin stated categorically that Russia's isolated socialism in one country could not be an end in itself and that victory could not be claimed until socialism had triumphed on the international level. Presumably this statement was meant to refute Trotsky and to serve as a placebo to impatient foreign revolutionaries.

## STALIN MANEUVERS WITH FASCISM

In the late 1930s all of Europe was under the pervasive menace of war. German rearmament and Hitler's threats made it ever more likely that an all-European conflict would again arise. The Nazi menace was used by many to rationalize Stalin's purges. Even the American ambassador to Moscow reported to the State Department that Stalin's purges were apparently cleaning out potential traitors. The debilitating effect of the purges on Soviet leadership—even the general staff was not immune, losing many top generals including the famous Mikhail Tukhachevsky—further diminished any commitment Stalin may still have felt toward agitating world revolution in the near future. From the point of view of revolutionary socialism, it is ironic that in the Great Depression of the 1930s, when the West suffered its greatest crisis of confidence in capitalism and democracy, that the Comintern, an organization ostensibly formed to generate revolution, met only once in 1935 for the purpose of ratifying the popular front, which hardly represented a revolutionary strategy.

But as had been the case with the German crisis of 1923, history refused to give Stalin's bowdlerized Comintern a total respite from revolutionary confrontation. This time the arena was not Germany but Spain, a country that unlike Germany had never enjoyed a high priority in Comintern planning.

Partially because of its geography Spain had long been ignored by much of Europe. Since the Renaissance it had been outside the mainstream of European events and had entered the twentieth century with an economy and a political system that could only be described as backward. In 1930, however, the monarchy abdicated and a struggling republic emerged in its place. Although all republics of the 1930s had difficulties, few had as many as Spain, which had no republican tradition to invoke. In 1936 a military rebellion, led by General Francisco Franco (1892–1975), attempted to overthrow the republic and the Spanish Civil War was launched.

The Spanish Republic was by no means a Communist regime, but it did have heavy representation from the Left, including quite a few anarchists. On the other hand, Franco's side quickly became identified with fascism as Mussolini and then Hitler began to intervene on his behalf with military assistance. If for no other reason than to preserve its important image as the center of antifascism, the Soviet regime had to aid the Spanish Republic, and by late 1936 Soviet aid arrived and played a role in preventing an early seizure of Madrid by Franco's forces.

The Spanish Civil War provided the Comintern with a new rationale for its existence; in its name Communists from all over the world flocked to Spain to fight on the side of the republic. But Spanish antifascists and the multinational volunteer army soon discovered the high price of Soviet aid. A disproportionate number of the Soviet personnel sent to Spain were secret-police officials who directed their attention to the various supporters of the republic. Mensheviks, Trotskyites, anarchists, and others fighting for Spain soon found themselves in more danger from Soviet police than from Franco. Many disappeared, never to be seen again, presumably executed or returned to the Soviet Union. The Comintern had indeed momentarily "saved" the republic, but at the price of destroying its leadership.

Having decimated the ranks of the Spanish Left and having limited the options of the Spanish leadership through his police officials, Stalin then abandoned the republic entirely at the end of 1938, withdrawing arms support and ordering (Communist) International Brigades out of Spain.

When Franco entered Madrid in triumph in May 1939 he announced that he had saved Spain from communism and anarchism. To this day there persists the question as to whether Stalin's quixotic policies toward the Spanish Left had not substantially helped Franco in his task of deterring Communist victory in Spain.

In 1939, however, Stalin had no time to mourn the death of the Spanish Republic. The international situation had so deteriorated that the overriding concern was now the defense of the Soviet Union from the growing menace of Hitler's Germany. Under Hitler, Germany had rearmed, cast off the restrictions of the Treaty of Versailles, and proceeded to challenge the Western powers repeatedly and with great success. In March 1938 Germany annexed Austria, but it was the fate of Czechoslovakia later that year that probably convinced Stalin beyond question that he needed a new course of action in international politics.

In the mid-1930s, Stalin had been persuaded that Soviet protection from Nazi Germany required outside help, and for that reason a Franco-Soviet military alliance had been negotiated. As a sequel to this treaty, the Soviet Union had also agreed to a supporting role in a Franco-Czech agreement that guaranteed the sovereignty and borders of Czechoslovakia.

The treaties with France proved worthless when in September 1938, yielding to Hitler's demands at the Munich Conference, France reneged on its obligations and agreed to the dismemberment of Czechoslovakia. Since France had failed to defend Czechoslovakia, the Soviet Union was not obligated to do so either. Realizing how worthless French guarantees were, the Soviet Union abandoned its faith in the treaty with France as protection against expansionist Nazi Germany.

In 1939 Stalin began to recast his foreign policy. The Western powers seemed to place little importance on the needs of the Soviet Union and were lackadaisical when it came to discussing mutual defense. Having just left behind the hectic period of the purges, with a weakened party and military leadership, Stalin was hardly in a position to fend off Germany. In a macabre decision, he decided that if he could not fight Hitler he might do well to join forces with him or at least pacify him. Hitler, despite his longstanding anticommunism, needed at that moment to assure his generals that the forthcoming invasion of Poland would not mire down the German Army on the Russian front. After both powers gently sought signals from each other, a so-called Nonagression Pact was negotiated in August 1939.

Within days of the signing, on September 1, 1939, Nazi Germany invaded Poland; England and France, finally realizing that Hitler could not be trusted or sated, declared war on Germany, and World War II had begun. For the moment at least it had begun without Soviet participation; Stalin had, at a heavy price, ostensibly bought neutrality.

Part of that price was credibility in the Communist world. During the 1930s Communists and Communist sympathizers had closed their eyes to the purges, rationalizing that the Soviet regime was the only regime in the world openly aligned against fascism. They tried to explain Soviet policies in terms of world imperatives and believed Stalin even when the facts told them otherwise. But for many, the Nazi-Soviet pact was the final challenge to their credulity and loyalty. As the American journalist Louis Fischer—never a Communist but highly sympathetic to the Soviet Union—put it "This was my Kronstadt"—an allusion to Lenin's suppression of the revolt of Soviet sailors at the Kronstadt garrison in 1921. By the thousands foreign Communists admitted that they had been misled and deceived. The American Communist Party, which had claimed over 75,000 members in 1938, never recovered the membership and public support it lost as a result of the Nonagression Pact.

The worst dilemma was that of the French Communists. Right up to the eve of the Nazi-Soviet pact they had been loud champions of a Soviet-led collective-security movement against the fascist menace. Now they were confronted with the spectacle of a Soviet alliance with Hitler and, moreover, the prospect of having to support Stalin and denounce their own government. The Communist leader Maurice Thorez, then in the French Army, tried to set a new example by deserting from the army and fleeing to Moscow. From there he sent word that capitalist France was unworthy of defense and that Communists should promote defeatism. Such a policy had little chance of success, and the French Communist Party suffered membership losses as well as public support. When France fell in 1940, some blamed national defeatism, although they might have been better advised to blame Stalin, who had guaranteed Hitler a peaceful Eastern front.

It was very difficult to be a Western Communist in the years of the Nazi-Soviet pact, that is, from August 1939 to June 1941. At best, it meant ignoring the Nazi reality, and at worst, excusing it; it was not a role most Communists relished. Less notice was given to the Soviet occupation, as part of a secret corollary to the Nonagression Pact, of East Poland, Lithuania, Estonia, and Latvia. This obvious act of high-handed imperialism was ignored while Communists wrestled with the task of rationalizing their vicarious alliance with Hitler.

The Soviet invasion of Finland in the winter of 1939–1940 hardly comforted Communists either. Although they tried to excuse this action with statements about Finland being an outpost of capitalist imperialism, they were in a very uncomfortable position. When the Finns successfully resisted for several months, the situation of foreign Communists grew even stickier, and they took little pride in the eventual Soviet victory in the spring of 1940, in which the Soviet Union annexed a portion of southern Finland.[3]

## THE GERMAN INVASION OF THE SOVIET UNION

In the long run it was, ironically, Hitler who saved the credibility of international communism. In 1940 the Nazi armies had enjoyed fantastic successes, defeating France, overrunning Belgium, Holland, Denmark, and Norway, and imposing profascist regimes in virtually all of the countries of Central Europe. Yet Hitler was unable to muster the naval capacity to invade England or the air domination to subdue it. Frustrated on the British issue he turned eastward, preparing for war against the Communist ally he had never really wanted.

When on June 22, 1941, without even bothering to declare war or offer any reason, Nazi units invaded the Soviet Union, World War II took on a whole new dimension. For foreign Communists, it meant a welcome reversal of roles. Now they could and did join resistance movements and became the greatest of patriots. Support of the Soviet Union became identified with the fight against fascism once

[3]The pressure on Communists to rationalize the Soviet invasion of Finland was not so much dictated by Moscow as by the defensiveness of Communists themselves. Even Trotsky, a few months before his assassination in Mexico, wrote a defense of the Soviet position vis-à-vis Finland.

again, a fight that made sense to both Communists and their putative supporters.

When the German war machine turned its guns toward Russia, the two years of neutrality that Stalin had purchased with the Non-aggression Pact proved to be of little use. Nazi units moved on a wide front, advancing almost at will, and in many cases, particularly in the Ukraine, they were greeted as liberators by a population that had been terrorized successively by collectivization and the purges. Whatever preparations the Soviet Union had made during the two years of neutrality proved to be inadequate in halting the Nazi advance. Only the onset of winter in 1941 saved Moscow from seizure, and only the barbaric behavior of the Nazi occupation forces turned the population toward stout resistance of the invaders. The Soviet people rallied to the cause of national defense, fighting bravely and, in the long run, successfully. The cost, however, was enormous; at least 20 million casualties and tremendous damage to factories, homes, fields, and livestock.

During the first two years of the Soviet involvement in World War II, while the very issue of survival was touch and go, Stalin made several conciliatory gestures toward the Western world, whose aid he desperately needed. For example, he recognized the Polish government-in-exile in London, despite Soviet collaboration in the destruction of Poland in 1939. And in May 1943 he formally dissolved the Comintern, which had long since ceased to serve any revolutionary function, but in so doing he offered its abolition as a symbolic act suggesting future coexistence with the capitalist West.

Once the tide of war turned, however, especially during the Soviet counteroffensive of 1943, Stalin's attitudes changed perceptibly. One early evidence of this change was his breaking off of relations with the Polish government-in-exile after they asked for an investigation of German charges that the Soviet Union had massacred thousands of Polish officers in the Katyn Forest area in 1940. At the time such a Nazi charge lacked credibility, and the Polish request did not imply an attack on the Soviet Union, but Stalin welcomed the opportunity to rid himself of any commitment to the prewar Polish government.

As the fortunes of war turned against Germany in 1943, both the Western powers and the Soviet Union had to reappraise the future of East Europe. Rightly or wrongly, Soviet leaders believed that they alone had stopped the Nazi onslaught. The lateness of the Western powers in making a commitment to land warfare in Europe led Soviet leaders to believe that the West had held back until the Nazis could inflict maximum casualties on the Soviet Union; Western hopes had been frustrated, the reasoning went, by the heroic Soviet defense of Stalingrad in the winter of 1942–1943 and subsequent Soviet victories. The Soviets, who believed that the victory dimly coming into view in 1943 was of their making, also believed that the peace, at least in East Europe, ought to be of their making.

The reasoning went a step further: with the exception of Czechoslovakia the countries of East Europe had been hostile to the Soviet Union and in some cases had even collaborated with the Nazi armies in the invasion of the socialist state. Therefore, considerations of revolutionary ideology aside, Soviet security could only be ensured by having friendly governments in these countries, governments which would not assist future enemies in attacks on Soviet territory. The implication was that "friendly" governments could be best defined as pro-Communist regimes.

Poland, because of its geographical position, proved to be the unfortunate touchstone of future Soviet policy. As the Red Army moved westward there was a very immediate problem as to who would assume the leadership of Poland after it was "liberated" from German occupation. At the end of 1943, a group of Polish Communists living in Moscow were formed into a so-called "Council on National Unity," and in the summer of 1944, as the Soviet offensive moved into Poland the council was installed in the city of Lublin as a sort of provisional government and named the Polish Committee of National Liberation. Stalin rejected Western suggestions that diplomatic relations now be reinstituted with the Polish government-in-exile in London. Thus, even while the war was still going on, the nucleus of a future Communist-led government was being installed in Poland, in a country where only a few years earlier the Comintern had dissolved the Communist Party entirely.

For the Soviet Union, however, the most-pressing issue was the defeat of Nazi Germany, a goal that was finally accomplished in May 1945 as the Red Army seized Berlin and all remaining German resistance crumbled. The war continued in the Far East, but the

Soviet Union was not involved in this area and only declared war on Japan in August 1945 after the atomic bomb was dropped on Hiroshima and the outcome assured.


## THE YALTA CONFERENCE


In May 1945 the war with Japan was at best a secondary issue for the Soviet Union; the crucial issue was the physical reconstruction of the Soviet Union and the reorganization of East Europe under Soviet occupation. There had been several wartime conferences to discuss the postwar arrangements for East Europe, but the most important and the most controversial by far was the Stalin-Roosevelt-Churchill meeting at Yalta on the Black Sea in February 1945. By this time victory over Nazi Germany was clearly in sight, and the issue of postwar settlement was urgent and pressing. At the Yalta Conference it was agreed that the postwar governments of East Europe would "broadly represent all democratic elements" and that the eventual future of each country would be determined by "free elections," with Stalin adding the important reservation that he expected such new governments to be "friendly," a proviso that eliminated almost all of the prewar East European governments.

For the next several years the Soviet Union proceeded to implement a program that while ostensibly carrying out the mandate of Yalta also created a Soviet-dominated East Europe. For some the process was viewed as a revival of the world revolution. Others saw it as crass Soviet imperialism, extending Soviet dominion militarily, politically, and economically over half the European continent.

In essence the process of "Sovietization," as it became known, started with the drive into Poland in 1944; it was finished by 1949. A pattern evolved in several countries of creating a coalition government of Communists and non-Communists, ostensibly in accordance with the Yalta agreements; underneath the veneer of broad representation, however, true power stayed with the Communists, who almost invariably controlled the ministeries of defense, interior (police), and communications. The added presence of the Soviet army of occupation further guaranteed Communist control. Life was made difficult for non-Communists, and the "free" elections, held in most countries in 1947, were a sham. The absence in most of these countries of a strong tradition of truly free elections worked to the Communists' advantage. By the end of the year, most of these governments were reorganized, anti-Communists were expelled, and other non-Communists restricted to meaningless posts, and the "Sovietization" of East Europe was essentially accomplished. There were, however, exceptions: Germany, Czechoslovakia, and Yugoslavia.

Although Germany had been totally defeated, the razor-thin margin by which Germany missed total domination of the European continent still frightened most of Europe, and especially the Soviet Union. In accordance with the wartime agreements, Germany was divided into Soviet, American, British, and French occupation zones. The city of Berlin, in the center of the Soviet zone, was itself divided into occupation zones (again, administered by the four powers) with access authorized along railroad, highway, and air routes. Soviet intentions regarding the reunification of Germany were at best unclear; for obvious reasons they preferred a weak Germany and may well have been deferring any decisive action there until the United States, which was demobilizing at home, withdrew its forces. Whatever the reason, the three Western powers were able to merge their zones in both western Germany and western Berlin but encountered difficulties in relations with the Soviet occupation authorities. Anxious to get local economies functioning, the Western powers in 1947 introduced a currency reform in western Germany; the Soviet Union retaliated by cutting off all ground access to Berlin on the pretext of "making repairs"; in effect, they launched a blockade of the city. The Western response was to supply Berlin by a massive airlift, which defeated the objective of the blockade. The eventual outcome was a division, in 1949, of Germany into two states: West Germany formed out of the western occupation zones and a so-called German Democratic Republic out of the Soviet zone (commonly known as East Germany). Unlike Poland, Hungary, and elsewhere, there was in East Germany no political mixing of Communists and non-Communists in a coalition government. The government was totally staffed by Communists and under the close control of the Red Army. The Berlin question remained unresolved, and the city has been divided and been a perennial crisis spot ever since.

The case of Czechoslovakia was far different. The prewar Czech government had been on friendly terms with the Soviet Union, and for this reason, it was allowed to return to Czechoslovakia after the war without dispute. Free elections were part of a long democratic tradition in Czechoslovakia, and in a genuinely open election in 1946 the Communists won 38 percent of the vote, properly entitling them to representation in the coalition government. The Communist success reflected both the discontent in the country over the Western acceptance of the 1938 Munich Pact and some peasants support for land-redistribution policies championed by the Communists. In the new government the Communists were awarded the all-important Ministry of the Interior, which enabled them to control the country's police forces. Using the Ministry to their own advantage, the Communists dismissed all non-Communist police officials and replaced them with their own supporters. A protest against this policy led by the anti-Communist Foreign Minister Jan Masaryk (1886–1948) was silenced when Masaryk either fell or was pushed from a window to his death in March 1948. The government, still living in the shadow of Munich, feared to challenge Soviet power, and it acquiesced in the reorganization of the country. Thus, in 1948, Czechoslovakia joined the other East European countries in the Soviet bloc and became a Communist-led country with non-Communists being gradually edged out of governmental positions.

Yugoslavia's experience in 1948 was truly unique. Here there was no experience with a coalition government installed under the auspices of the Red Army—although there had been a brief Soviet occupation of northeast Yugoslavia—instead a native Communist movement rose to power led by Joseph Broz Tito (1892–1980). Tito owed the Soviet Union far less than any other East European Communist leader. The others had spent the war years in Moscow and had only returned to their native countries under the protection of the Red Army. Tito had led a resistance movement during the war against both the Nazis and other anti-Communist resistance forces. He had become somewhat of a national hero, at least to Yugoslav Communists, and could exercise power without Soviet help.

Stalin found Tito's independent position to be intolerable.

Much preferring leaders who were totally dependent upon him, he shortly began to pick quarrels with the Yugoslav leadership; these culminated in June 1948 with the expulsion of the Yugoslavs from the Communist Information Bureau (Cominform), the official international organization of European communism since 1947. The expectation was that the Yugoslav Communists, alarmed at being cut off from the Communist bloc and left at the mercy of the anti-Communist West, would depose Tito and present Stalin with a repentant leadership ready to do his bidding.

Nothing of the sort happened. Tito's regime had been handpicked by him and was further bound by the loyalties developed during the long wartime resistence to the Nazis. In the crisis, Yugoslav Communists rallied to Tito and rejected Stalin. Perhaps Stalin could have ordered the Red Army to depose Tito, but such a step would have generated a new resistance movement in Yugoslavia, this time with Communist against Communist; Stalin bitterly gave in.

The combination of the various events of 1948 convinced Stalin that the time had come to cease looking for new acquisitions in Europe and to consolidate the Soviet position.[4] Recognizing the new monolithic nature of the regimes in East Europe, the various countries of the Soviet bloc were reorganized as "People's Democracies" in which non-Communist elements had no further legal standing. In each country, the Communist leadership was purged, especially of any leaders suspected of "Titoism," a new euphemism for national communism. A number of trials were held in 1951 and 1952 in East European countries which resulted in the execution, at Stalin's behest, of several Communist leaders whom he had himself installed in power just a few years earlier. The Communist "revolution" had now come full scale to East Europe, in a form that displayed more repression than reform.

Within the Soviet Union itself, prospects were equally gloomy. Despite genuine progress in the reconstruction of wartime damage, the political climate grew harsher. Several trials of erstwhile high officials portended a new round of purges. The forced deportation of

---

[4] There had been a Communist-led general strike in France in 1947, but it had been broken by the government. An attempt to secure an electoral victory in Italy in 1948 had fallen far short of its goal.

nationalities and the emergence of an official anti-Semitism further suggested that Stalin's late years might revive the bloody scenario of the 1930s. When Stalin suffered a massive stroke and died a few days later, on March 5, 1953, Communists may have been as relieved as non-Communists. In various ways, Stalin had come to symbolize the harshest expression of Communist revolution; many hoped that the worst of repressive communism had died with him.

# SELECTED READINGS

FEDOR BELOV, *A History of a Collective Farm* (New York: Praeger, 1955).
> This is a personal account of life on a collective farm and the problems facing its residents.

ROBERT CONQUEST, *The Great Terror* (New York: Macmillan, 1968).
> Conquest's book is by far the most-comprehensive analysis of Stalin's purges of the 1930s, detailing the individual trials and attempting to estimate the incredible dimensions of the purges.

MERLE A. FAINSOD, *Smolensk Under Soviet Rule* (Cambridge: Harvard University Press, 1958).
> A unique account, based on archives captured during the war, of life in Smolensk in the 1930s.

*History of the Communist Party of the Soviet Union/Bolsheviks* (Moscow: Foreign Language Publishing House, 1943).
> Stalin was rumored to be the author or at least supervisor of this volume which blatantly distorts history to justify Stalin.

ARTHUR KOESTLER, *Darkness at Noon* (New York: Signet, 1961).
> Koestler skillfully uses the vehicle of historical fiction to offer a rationale for the behavior of the prominent victims of the purges.

ROBERT H. MCNEAL, *The Bolshevik Tradition,* 2nd. ed. (Englewood Cliffs, N.J.: Prentice-Hall, 1975).
> Although this book is an attempt to show the role of all primary leaders of the Soviet regime (Lenin, Stalin, Khrushchev, and Brezhnev), it is particularly strong on Stalin and his impact on Soviet society.

ROY A. MEDVEDEV, *Let History Judge* (New York: Knopf, 1972).
> This is an extraordinary glimpse of Stalinism since it was written by a Soviet dissident still living in Moscow.

HUGH SETON-WATSON,*The East European Revolution,* 3rd. ed. (New York: Praeger, 1956).
> This book is probably slightly out of date, but it is still the best and most-original analysis of how Communist rule was imposed on East Europe.

ALEXANDER SOLZHENITSYN, *The Gulag Archipelago I* (New York: Harper & Row, Pub., 1974).
> This is an extraordinary memoir of life under Stalinism by the

Nobel-laureate writer who personally experienced the trauma and injustice of the system.

ROBERT TUCKER, *Stalin as a Revolutionary, 1879–1929* (New York: W.W. Norton & Co., Inc., 1973).

Tucker skillfully employs the tools of psychohistory to explore the rationale for Stalin's behavior and the motives that impelled him to seek absolute power.

# 9

# The Divisions in the Communist World

## THE RISE OF ANTI-STALINISM

With the death of Stalin there appeared to be no single Soviet leader who could exercise total mastery and control over the Soviet regime and the Soviet bloc in East Europe as he had done. At first, Georgi Malenkov (1902–), who had apparently been quite close to Stalin during the last several years of Stalin's life, was announced as his successor. He was to fill two posts: that of prime minister, which Stalin had held since 1939, and that of General Secretary of the Communist Party, which had been Stalin's base of power since 1919. However, Malenkov never had any real chance to exercise this dual power. In an arrangement that was reminiscent of the situation after the death of Lenin, a triumvirate emerged consisting of Malenkov, Lavrenti Beria (1899–1953; the dreaded head of the secret police), and Vyacheslav Molotov (who again took charge of foreign affairs). Despite some rhetoric about the heritage of Stalin, the edifice of Stalinism began to crack at once. Arbitrary arrest—an everyday occurrence under Stalin—ceased, and, in one major case in process involving Soviet leaders, it was announced that the charge was based on a hoax and the prisoners were released.

Almost at once it was clear that Malenkov would not be able to hold onto the reins of power. Less than two weeks after Stalin's death, Malenkov relinquished his post as Party general secretary while remaining prime minister. The lesser-known Nikita S. Khrushchev (1894–1971) was designated to replace Malenkov in the Party post, but this position now received a new designation: instead of general secretary, Khrushchev became *first* secretary of the Communist Party. This change suggested that the power of the Party's Secretariat was no longer to be concentrated in the hands of one man. There was to be no "new Stalin," and the Party confirmed this by referring to the "collective leadership" of the Soviet Union.

The triumvirate was shattered in July 1953 when Beria was arrested and denounced by the new leadership. As the Stalin associate most commonly identified with terror, Beria was a popular target, and his arrest brought open public approval, as did the announcement in December 1953 that he and several of his top aides had been executed on charges of treason.

Soviet policy toward the outside world, both Communist and non-Communist, took a new and somewhat conciliatory direction. Some of the worst Stalinist types were removed from leadership in several of the East European countries and replaced with more moderate leaders. Relations were reestablished with Yugoslavia, relations that originally had been severed in the name of Stalinism. On the other hand, worker demonstrations in East Germany and in Czechoslovakia were harshly repressed, a reminder that the system of tight control was to be maintained. In a prison camp at Vorkuta in the Soviet Union, a prisoner strike was not only squelched but followed by mass executions of the prisoners involved.

And yet it still wasn't Stalinism. The "collective leadership" was capable of reacting repressively to challenges to its power, but, unlike Stalin's time, there was no premeditated terror designed to keep the population permanently cowed. Just who was making the major decisions for the Communist Party in 1953 was not at all clear. It was evident that Khrushchev was a major figure but not, at least at that time, a dominating one. His prominence seemed to be largely vested in agrarian affairs. In February 1955 the "collective leadership" underwent another shuffle when Malenkov resigned his post as prime minister and was replaced by Nikolai Bulganin (1895–1975). It appeared now that the triumvirate had been replaced by a dual leadership of Khrushchev and Bulganin. For the time being, the responsibility for state security was split into two functions so that no new Beria could arise and challenge the Party leadership.

In the next year Bulganin and Khrushchev traveled all over the world, visiting non-Communist countries as well as Communist ones and generally purveying the idea, discreetly, that the Soviet Union had mellowed considerably since Stalin's death. In what seemed to be an auspicious omen for foreign affairs, the Khrushchev-Bulganin leadership, at a conference in Geneva in April 1955, negotiated an Austrian treaty providing for the evacuation of Austria by all foreign troops and for Austria to be independent and neutral. The euphoria induced by what was then known as "the spirit of Geneva" raised hopes that more-basic issues could also be negotiated in the future.

The denouement of the new leadership came in February 1956 at the Twentieth Party Congress of the Communist Party, the first congress held since the death of Stalin. In a secret session Khrushchev denounced Stalin as a vain egoist who had murdered good comrades and whose incompetence had almost cost the Soviet Union victory in World War II. Eventually the text of Khrushchev's speech became available to the outside world. Some Communists, particularly those most associated with Stalinist measures, were shocked; others regarded the speech as a signal that the time had come to end Stalinism in their own countries.

## CRACKS IN THE COMMUNIST BLOC

All Communist leaders were affected by the anti-Stalin campaign, but nowhere were the repercussions as sharp as in Poland and Hungary. Both countries had been chafing under leaders molded in the Stalinist image who were involved in the suppression of not only anti-Communists but of Communists who were supporters of "national communism," or Titoism. In both countries but most particularly in Poland, the stirrings of an anti-Stalin movement had long predated the Twentieth Party Congress.

The disquiet amongst Polish youth and intellectuals, which had been simmering below the surface for some time, burst into the open in the summer of 1955 when the Communist poet Adam Wazyk published in a Communist literary journal a remarkable piece entitled *Poem for Adults*. The poem satirized both the harshness and the bungling of Polish communism, accusing it of ruining the country and especially of corrupting and betraying its youth. In his closing stanzas, Wazyk boldly demanded that the Communist Party of Poland forswear false promises and begin to deliver on the legitimate expectations of a socialist society.

> We make demands on this earth
> . . . . . . . . . . . . . .
> for a clear truth
> for the bread of freedom
> for burning reason
> for burning reason
> We demand these every day
> We demand these through the Party.*

That such a poem could be published by a Communist poet in an official Communist journal was astounding. Some Party officials reacted sharply, criticized Wazyk, and dismissed the editors who had dared to print his challenge. Other leaders recognized that Wazyk had opened a discussion of a very real problem and that the Party might do well to heed his advice.

The old-line Communist leadership of Poland, installed in the days of Stalin, were more alarmed by Khrushchev's secret speech of February 1956 than by Wazyk's poetry. The leader most discomforted by Khrushchev's words was Boleslaw Bierut, who had been placed in charge of Poland by Stalin in 1944, but he never had to face the consequences of the anti-Stalin revelations because he became ill at the Twentieth Party Congress and never recovered, dying several weeks later in a Moscow hospital. Bierut's death did not alter the trend toward internal criticism, however, for as far as Wazyk and his followers were concerned the entire old Party leadership was discredited.

There were those in Polish communism who recognized the wisdom of change and the message of the Soviet anti-Stalin campaign. Premier Jozef Cyrankiewicz and Edward Ochab, who had replaced Bierut as first secretary of the Polish Communist Party,

---

*Adam Wazyk, "Poem for Adults" in *National Communism and Popular Revolt*, Paul Zimmer (ed.). New York: Columbia University Press, 1956. By permission.

were the most important of this group, and they were anxious to ensure an orderly passage to a reform program. Those too deeply committed to Moscow could not, however, admit that basic change was needed. General Constantine Rokossovski, one of the leading Soviet generals during World War II, was an important example of this group. Because of his Polish birth, he had returned to Poland in 1949 and had become its minister of defense. To many Polish Communists he was the symbol of Moscow's interference in Poland's internal affairs, and in the summer of 1956 the Polish Communist Party denied him membership on their Politburo. This action, a clear challenge to the Soviet Union's authority over Poland, was not taken lightly.

As a further expression of their newly found independence, the Polish Communists chose as their new party secretary Wladyslaw Gomulka (1905–) who had been arrested and jailed in 1952 during Stalin's purges of "national Communists" and Titoists in East Europe. The very fact that Gomulka had been imprisoned by the Stalinists made him a hero, especially to student activists who in the spring of 1956 had held repeated demonstrations against Rokossovski and other people who were symbols of Soviet control. Cyrankiewicz and Ochab saw the potential in Gomulka as a suitable leader for a transition to national communism. Ochab yielded to Gomulka his party post as first secretary, but he remained on the Party's Politburo to aid in the recomposition of the Party along the line of national communism. Virtually by acclamation, therefore, Gomulka became the leader of the Polish "revolution" and the hope for a new kind of communism.

Gomulka was a highly pragmatic, committed Communist and, in many ways, a Polish patriot. Polish history is replete with heroic revolts against Russian domination (every generation since the eighteenth century has launched such a revolt), but they all have followed a tragic pattern of heroism, martyrdom, and ultimate failure at the hands of a superior Russian military. Gomulka had no desire to add one more such failure to Poland's history. Instead, in October 1956 when Khrushchev and other Soviet leaders flew to Warsaw to discipline Polish Communists, Gomulka persuaded the Soviet leaders of the mutual benefits to both countries in avoiding a showdown. Convincing the Polish people that the Soviet Union had yielded to Polish demands, Gomulka was able to restrain the demonstrations, avoid any clashes with Soviet troops, and take charge of the revolution. He announced a new kind of communism for Poland, one which would be more responsive to the needs of the Polish people and, by inference, less responsive to the demands of Moscow. For the next several years the euphoria generated by Gomulka's "controlled revolution" served to placate the country and even to convince the anti-Communist Catholic Church to support Gomulka's regime as the lesser evil.

Although the Polish "revolution" of 1956 can be viewed as a limited success, its Hungarian counterpart was an enormous tragedy. Throughout modern history there has always been a certain empathy between Hungary and Poland, partly derived from a shared belief by both countries that they are the only truly historic kingdoms in East Central Europe and that other East European countries are relatively recent geographical upstarts. The events in Poland leading to a liberalized regime were followed with great sympathy in Hungary, but attempts to emulate the Polish example unfortunately had quite different consequences.

There was no Hungarian equivalent of Wazyk's *Poem for Adults*, which had served as a credo for the Poles, although there had been increased activity by dissident writers challenging the curbs imposed by Stalinism. In the summer of 1956 Matyas Rakosi, who had a long Stalinist past, was forced to resign as first secretary of the Hungarian Communist Party. Like Gomulka in Poland, Imre Nagy (1896–1958) now emerged as the symbol of anti-Stalinism in the Hungarian Party. In fact Nagy in some ways outdid Gomulka in this regard. He had been identified publicly with a policy known as the "new course" which sought to ameliorate life for Hungarian peasants and workers in the months immediately after the death of Stalin. The fact that he had been deposed in 1955 by the Stalinist Rakosi had made Nagy even more of a hero to Hungarian dissidents, who in the fall of 1956 began to urge that he become the leader of Hungarian communism.

There were, however, critical differences between both the events and the personnel involved in Poland and Hungary in 1956, ones which ultimately were more important than the similarities. For one, whereas Gomulka, with the consent and cooperation of the Communist Party, took charge of the Polish "revolution," Nagy never established control over the street demonstrations in Budapest or over the Hungarian security forces. The latter challenged the demonstrators and thus escalated the confrontations to the point where Soviet occupation troops were called in. Unlike Gomulka in Poland, Nagy was never fully successful in persuading Church authorities that his regime would represent dramatic progress for the people of Hungary. The fault was not exclusively Nagy's. In Poland the leader of the Catholic Church was Cardinal Wyszynski, who, although a resolute anti-Communist, had made a pragmatic choice between Gomulka and the Stalinists, openly throwing the considerable prestige of the Church behind Gomulka in the winter of 1956. The leader of the Hungarian Church, Cardinal Joseph Mindszenty, only recently freed from prison, did not fully comprehend the nature of the revolution and made several pronouncements that confirmed his lack of understanding. Finally, confused by events, he sought asylum in the United States Embassy.

The most crucial difference, however, was the role of the Soviet Red Army. In Poland, the Soviet Union had restrained the Red Army when it became apparent that Gomulka was in charge, had the nation behind him, and had demonstrated his clear awareness of how far he could go. In Hungary, Nagy never established the level of control that Gomulka had. On November 1, 1956, under pressure from the demonstrators, Nagy declared Hungary to be a neutral country and asked for support for that position from the United Nations. He took the step that Gomulka had been able to avoid: withdrawal of his nation from the Soviet Union's military perimeter. The Red Army, which a few days earlier had withdrawn from Budapest, now returned in full force, and bloody fighting ensued. Pitched battles were fought in the streets of Budapest, particularly in the worker sections of the city where the resistance was extremely fierce. In the first days of November, well over 100,000 people fled Hungary, most of them into neighboring Austria. Nagy and some of his top aides were arrested, held in prison for quite some time, and eventually executed. Whereas the Polish revolution had ended in triumph, the Hungarian revolution had produced a tragedy that neither side had really wanted. It also raised serious questions about how dead Stalinism really was in the Soviet Union.

# THE SOVIET UNION'S RECOGNITION OF POLYCENTRISM

World communism reacted sharply to the Hungarian revolution, to the challenges it presented, and most of all to the harsh suppression of the revolution by the Red Army. Individual Communists openly broke with the movement, declaring that they could not be part of a movement that suppressed workers. In France, the noted writer Jean-Paul Sartre publicly tore up his Party membership card, as did the American novelist Howard Fast. Several staff members of the American Communist newspaper, *The Daily Worker*, resigned rather than invent apologies for the suppression of the Hungarian revolution. There were well-founded rumors that even in the Soviet Union Communist Party "agitation" (indoctrination) sections were challenged by sharp questioning by party members on the Hungarian revolution. The official Soviet line that the Red Army had invaded (to crush "fascist counterrevolutionaries") at the invitation of their Hungarian comrades met with widespread disbelief. Yet some did believe it, and even President Tito of Yugoslavia justified Soviet intervention, thereby shocking many observers who felt his willingness to promote his new accommodation with the post-Stalin leadership had gone too far.

Western Communists were not as sanguine about the claim that resurgent fascism necessitated Soviet suppression of the Hungarian revolution. The large Italian Communist Party was extremely agitated over the Hungarian events and what they portended. Palmiro Togliatti (1893–1964)—one of the few major Communist leaders remaining who had also been active in the old Comintern of the 1920s—publicly defended the Soviet invasion as a "painful necessity," but privately he insisted to the Soviet leadership that the viability of European communism required the end of monolithic Moscow control and the building of a new system of world communism ("polycentrism"), a system which Togliatti had been urging since Khrushchev's anti-Stalin speech.

As the word implies, *polycentrism* meant the establishment of more than one center of power in the Communist world; Moscow would have to accept the right of native Communist regimes to make their own decisions in internal affairs. During the summer of 1956

Togliatti had engaged in open argument with the French Communists about the merit of polycentrism. After the Hungarian episode he avoided publicly calling again for polycentrism, but privately he urged the policy on Khrushchev. Although Khrushchev made no public pronouncement in its support, he did begin to pursue a policy with the East European states that essentially promoted polycentrism. Over the next several years Khrushchev, anxious to avoid a repetition of the Hungarian invasion, encouraged the development of strong native Communist leadership in the countries of East Europe, but he reserved for the Soviet Union the special right of correction should any Communist regime stray too far from Moscow's ideals.

Khrushchev's favorite example of a Communist leader became the man who had successfully challenged him in 1956, Waldyslaw Gomulka. It quickly became apparent that, despite his stand for Polish rights in 1956, Gomulka was still a hard working, loyal Communist who had no intention of breaking up the Communist bloc. Furthermore, by defusing many of the internal complaints in Poland, Gomulka had for the time being made Poland a more reliable member of the bloc. Considering the histories of the two countries there was no policy Gomulka could promote to make the Poles pro-Soviet, nor was such a policy attempted. Until Khrushchev's forced retirement from office in October 1964, he continued to exhort East European Communist leaders to follow Gomulka's example. Even in Hungary the new leader installed by the Soviet Union, Janos Kadar, was encouraged to ameliorate the harshness of Communist rule so as to avoid a repetition of 1956.

## THE BREZHNEV DOCTRINE

In some East European countries this reform policy was implemented more forcefully than the Soviet Union might have wished. Rumania, which had had one of the most Stalinist leaderships, started changing its policies in the 1960s to the extent that it began to challenge the dictates of the Soviet bloc in foreign affairs, especially in the Middle East. But it was in Czechoslovakia, after the fall of Khrushchev, that the tempo of change grew so rapidly that the Soviet leadership felt constrained once again to use its military prowess against a Communist regime.

There, with Soviet acquiescence, Alexander Dubcek had replaced the Stalinist Novotny as first secretary of the Communist Party. In the first half of 1968 Czechoslovakia underwent a policy of liberalization in internal affairs that far exceeded anything that the Soviet leaders had intended. During 1956, when Poland and Hungary had challenged Soviet hegemony of their communist parties, the Czech Communists had been totally uninvolved with the events taking place on either side of them and had thereby suggested to the Soviet Union their leadership could be trusted to develop change on a basis that would not harm Soviet interests.

Prior to 1968, there had been several harbingers of a changing atmosphere in Czecholsovakia. In the Czech film industry, a group of young directors made several films—"Loves of a Blonde," "Shop on Main Street," "Closely Watched Trains"—which were completely out of keeping with the didactic themes of "socialist realism" that the Soviet Union had imposed, not only on its own intellectuals, but on those of East Europe as well. These Czech films, which explored the human condition and all its frailties, coincided with a concurrent development in Czech literature, suggesting that the arid themes of mechanistic socialist heroes had become incompatible with the interests of the generation of the late 1960s. The free expression of the arts now began to spread to all aspects of Czech life, even many of the leaders of Czech communism seemed sympathetic to the new liberal spirit.

This newly liberalized atmosphere in Czechoslovakia came to be known as the "Prague Spring." Czech Communists began openly to discuss new political options including other varieties of communism, a free press, and even a reinvestigation of the death of Jan Masaryk during the communist takeover. Soviet leaders were deeply disturbed by these developments. Other Communist leaders, especially those from East Germany, also expressed alarm at the direction the Czech regime was taking. In July the Soviet leadership, supported by several other major Communist leaders, issued a warning to Czechoslovakia that it not wander off "the road to socialism." On August 20, 1968, just when it seemed that Dubcek had succeeded in pacifying the Soviet leadership, the Red Army, reinforced by troops from East Germany, Poland, Hungary, and Bulgaria invaded Czechoslovakia "to save the country from counterrevolutionaries." Unlike the Hungarian revolution of 1956, very little resistance was encountered; the Czechs recognized the futility of fighting such massive forces. Dubcek, first removed to Moscow where he was bullied into acquiescing in the Soviet occupation, was later returned to Prague; however, he was replaced by Gustav Husak, Moscow's nominee, as leader of the Czech Communist Party. Under Husak's leadership, the Prague government now agreed to an indefinite occupation by Soviet troops and began to curtail the freedoms which Czech communists had enjoyed during the "Prague Spring."

Very quickly, the Czech political climate changed from an outgoing, experimental quest for a humanistic form of Marxism to a harsh, no-nonsense, monolithic regime. Once again the slightest dissent could lead to imprisonment, and the recent free exchange of ideas was all but eliminated. Czech intellectuals who had the good luck to be out of the country when the Soviet invasion took place became permanent exiles; a few others were able to leave after the invasion and joined the growing exile community. For the majority of Czechs the exhilarating hopes of early 1968 were permanently eliminated.

For the Soviet Union, the squelching of the "Prague Spring" had hardly been a triumph. Once again Moscow had to explain a military action against a Soviet-bloc nation both to other Communists and to non-Communists throughout the world. Leonid Brezhnev (1906–), who had replaced Khrushchev as the leader of Soviet communism in 1964, responded to world concern with a clarification of the meaning of the Soviet policy of nonintervention. In what subsequently became known as the "Brezhnev Doctrine," the Soviet Union publicly reserved the right to intervene in any Communist country where it considered such action necessary to save Communist rule. It now appeared that any dissent from Soviet policies, especially in East Europe, would be vetoed, by military force if necessary.

# THE REBIRTH OF NATIONAL COMMUNISM
IN POLAND

The march into Prague sufficed to preempt any independent internal actions by East European Communist regimes, but it did not eliminate any of the perennial discontents amongst the populations of these nations. This was particularly true in Poland, where continued economic problems, chronic Russophobia, and various other conditions peculiar to Poland repeatedly undermined the uneasy "independence" Gomulka had charted for Polish Communism in 1956.

Late in 1970, economic difficulties led to widespread demonstrations and strikes in northern Poland. Gomulka, mindful of what had happened in Czechoslovakia, was not anxious to provide another test of the Brezhnev Doctrine. Whereas in 1956 he had used the loyalty of the Polish army to persuade the Soviet Union not to intervene in Poland, he now turned the army on the demonstrators. Casualties included at least forty–five workers dead and well over a thousand wounded. The demonstrations were suppressed and the Soviet Union deterred from intervention, but at a price that suggested that the "national communism" that Gomulka had helped to create in 1956 was dead. Indeed, although Gomulka had kept the situation under control, his actions cost him his political career. The Party demanded his resignation, replacing him with Eduard Gierek (1913–) whose appointment was meant to reassure both the Soviet authorities that control was reestablished and the traumatized demonstrators that a more flexible leadership would ensue.

Throughout the 1970s, Gierek attempted to keep Polish affairs on an even course. He had to deal with the continued economic problems of the country; the revival of political demonstrations, especially in 1976 when for a brief time the situation evoked memories of the 1970 showdown; and the ever-present danger of his Soviet neighbor. For a while his regime tolerated the virtually open publication and discussion of dissident political views, hoping that this policy would serve as a safety valve for discontent. However, the Polish workers, whose continued unrest was based on the persistence of economic hardships, were not appeased, and the economy's sharp downturn in 1979 further exacerbated an already difficult situation.

Early in 1980, as worker discontent manifested itself in various incidents of labor unrest, a rapprochement began to develop between a group of dissident intellectuals known as the Committee for Worker Defense (KOR) and various other worker groups. Both workers and intellectuals had been involved in the 1956 events in Poland, but not as part of a truly coordinated effort. This time KOR addressed itself to worker issues by urging that workers not restrict their battle to specific economic grievances but instead to demand free trade unions, which could effectively and continuously represent worker interests. Such trade unions were unknown in Communist societies, having been denounced in the early years of the Soviet experience as useless organizations in a society where the workers presumably owned the means of production.

All of this came to a head on July 1, 1980 when the Polish government announced massive food-price increases. Meat virtually doubled in price. The pent-up resentments among Polish workers triggered strikes throughout the country, the most important of which took place at the Lenin Shipyards in the Baltic seaport of Gdansk. There the workers closed down the yards and virtually defied the government to do anything about it. After initial vacillations, the Gdansk strikers chose fellow worker Lech Walesa (1943–) as their leader and began to issue political demands as well as economic ones. The government tried to crack down on them but found that this merely enhanced the strikers' prestige amongst all Poles. When Walesa demanded the institution of free trade unions, the politicization of the strike became complete. Then early in September it was announced that Gierek had been stricken with a heart attack. The irony of the situation led many to openly voice the suspicion that his illness was as much political as medical. After all, Gierek had come to power a decade earlier on issues similar to those now confronting him; the threat to his political career was the same as the one that had made him Gomulka's successor.

In the moment of crisis, the Polish Communist Party replaced Gierek with Stanislaw Kania (1927–), a party leader known for his commitment to discipline and order, and presumably a choice made to reassure Moscow that the Communist Party was not going to lose control over the situation. Kania, with an extensive background in state security, was cognizant of both the deep-rooted causes of the disturbances as well as the importance of reestablishing authority. Over it all, the impending threat of Soviet intervention spurred Kania to attempt to resolve the situation as quickly as possible with as little diminution of the Party's position as could be managed.

He recognized the legitimacy of all concessions negotiated with Walesa to that point, yielding on most of the strikers' demands: wage increases, televised Sunday masses, release of jailed dissidents, relaxation of censorship, and most importantly, free trade unions responsible to the workers and not to the government.

Throughout the rest of 1980 and into 1981, the restless workers continued to make further demands, while the government sought to moderate these demands, some of which were beyond the capacity of the Polish economy. The government struggled to retain its control, continually reassuring the Soviet Union of its effectiveness in coping with the situation. Various groups of workers formed a federation that coalesced in a workers' organization known as Solidarity. Walesa quickly emerged as the most visible leader of Solidarity and began to be treated as such by the government which begrudgingly had to acknowledge that he now spoke for millions of workers. Walesa himself perceived his responsibility as more than that of a spokesman, but as a voice of moderation. He shared with Kania the desire to avoid a situation in which the Soviet Union had a cause to intervene militarily; and this bond between the two men was often enough to allow them to bridge their differences.

Thus, for example, early in 1981 when workers demanded a five-day week, an impasse was avoided when a compromise was developed. The government argued that such a concession would entail an unacceptable curtailment of worker productivity; the workers, for their part, saw no reason why they should have a lesser advantage in a socialist society than their counterparts in capitalist societies, where the five day work week was the norm. Dealing directly with the government, Walesa accepted, in the name of Solidarity, a compromise whereby the workers would get three Saturdays off a month, the kind of concession that only a free trade union could extract.

Poland had, in the span of less than a year, undergone a peaceful revolution that portended a basic change in the political and economic life of the nation. Polish workers had asserted their primacy and essentially justified the tactic of the mass strike championed by Rosa Luxemburg almost eighty years earlier.* Solidarity was in all respects a worker organization, defending the workers, espousing their cause, and representing their interests. Communism has always claimed to be a society of the workers but, with quite limited exceptions in Yugoslavia, in no communist society have free trade unions, which are responsible only to the workers, successfully functioned as yet. Should they survive in Poland for a decisive period of time, Solidarity will have wrought the most important change in European communism since de-Stalinization.

*It could be argued that Rosa Luxemburg had urged the mass strike against capitalist societies and that the Poland of 1980 professed to be a socialist society. However, one might also note her 1918 criticism of the Bolshevik Revolution for Lenin's refusal to allow the workers to participate in the decision-making process. Although her name has not been invoked by Solidarity, they have been remarkably faithful to her principles and her tactics.

# SELECTED READINGS

GALIA GOLAN, *The Czechoslovak Reform Movement: Communism in Crisis, 1962–1968* (New York: Cambridge University Press, 1971).
Golan's work is a scholarly reconstruction of the development of a reform movement in Czechoslovak communism and its unhappy fate in the summer of 1968.

NIKITA S. KHRUSHCHEV, *Khrushchev Remembers* (Boston: Little, Brown, 1970).
Khrushchev's memoirs include little important information that was not already known but do shed some light on the man's character and the motives that underlay his policies.

M (pseudonym), *A Year Is Eight Months* New York: Anchor Books, 1971).
An anonymous journalist, presumably a well-placed Czech communist, offers a personal account of the attempt to humanize communism in Prague in 1968.

IMRE NAGY, *On Communism: In Defense of the New Course* (New York: Praeger, 1957).
In this highly tentative analysis, the ill-fated leader of the Hungarian revolution suggests a more moderate course for East European communism.

HARRY SCHWARTZ, *Prague's 200 Days* (New York: Praeger, 1969).
A member of the *New York Times* staff with long experience in evaluating Soviet policies, Schwartz has attempted a highly impressionistic account of the fateful "Prague Spring."

KONRAD SYROP, *Spring in October: The Polish Revolution of 1956* (New York: Praeger, 1958).
Each revolt in East Europe has spawned a number of books. Syrop's work serves to illuminate the forces involved in a national communist revolt.

MICHAEL TATU, *Power in the Kremlin: From Khrushchev to Kosygin* (New York: Viking, 1969).
Despite the choice of leaders in the subtitle— why Kosygin rather than Brezhnev?—Tatu's book is one of the better analyses of the leadership struggle in Moscow after the Stalin years.

PAUL E. ZINNER, ed., *National Communism and Popular Revolt in Eastern Europe* (New York: Columbia University Press, 1956).
Zinner offers a valuable collection of documents on the Polish and Hungarian events of 1956.

# 10

# The Development of Chinese Communism

## THE EMERGENCE OF MAO ZEDONG AS LEADER
## OF CHINESE COMMUNISM

Soviet relations with Chinese communism have always been delicate. During the 1920s, when the Chinese Communist movement was in its developmental stage, Soviet policy had almost ruined the movement and had certainly cost it whatever chances it then had at victory. The Chinese Communists, badly mauled by Chiang Kai-shek in the previous decade, and receiving a flow of unrealistic and sometimes contradictory orders from Moscow, spent much of the 1930s simply trying to survive. After the collapse of an ill-fated "Soviet Republic" in Southeast China, Mao Zedong emerged as the most capable of the Communist leaders; his success came from disregarding unrealistic orders from Moscow. Other Communist leaders had either been captured by Chiang Kai-shek's forces, had dissipated their strengths in factional squabbling, or had simply abandoned Chinese Communism because it seemed to have insufficient prospects for success.

Mao realized that direct confrontation with Chiang's superior military force was suicidal. Consequently he regrouped his forces, at that time numbering less than 100,000 men, and in 1934–1935 led them on a long and difficult march to Yenan province where the terrain offered some protection from a direct attack. The strains of the march depleted his forces, and he concentrated his efforts on rebuilding his army, content to wait for a more propitious opportunity for revolutionary activity.

In 1937 when full-scale war broke out between Japan and China, Mao's moment arrived. He formed a united front with a reluctant Chiang Kai-shek, who was at that time desperate for any help he could get in repelling the Japanese invasion. When the war finally ended in 1945, Mao's forces held much of northwestern China, while Chiang's armies were confined to the southern regions. The Japanese had earlier controlled much of the urban areas, and the industrial province of Manchuria in northeast China had been occupied by Soviet troops in the closing days of the war.

There was considerable dispute about the reestablishment of Chinese authority. Chiang demanded that his forces take charge of disarming the Japanese and establishing a central government, while Mao insisted on basic changes in the way China was governed. While each group was maneuvering for position, the Soviet Union ostensibly refused to commit itself to Mao's cause and asserted that it recognized Chiang Kai-shek's government as the legitimate government of China. The Soviet Union in many ways, seemed in no hurry to assist Mao. In August 1945, Stalin signed a treaty with Chiang's regime, in which the Soviet Union recognized it as the legitimate government of China. Although Soviet forces did allow abandoned Japanese weapons to pass to Mao's forces, Stalin was in no hurry to evacuate Manchuria, the industrial area that Mao considered so vital to his strength.

At first, the Soviet Union seemed to be in accord with the United States that a truce be arranged between the competing Chinese forces of Mao and Chiang. Early in 1946, when the Soviet Union began its phased withdrawal from Manchuria, it was more cooperative than it needed to be in enabling Chiang's forces, who by now were once again battling Mao, to move into parts of Manchuria. Mao's troops, interested in Manchuria's industrial capacity, challenged Chiang for supremacy there, eventually trapping his forces in an important communist victory. However, the Manchuria Mao inherited had been stripped of its industrial plants by his ally, the Soviet Union, which had dismantled most of the machinery and taken it back to Russia.

The United States, which had been attempting to mediate between Chiang and Mao, now understood that Mao's communist forces were much more formidable than had been realized, as was

Chiang's vulnerability. In January 1947, the United States withdrew its mission and glumly watched as the spreading civil war turned against Chiang's Kuomintang. The Communists, after first establishing their total control over Manchuria and northwestern China, turned southward and gradually drove Chiang's forces out of one area after another. The war came to an end in the fall of 1949 as Chiang withdrew from the Chinese mainland to the island of Formosa (Taiwan). Mao proclaimed a Chinese People's Republic with its capital at Beijing (Peking) on October 1st. Mao's victory was not a sign of popular support of communism but a lack of popular confidence in Chiang's Nationalist regime, which was widely considered corrupt, self-serving, and oblivious to the dire straits of the Chinese people. Mao had relied on the spirit of defeatism and lack of confidence in the Kuomintang rather than on ideological issues to gain popular support. The communism installed in China in 1949 remained a doctrine unknown and unfamiliar to the vast majority of the Chinese.

One of the first steps taken by Mao as the new leader of China was to go to Moscow in the winter of 1949 and to attempt to establish a peer relationship with Stalin. Ostensibly the talks went well, and before Mao returned to Beijing a Sino-Soviet treaty was announced providing for economic and political aid from the Soviet Union; Mao reciprocated with some appropriate statements on the role of the Soviet Union as the leader of world communism.

In June 1950 military forces of the Soviet-installed Communist regime in northern Korea, now called North Korea, invaded the south, and for a few months the Communists seemed likely to unite all of Korea under their control. However, an American-led counteroffensive drove the North Korean forces all the way back to the Chinese border. Mao, interpreting remarks made by General Douglas MacArthur as the harbinger of an American drive into China, entered the war with a Chinese "volunteer" army and succeeded in driving the American forces back approximately to the frontier existing at the time of the North Korean invasion. There the war stalemated until protracted armistice negotiations finally ended it in the spring of 1953. For Mao, the Korean episode was a necessary but costly diversion. The weight of evidence suggests that it was the Soviet Union that equipped and approved the North Korean invasion; however, it was Mao who had to physically intervene and save the day for North Korea, at a much greater cost to China than to the Soviet Union. Whatever the true responsibility for the initiation of hostilities, the war apparently strengthened Mao's resolve to build a viable Communist society at home and to do it with dispatch.

## THE SINO-SOVIET ALLIANCE AND CHINA'S "GREAT LEAP FORWARD"

The initial years of the People's Republic of China were extraordinarily harsh and repressive. The government confiscated private holdings in both the cities and rural areas and carried out widespread arrests and executions. Eventually the purges reached far beyond the formerly well-to-do and began to embrace any segment of the population considered to be out of step with the "thought struggle" encouraged by the new regime. The total number of casualties will never be known, but countless millions perished or were imprisoned in the transition to a Communist society.

Relations with the Soviet Union remained correct but not warm. Remembering the years that Mao had defied Comintern instructions, Stalin never fully trusted him and probably considered him another potential Tito. Mao, for his part, could not be expected to forget the cost that Stalin's follies had inflicted upon the pre-war Chinese Communist movement.

The death of Stalin in 1953 was hardly a blow to Mao; he did not attend the funeral, although he did pay proper tribute to him in a public eulogy. However, the second-ranking Chinese Communist leader, Zhou En-lai (1898–1976), who did go to Moscow, was struck by the extremely warm reception he was accorded by the new Soviet leadership. The following year Khrushchev himself came to Beijing to sign a revised Sino-Soviet treaty that considerably expanded Soviet aid to China, especially in the area of technological assistance and in the training of Chinese students at Soviet universities. In view of the industrialization needs of the Chinese Five-Year Plan, technological expertise was worth more than any direct financial aid the Soviet Union might have offered.

The new close ties between the Soviet Union and China proved to be shortlived. The first major strains on the alliance came with the anti-Stalin drive launched by Khrushchev in 1956. Mao, who had ample cause to regard himself well rid of Stalin, was nonetheless clearly annoyed that a decision with such momentous implications for world communism as well as for the Soviet Union had been undertaken without consultations with the Chinese leadership.

Later that year, during the hectic events in East Europe, the Chinese openly backed Gomulka in Poland, causing considerable tension with the Soviet leadership, who believed that all affairs in East Europe were the Soviet Union's exclusive concern and no business of China's. When Zhou En-lai made an "information" trip to Moscow, Warsaw, and Budapest, Soviet annoyance was hardly concealed. Soviet pride was badly served by Zhou's obvious eagerness to be a mediator between East Europe and the USSR.

Of even greater consequence was a divergence in Soviet and Chinese outlook regarding both internal policies and foreign affairs. In October 1957 the Soviet Union enjoyed a spectacular technological triumph when it launched the first space satellite. This feat not only established the Soviet Union's supremacy in space but, by implication, in missiles as well, since missiles were propelled by rockets. Secure in its new-found strength, Soviet policy now became a campaign for "peaceful coexistence" with the non-Communist world. The Chinese regime, on the other hand, humiliated by international ostracism and believing itself under perpetual danger from American attack, argued that if there was a new Soviet superiority in rocketry it ought to be used to advance the cause of world communism and not to promote peaceful relations with capitalist imperialism. The American fleet that patrolled the waters between China and Chiang's regrouped forces on the island of Taiwan was considered by China an immutable barrier to "peaceful coexistence," since its function was to prevent the "unification" of mainland China with Taiwan. Thus China was offended by the Soviet Union's newly accommodating foreign policy which seemed to ignore revolutionary solidarity and the common bonds of Communist regimes against capitalism.

## THE GREAT LEAP FORWARD

Chinese and Soviet economic policies had also taken divergent paths. After several years of chaos in the economy, marked by the displacements of millions of people, the "reeducation" of intellectuals, the jailing or execution of former landlords, factory owners, and others, Mao's regime became acutely aware of the lag in China's productivity compared with the rest of the world. In the middle 1950s, the Chinese began to formulate plans for a major new effort to catch up industrially with the Western powers. For the purposes of propaganda, Great Britain's level of productivity was the immediate target they set for themselves, since catching up with the United States seemed too unrealistic. The Soviet Union, on the other hand, was seeking to mollify its population with an increased commitment to a consumer economy, a commitment the Chinese felt to be incompatible with revolutionary communism.

Early in 1958, Mao proclaimed a new economic program boldly named "The Great Leap Forward," whose slogan was, "Twenty Years in a Day!" The plan had features reminiscent of Stalin's introduction of the First and Second Five-Year Plans. It called for the moving of millions of peasants into rural communes and for mobilizing the population toward making a personal contribution to industrialization by producing "pig iron" in their back yards. At the same time, the leadership of the Chinese Communist Party was beset by new factionalism. Liu Shaoqi (1898–1974) led a faction which sought to mitigate the unrealistic goals of the "Great Leap Forward." For a short while Liu held the title "head of state," but his efforts were insufficient to offset the dislocations that had occurred in the economy. As the poor prospects of the plan became evident, Chinese communists developed great resentment of the Soviet Union which seemed disinclined to help China if it meant any sacrifice at all for Soviet citizenry. What especially bothered the Chinese leadership was the Soviet introduction in 1959 of a new Seven-Year Plan which greatly increased the targets for consumer goods. Although the Soviet Union also simultaneously announced more aid for China, the Chinese were openly unhappy about Khrushchev's commitment to consumer goods at a time when the Chinese were so desperately trying to create an industrial base. The concurrent Soviet campaign for improved relations with the West further aggravated tensions. China, boycotted by most western powers, contended that the Soviet Union had acted in a manner not suited for the professed leader of world communism.

More and more, the Chinese began to speak of a Maoist approach to communism as being inherently different from that pursued by the Soviet Union. Although the term *Maoism* is used more in the West than in China, there was clearly a Chinese approach to communism that emphasized commitments to international revolution, to building a communist society at whatever price, and a readiness to adopt tactics of confrontation against the non-communist world.

The dispute simmered below the surface until 1960 when the small East European country of Albania began to criticize the Soviet Union and to applaud China as the kind of Communist regime fit to lead world communism. At the 1961 Congress of the Soviet Communist Party, an enormous amount of time was devoted to attacks on Albania. The Chinese delegation, recognizing that they were the true target of the attack, walked out of the hall. In a bizarre sequel to these events, when the Congress voted to remove Stalin's body from the mausoleum in Moscow's Red Square, the departing Zhou En-lai placed a wreath there, honoring Stalin in a symbolic act of defiance. From that point on relations between the Chinese and the Soviets became increasingly acrimonious. The Soviet Union, in retaliation, began to withdraw the thousands of technicians it had sent to China in the 1950s. The two countries engaged in open criticism of each other after 1961.

## RADICAL COMMUNIST CHINA DURING THE CULTURAL REVOLUTION

Within China Mao still faced a difficult situation. The country's economy had not improved; Chinese leaders ceased to speak of "The Great Leap Forward" as a solution to economic ills. The ranks of the party leadership were constantly being revised as various people were accused of failing to perform the tasks assigned to them; leaders were demoted, arrested, or even executed. The Soviet Union was now openly denounced as a traitor to Marxism-Leninism and a collaborator with Western imperialism.

The ascending tempo of the dispute with the Soviet Union concealed a much more fundamental dispute within China itself. There the failure of various government plans for economic development, the varying receptivity of social groups to the changes of the new regime, internal bickering amongst Communist Party leaders, and demands of an impatient youth, led Mao to launch one of his most-dangerous strategies: "The Cultural Revolution," an attempt to purify the Chinese Revolution by cleansing it of all presumably decadent elements.

Mao's sense of disquiet over the situation in China in the mid-1960s was evident to all observers. Moving into old age—he was now in his midseventies—he had witnessed the opening of an apparently irreparable rift with the Soviet Union, a collapse of his economic program, "The Great Leap Forward," and a prescience that he would not live to see the Chinese Revolution fulfill its destiny. He was further encouraged in this view by his wife, Jiang Quing (1910–), a political figure in her own right, who now emerged as a leading advocate of a radical program that called for a rededication of Chinese Communism to its revolutionary mandate. Mao now publicly admitted the failure of "The Great Leap Forward," attributing it to a lack of revolutionary commitment; many Communist leaders were purged following this public criticism. Jiang Quing and her fellow radicals, however, had a program in mind that was more far-reaching than finding scapegoats for economic failures.

In the summer of 1966, a youth movement known as the Red Guards was launched. Posters began to emerge in the major cities calling for a new dedication to the revolution, elimination of "bad elements," reliance on youth rather than age (presumably with the exception of Mao whom they treated with great reverence), and the elimination of alien and impure influences. Some observers' initial impressions was that the colorful posters reflected no more than the exuberance and immaturity of their authors. However, as the Red Guards swelled their ranks, proclaiming the Cultural Revolution in the name of Mao, they displayed an awesome amount of power, and were able to effectively attack any political leader they found wanting. One of their major targets was Liu Shaoqi who had, a few years earlier, appeared to be both Mao's possible rival as well as his designated successor. However, Liu's attempts to restrain "The Great Leap Forward" had constituted an unacceptable challenge to Mao. Liu's criticism of the program—that it was too heavily laden with ideological issues and wanting in economic realities—had proved correct. His perspicacity was intolerable to the Red Guards and their mentor, Jiang Quing. Liu and others like him, became the primary targets of the Red Guards, and by the end of 1966, under the pressures of the Cultural Revolution, Liu was "confessing" his errors while being relieved of all of his party positions.

The Red Guards were not satisfied with the mere fall from grace of the man who was now described as the "Chinese Khrushchev." The disruptions of the Cultural Revolution continued; numerous party and military figures were singled out as enemies of the regime. By now, however, Mao was alarmed by the "Frankenstein monster" he had created. The Red Guards in their overexuberance had disrupted the entire country, and he feared that if they were left unchecked they might well ruin the Party and leave China vulnerable to its enemies. In April 1969, at the Ninth Congress of the Chinese Communist Party, it was announced that the Cultural Revolution had achieved its aims and was, by implication, completed. Had the Communist Party not taken this step it was possible that the Chinese Army, never sympathetic to the Cultural Revolution, might have taken military action to end the chaos. With the Party's announcement the flamboyant posters disappeared, the Red Guard units were disbanded, and some  semblance of order returned to China.

The Cultural Revolution had brought China to the brink of a new civil war, forced a severance of all but skeletal contacts with the outside world, terrorized intellectuals, almost generated an army mutiny, and decimated party ranks. That the Red Guards could be disbanded testifies to the strength of both the army and the Communist Party, but a dangerous situation had existed for some time. A permanent result of the Cultural Revolution was the deification of the elderly Mao, who was now regarded with such reverence that it became difficult for him to engage publicly in mortal day-to-day activities. He retreated into semiseclusion, emerging only occasionally to belie rumors of his death or incapacity, while Chinese officials attributed every positive act, from diplomacy to athletics, to his superior wisdom and insight. Public leadership was taken over by several others; of these, Zhou En-lai was the most notable in his post as prime minister.

At the close of the turmoil of the Cultural Revolution, China encountered a sobering experience in its deteriorating relationship with the Soviet Union. In the spring and summer of 1969, a border dispute had erupted into open clashes. Soviet armed forces used heavy firepower to inflict substantial casualties on the Chinese. It was clear that the Chinese Army could not afford another Cultural Revolution, especially since the Soviet Union suggested that it was not loath to use stronger weapons if necessary or even to invoke the Brezhnev Doctrine if China's instability continued.

## CHINA REENTERS THE WORLD COMMUNITY

China now sought to build a new image in world affairs, one that would ensure its safety from Soviet attack. In 1969 it began to make overtures to Yugoslavia, a Communist country it had hitherto denounced as "revisionist" and considered more a menace to world communism than a help. Conciliatory signals were also sent to the United States, and in February 1972 President Richard Nixon, who had built his political reputation on his anticommunism, was invited to visit China and discuss a rapprochement between China and the United States.

The building of this new relationship with the United States, an undertaking still in progress, was followed by new contacts with other non-Communist nations such as Japan, China's old enemy in World War II. Although Mao Zedong often granted audiences to visiting dignitaries, he essentially played the role of revered elder statesman rather than negotiator. The personality cult continued, but serious dealings with non-Communist leaders continued to be handled by Party and government officials, especially by Zhou En-lai until his death in 1976. Mao himself died in the fall of 1976, but no great upheavals or succession crises took place. The new leader of Chinese communism, Hua Guofeng (1920–), enjoyed the confidence of both the Communist Party and the army. As one who had almost been a victim of the Cultural Revolution, he showed no interest in launching any radical or violent changes. Quite to the contrary, he set about eliminating those who were usually associated with the most radical measures in the 1960s, condemning the so-called "Gang of Four," which included Jiang Qing and her closest associates. Hua was loath to direct any of the criticism at Mao himself, implying that the "Gang of Four" had deceived and misled the aging Mao. Hua's ascendancy proved to be short-lived, however, and as his power waned so did Mao's posthumous reputation.

In 1978, Hua's colleague and sometimes competitor, Deng Xiaopong (1904–) initiated a downgrading of Mao himself, and by 1980 it seemed that Deng was exercising as much power as Hua, if not more. Then on September 7, 1980, Hua resigned his post as Premier and was replaced by Zhao Ziyang (1918–), a long-time support of Deng Xiaopong. Nominally, Hua was still Chairman of the Communist Party, Mao's old position, but he began to spend less and less time in the public eye and was evidently being eased into total retirement by 1981 with Deng's protege Hu Yaobang (1915–) acting as the real party secretary without benefit of title. The changes further confirmed Deng's course of moderation, including deemphasis of Mao and his cult.

Anxious to break as much as possible with the values of the Cultural Revolution, Deng once again reiterated the need to punish the "Gang of Four," and their trial was energetically pursued as a national catharsis. The trial concluded early in 1981. Jiang Qing was sentenced to death and then reprieved with a two year suspension of the sentence to see if she might be "rehabilitated" after she had the opportunity to reflect on her evil deeds. Although Mao was not directly criticized, the verdict against the "Gang of Four" was all too obviously a judgment against the excesses he had imposed on China.

China of the 1980s still seemed to be a society that had not resolved its own destiny. One could be deceived that an ideological retreat was in progress by such surprising developments as the rush of American businesses to establish a foothold. In fact, however, China was still very much a communist society. More than the Soviet Union, it appeared to have created an egalitarian social structure with fewer socioeconomic disparities. Some of the worst problems of the old China: famine, begging, the inferior status of women, had been eliminated, albeit sometimes—especially in the 1950s—by traumatic methods. China appeared to have mellowed, both internally and externally. Public executions no longer took place, foreign diplomats and other visitors were no longer abused, and a Chinese presence was established in the world capitals. In 1972 China joined the United Nations, and in January 1979 delicate negotiations were completed that led to diplomatic recognition of its erstwhile nemesis, the United States. Yet on the other hand, China continued to be a more repressive state than the Soviet Union. Governmental control over Chinese society was carefully and efficiently exercised despite the limited access now afforded to non-Communist visitors, who began to arrive in ever-increasing numbers in the late 1970s. China's suspicions of the Soviet Union intensified and relations continued at levels that ranged from distant to acerbic. It even fell into the remarkable position, for a Communist state, of urging the United States to maintain a strong military posture versus the Soviet Union and to be cautious not to place too much trust in Soviet professions of peaceful intent. Although to date no Chinese-American military arrangement has emerged, the spectacle of the decidedly non-Communist United States aligning itself with Chinese communism against the Soviet Union has constantly hovered in the background of world affairs and colors the alignments and realignments within the Communist world.

# SELECTED READINGS

ARTHUR A. COHEN, *The Communism of Mao Tse-Tung* (Chicago: Phoenix Books, 1964).
Cohen seeks to appraise the various components of Mao as a leader, philosopher, and revolutionary.

ANNE FREEMANTLE, *Mao Tse-tung* (New York: Mentor Books, 1962).
Ms. Freemantle offers an anthology of some of Mao's writings as a clue to understanding his political philosophy and aspirations.

WOLFGANG LEONHARD, *Three Faces of Marxism* (New York: Capricorn Books, 1970).
A former German Communist compares the politics and ideology of the Soviet Union, Maoism, and various socialist humanists.

MAURICE MEISNER, *Mao's China: A History of the People's Republic* (New York: Free Press, 1977).
Meisner attempts to present the zig-zag course of Mao's China, particularly the hectic years before, after, and during the Cultural Revolution.

JAMES R. TOWNSEND, *Politics in China,* 2nd. ed. (Boston: Little, Brown, 1980).
Townsend's book tries to reconstruct the changes in China during Mao's late years and after his death. After charting these changes, he constructs a framework for the institutional operation of contemporary China.

DONALD S. ZAGORIA, *The Sino-Soviet Conflict, 1955–1961* (New York: Antheneum, 1967).
Although the author stops with the open break of 1961, the book is still an exhaustive and convincing analysis of how relations deteriorated after the presumed reconciliation of the two powers after the death of Stalin.

# 11

# Socialism and Communism in the Contemporary World

By the beginning of the 1980s the professedly socialist world had become so diverse that socialism could mean the total integration of socialist ideas into democratic society or a rationalization for the monopoly of political power in a highly monolithic and oftentimes repressive regime. In the West, especially in West Europe, the democratic-socialist movement had made enormous gains and had become in many instances not only part of the political activity of the nation but often the dominant political force. The success of democratic socialism and the advent of a new generation of leaders after the death of Stalin facilitated the acclimation of Western Communists to the democratic process. They now launched a major campaign to convince the electorate not only of their independence from Moscow but of their identification with democracy in accordance with Western standards.

## THE BRITISH LABOR PARTY AND THE GERMAN SOCIAL DEMOCRATIC PARTY

There had long been a significant socialist involvement in governmental politics in Europe, dating back to Millerande's joining the French cabinet in 1901. Since the 1920s socialists had achieved electoral triumphs as well, chiefly in the Scandinavian countries where the dominance of social democrats had made possible an extensive program of social-welfare legislation. However, prior to World War II socialist triumphs in major powers had been possible only through the formation of coalition governments, a tactic which inhibited the mandate any socialist leader might derive from an electoral plurality. Leon Blum's short-lived "Popular Front" government in France (1936–1937) was one example of this strategy; for many socialists it was an example they would prefer not to emulate.

The first clear-cut electoral mandate for a socialist program in a major country came with the decisive triumph of the British Labor Party in the elections of July 1945. The new government formed from these elections was in no way Communist or Marxist; many of its leaders came from the London School of Economics, which had been propagating for more than a generation a Fabian approach to socialism. Although many of the programs introduced by the new government seemed as far reaching in the direction of socialism as those attempted by more-professedly Marxist movements, the programs were couched in terms of the British experience and sought to meld British history and socialist aspirations in a manner that had always been espoused by the Fabians.

Anxious to avoid the economic doldrums and chronic unemployment that had beset Britain after the First World War, the Labor government, led by Clement Attlee (1883–1967), declared that with the economic and social problems facing postwar Britain, unrestricted capitalism was simply too self-serving to provide equity and social justice. While not seeking the total elimination of capitalism, Attlee's government proposed to remove from private ownership those sectors of the economy which were most critical to the population's well-being, namely public utilities, transportation, the Bank of England, and the basic production facilities of the iron and steel industries. The nationalization of these sectors affected less than a quarter of Britian's economy, but it was an awesome beginning in the country that had in Marx's time been viewed as the paragon of capitalism.

Attlee also devoted considerable attention to social welfare, guiding through legislation covering such matters as pensions, unemployment insurance, and, most controversial of all, a comprehensive plan of free health care. All of this activity, the Labor government presumed, would convince the population that it was responding to the demands for social and economic justice but would proceed in a manner consistent with British democratic traditions and avoid, in any manner whatsoever, the repression that had characterized the rise of Communist societies.

Yet at the next election, in February 1950, the Labor Party's margin of victory was dramatically reduced. A year later, Attlee, unable to control either the Left in his own party, which wanted further social and economic initiatives, or the Right, which to keep the economy in balance had proposed some modest retreats from the socialist welfare program (such as charging for eyeglasses and dentures), was forced to call for new elections in line with the British parliamentary tradition. In October 1951 the Labor Party lost its majority to the Conservatives and gracefully retired to the role of "loyal" opposition, biding its time till the next elections.

The changes the Labor Party had introduced during its six years in power were not canceled, although they were modified, particularly the nationalization program. In the iron and steel industries "denationalization" proceedings were initiated. Except for the restoration of a privately owned trucking industry, public ownership of transportation and utilities continued. Most of the social-welfare programs were also maintained with some minor changes, such as a nuisance charge for prescription medicines. Both the Labor and Conservative parties seemed to have recognized that the public wished to maintain a certain level of government involvement in social and economic life. For the next three decades the country alternated between Labor and Conservative governments with only minor differences in socioeconomic programs, although Labor still retained an ideological commitment to the gradual building of socialism. When Labor did form governments after 1951—usually with the help of the small Liberal Party—it eschewed a return to the policies of 1945 and disclaimed any renewed commitment to wide-reaching socialist change. Similarly, the Conservatives treaded gently on the issues of social welfare, although their campaign verbiage often suggested more differences in economic policy than existed.

Britain had not become a socialist society in any absolute sense, but neither could its economic system any longer be considered unfettered capitalism. For better or for worse, Britain had become the first major Westen power with a "mixed economy" combining elements of socialism and capitalism. Its economic record was not easy to assess, since negative factors to be considered included the severe toll of World War II and the legacy of an antiquated industrial plant, but its system of parliamentary democracy remained unchanged, and this feature greatly impressed other European socialists.

After Britain the major victory for democratic socialism in a non-Marxist form came in West Germany. Rising from the wartime destruction, with considerable American economic and political encouragement, the West German government, led by the mildly conservative Christian Democratic Party, had restored reasonable economic prosperity to the country within a decade of the end of World War II. The German Social Democrats, the oldest Marxist party in the world, seemed unable to challenge the Christian Democrats except in local elections, most notably the mayoralty of West Berlin. The presence of a repressive regime in East Germany, backed by a Soviet occupation army, greatly enhanced support of the Christian Democrats, although the Social Democrats could hardly be blamed for that phenomenon.

In the 1960s the Social Democrats belatedly became the major political force in West Germany. Part of the price paid for this political success was disavowal of the party's old Marxist heritage. In 1959 the Social Democrats adopted a new political program that divorced the party from the Marxist past, accepted the existence of a free market in the economy, and concentrated its energies on issues of economic justice, social welfare, and the involvement of workers in economic decision making. With a new charismatic leader, Willy Brandt (1913–), the Social Democrats gained rapidly amongst the German electorate, forcing the Christian Democrats first to accept a coalition government and then culminating with an electoral triumph that made Brandt chancellor in 1969.

In the ensuing decade, although the Social Democrats were able to retain the Chancellorship, they moved with great caution in all areas that might be described as socialist innovation. Although social-welfare legislation was expanded, nothing on the scale of Attlee's program in England (1946–1951) was even discussed, much less attempted. The Social Democrats governed a West German state that provided full employment, wide-ranging social welfare, and flexibility toward Communist East Europe, but it was a state that had disavowed revolutionary Marxism. The one major change in economic relationships introduced by the Social Democrats was a policy known as "codetermination," in which half of a major corporation's board of directors were to be representatives of the workers. Whether or not this has achieved a serious measure of worker control of industry is still debatable. If prosperity and security are the measure of a regime, the German Social Democrats have succeeded handsomely. Few would call the result socialism, however, and within the ranks of the Social Democratic Party there has remained a disaffected left, known as the Juso's (*Jungsozialisten* [Young Socialists] )that has accused the party of selling out its socialist heritage for a prosperity that in the long run might prove to be transient and unstable. There has also been an alarming opposition from radical youth groups that have attempted to assail the complacency of the regime by acts of political terror, especially the notorious Baader-Meinhof gang. Despite some frightening assassinations, the terrorists have neither changed the objectives of the Social Democrats nor attracted a major following from any socialist group, whether from the Right or the Left.

The political terror and violence of professed radicals has not been confined to West Germany. Other countries as well have experienced it. In Italy in 1978 the so-called Red Brigades carried out several assassinations, including that of a recent prime minister, but the terrorists were repudiated by both socialists and Communists who were more interested in furthering their political fortunes through the electoral process.

## THE ROLE OF MARXIST MOVEMENTS
## IN THE UNITED STATES

Only in the United States did socialists and Communists remain outside the mainstream of politics. American socialism has had a long and interesting history of its own—with virtually every European variety of socialism developing some following—but it has had only marginal impact on American history and even less impact on the history of international socialism. American socialists have always been restricted to the fringes of political movements and, except for a rare triumph in a municipal election, have never been able to achieve election to major positions of government. In its peak years, that is to say in the decade prior to World War I, the American Socialist Party barely topped 100,000 members, and it was already in a period of membership decline when the war broke out in 1914. The Bolshevik Revolution and the antiwar movement combined to give the socialist Left in the United States a new momentum, and the American Communist Party was created in 1919.

The fledgling Party was beset by factionalism from the very beginning, and the "know-nothing" directives that emanated from Moscow increased this. Even those sympathetic to the Bolshevik Revolution were alienated by the Twenty-One Points and the subsequent harsh measures employed by the Soviet Union against its own population. During the early years of American communism, the Communist Party was better known for those who left it than those who joined it. The low esteem of the party was mirrored in the presidential elections of 1932—a year when the United States had millions of workers unemployed and an apparently collapsing economy—in which the Communist candidate, William Z. Foster, polled a mere 103,151 votes out of a total of almost 40 million votes cast. The Party did succeed in attracting some support from American intellectuals and established bases in certain unions, notably in the newly formed Congress of Industrial Workers (CIO), but the formation of a political movement seemed to remain outside its competence. The socialists, somewhat eclipsed by the reform legislation of Roosevelt's "New Deal," fared no better.

The Socialist Party, for all practical purposes, ceased to exist after World War II. A small group of intellectuals, most notably Norman Thomas (1884–1968) and Michael Harrington (1928–) continued to articulate a doctrine of democratic socialism but were unable to form any viable political grouping. The Communist Party had better fortunes. The wartime alliance against fascism recouped some of the losses from the membership rolls, and the Party succeeded in dominating the third-party candidacy of Henry Wallace in the 1948 presidential elections. But punitive legislation at both the national and state levels scared away some supporters, as did the anti-Communist crusade launched by Senator Joseph McCarthy in 1950. And even the faithful who withstood the harassments were unnerved by the Soviet invasion of Hungary in 1956, and Party ranks were again thinned.

In the 1960s prospects changed for the American Communists. Senator McCarthy had died in 1957, and some of the anti-Communist hysteria died with him. The civil-rights movements of the early 1960s and then the growing popular discontent with American participation in the Vietnam War gave the Left new opportunities to develop a following. Yet the Communist Party surprisingly profitted little from these developments. The major civil-rights leader of the time, Martin Luther King (1929–1968), was not interested in entangling his movement with the Communists, and the more militant groups such as the Black Panthers considered the Communists too pusillanimous to be an ally. The antiwar movement, especially amongst young people, spawned its own "New Left." This grouping, too amorphous to be described as a party or even a true movement, spouted a classical anticapitalist, antiimperialist vocabulary and for a while enjoyed dynamic leadership, particularly from the well-known Students for a Democratic Society (SDS) in the 1960s. However, the New Left was only marginally interested in the socialist heritage; the slogan of the time was: "Trust no one over thirty!" and it was as applicable to Communists as to others. What was most important was the inability of the New Left to establish any sort of cohesion amongst its diverse adherents. By 1970, the potentially unifying force of antiwar and antiracist causes had proven insufficient for this purpose. Factionalism became the rule as various youth groups, terrorist groups, Maoist groups, Trotskyite groups, and neoanarchist groups emerged. Although the Communist Party USA, as it now titled itself, acquired more confidence and once again began to put forward candidates for office, it could not harness or cope with the New Left.

At the beginning of the 1980s factionalism was still the dominant feature of the radical Left. One radical group, the Communist Workers Party, achieved an unwanted form of national prominence when, in November 1979, five of their leaders were killed in an altercation with Ku Klux Klansmen and American Nazis in Greensboro, North Carolina. Although there was widespread indignation against the Klan and the Nazis, the indignation did not translate into support for the Communist Workers Party.

Sixty years after its founding, American communism remains unable to attract adherents among American workers or any major sector of the American populace. Its major achievement has been survival—sometimes through difficult periods—and its ability to enter the decade of the 1980s with as much faith in its future potential as ever. Overall, however, it has still failed to develop its ranks beyond the basic core of true believers or to discipline and control the myriad radical groups that claimed to be the "true" communists.

## THE DEMOCRATIC COMMITMENT
## OF MODERN EUROCOMMUNISM

By contrast, West European Communists have shown considerably more imagination and insight in developing new images for themselves and in presenting a fresh approach to their respective populations. In Stalin's day, and even before, European Communists had been hampered by self-serving policies dictated by Moscow that often bore no relation to the situations that existed in various countries and, in some cases, were politically suicidal. The Nazi-Soviet pact and the resultant mandate to Communists not to oppose Hitler was but one example. In the past two decades there has emerged a new leadership among West European Communists with minimal ties to the Stalin era and with a strong appreciation of the Western political tradition and its importance to the Western electorate. Prominent amongst these new leaders are Enrico Berlinguer (1922–) in Italy, Georges Marchais (1920–) in France, and Santiago Carrillo (1915–) in Spain. The political outlook of this new leadership was expressed in a joint statement issued in late 1975 by the French and Italian Communist parties; it guaranteed the recognition of opposition politics and the Communist commitment to "democratic alternation between majority and minority."

This acceptance of democratic principles by Western Communist leaders was the culmination of several years effort toward developing an "independent" course, evident as early as 1968 when the French and Italian Communists denounced the Soviet march into Prague as "illegal." Carrillo was a latecomer to the group—the Spanish Communists had no legal existence prior to 1976—but he became even more articulate than the French and Italians in criticizing the Soviet Union's lack of appreciation for democracy, so much so that on one occasion he was denied the right to address a Communist meeting in Moscow.

The assertion by European Communists that they accept democratic principles—including their claim that if they ever win a national election, form a government, and then subsequently lose the next election, they would step aside—has never been tested. Non-Communists have remained skeptical, especially since the experience in Portugal, where the Communist Party after decisively losing the elections of 1976 refused to abide by the results and attempted to overthrow the newly elected government.

This strategy of Communist participation in democratic politics and acceptance of the rules of democratic procedures has generally been known by the name of Eurocommunism. How and where the term "Eurocommunism" originated is uncertain, but by the mid-1970s it had wide currency.[1] Its most common line is that Communists are loyal to their native countries rather than to Moscow. In France, since 1978, there has been some backtracking on the strategy of Eurocommunism. This was particularly evident when the French Communist Party defended the December 1979 Soviet invasion of Afghanistan, while the Spanish and Italian Communists denounced it. Overall, however, Eurocommunism still seems to hold the most attractive political strategy for West European Communists.

Eurocommunism is in many ways not only a strategy devised to enhance Communist electoral appeal but a response to European perceptions of the internal state of the Soviet Union. In the 1980s the Soviet Union has once again become a feared power in Europe—particularly as doubts have developed about the seriousness of American commitment to defend its allies—but in no sense has it been an admired power. Few Europeans envy the political or economic status of their Soviet counterparts. Many Western Communists have prudently come to believe that it would be self-defeating to attempt to vend at home a political program that promises a replica of Soviet society. Thus there has been a quiet reconsideration of the value of the Soviet

---

[1] It should be noted that the term did not originate with European Communist leaders and is rarely invoked by them. It is, however, commonly used by Western analysts in lieu of any more commonly accepted designation.

regime as a model for socialist society. To the Western observer, Soviet communism—or, as it describes itself, Marxism-Leninism—has retained the political format of the dictatorship of the proletariat far longer than any conscionable period would allow. Western Communist leaders have firmly maintained that they do not aspire to any dictatorship of the proletariat, even a short-lived one, for their own countries. Rosa Luxemburg's warning in 1918 that the Bolsheviks were making the dictatorship of the proletariat an end in itself rather than a transition to socialist democracy seems particularly cogent sixty years later.

Since 1964 the Soviet Union has been under the leadership of Leonid Brezhnev, a Communist who has long been in the front ranks of the party apparatus. Although the personal position of Brezhnev has never been jeopardized, there have been important changes in the exercise of collective decision making. For instance, whereas in the immediate post-Stalin years the role of the security police was diminished, in the 1970s the head of the reorganized state-security agency (KGB) Yuri Andropov (1914–) has obviously increased his power and influence, as demonstrated by his appointment to the Politburo. The political rise of KGB officials has been accompanied by a heightened intolerance for dissident viewpoints. Whereas in the early 1970s some public dissent was possible and to a point tolerated, by the late 1970s the Soviet Union, risking erosion of its ties to Western countries, cracked down on dissidents. In 1978, in a series of highly publicized trials, several well-known dissidents were charged with "slander" and given harsh sentences. This by no means represented a return to Stalinism or the era of the purges, but it caused alarm amongst Western Communists, who were not at all eager to defend such a policy.

Of great importance in shaping the development of Eurocommunism has been the embarrassingly slow rate of growth within the Soviet Union. In the Khrushchev years as consumer goods finally began to appear in significant quantities, there had been a phenomenon of rapidly rising Soviet expectations. The surprisingly good harvests of the late 1950s and the phasing out of an "old generation" of military hardware—an action which temporarily reduced military expenditures—enabled a genuine rise in the Soviet standard of living to take place. In 1961 the Communist Party adopted a new economic program, its first since 1919, in which Soviet citizens were promised a dramatic upswing in the quality of life. Within two years, however, problems in the economy had become severe once again; military expenditures rose and a poor agricultural yield forced the Soviet Union to import grain in 1963. These economic setbacks were an important factor in the sudden fall of Khrushchev in October 1964.

In the next decade, under the Brezhnev leadership, productivity rose but still did not come close to the expectations encouraged by the 1961 program. The hard fact was that Soviet citizens did not enjoy the improved living standard being achieved by most of their West European counterparts in the 1970s. Western Communist leaders could hardly point with pride to the achievements of the Soviet bloc under these circumstances. The only Western Communist leaders still loyally looking to Moscow were the erratic and volatile leaders of communism in Portugal, a country which for myriad reasons had not shared in general West European prosperity and still remains a country of great poverty.

## MARXISM IN THE THIRD WORLD

If the Soviet Union has retained any positive image it is with those countries that comprise what is known as the Third World. The grouping of nations under the Third World concept implies a commonality amongst the countries of Africa, Asia, and Latin America that is disputable. Obviously Saudi Arabia, with its conservative monarchy ruling an oil-rich country, looks at political and socioeconomic problems from different perspectives than a poor country such as Tanzania, where the leadership is avowedly socialist and regards living socialistically as a greater virtue than having riches. For this reason, the varieties of socialism or protosocialism among Third World countries need emphasis.

The greatest Soviet triumph in the Third World has been its special relationship with Cuba. Fidel Castro came to power in 1959, and from the beginning the Soviet Union strongly courted the new regime at a time when its political values, then apparently some sort of vague socialism, were still quite volatile. As Castro's relations with the nearby United States deteriorated, particularly after his expropriation of American firms, his dependence on the Soviet Union grew.

In April 1961, an abortive American-backed invasion of Cuba by political exiles further exacerbated Cuban-American relations and enabled the Soviet Union to increase its military presence there. The denouement came in October 1962 when it became known to the United States that the Soviet Union was installing missile bases. In the ensuing showdown, the Soviet Union removed the missiles but ties between Havana and Moscow remained firm. In fact, the American economic blockade led Castro to seek further support from the Soviet Union for Cuba's shaky one-crop economy, sugar, and a relationship thereby was established between the two countries that was unmatched anywhere else. Cuba not only became a committed Communist society but the Soviet Union's surrogate in Latin America and elsewhere throughout the Third World. The financial cost to the Soviet Union was enormous; estimates range as high as 10 billion dollars in subsidies over the years, a largesse that the Soviet Union has not offered to any other Communist nation.

Ironically the Soviet tie with Cuba has had only minimal effect on the spread of revolution in Latin America. Communist prospects amongst Cuba's most-immediate neighbors, for instance Haiti, remain as remote as ever. Some small Carribean islands, Grenada for example, have been influenced by the Cuban experience, but elsewhere in Latin America campaigns to promote revolutionary movements in emulation of the Cuban example fared badly. At first, the responsibility for exporting the Cuban revolution belonged to an emigrant Argentine, Che Guevara (1928–1968); after several hit-and-run escapades in various countries, Che was slain on a futile mission to build up Communist support in the interior of Bolivia. Only in Chile did some sort of socialist regime emerge, and this was without initiative from either the Soviet Union or Cuba, although both countries enthusiastically identified with the new regime.

In Chile in the fall of 1970, Salvador Allende (1908–1973), the Social Democratic candidate for president, formed a united front of socialists, Communists, and other radicals and wor. a plurality in the presidential elections. His party did not win the congressional elections, however, and this factor, along with an army that was dubious about Allende's program, inhibited his ability to promote drastic social change. Moving gradually and, as he had hoped, legally, Allende still sought to bring about socialist change by nationalizing foreign corporations and attempting some redistribution of wealth. In retrospect, it seems that Allende never had any chance to convert Chile into a socialist society; the open support of Cuba and the Soviet Union was insufficient to offset the economic hardships wrought by the withdrawal of American economic credits as well as the conscious attempts by American officials to sabotage the prospects of the Allende regime through various forms of subterfuge and diplomatic pressure. The economy deteriorated rapidly, the Chilean congress remained hostile to Allende's program, and finally in September 1973 the Chilean army moved to oust what had been touted as the only democratically elected Marxist regime in the world. The actual seizure of power by the military was a bloody affair; Allende himself was one of the casualties. The military regime that replaced him allowed no serious opposition, and the hopes for a new Cuba on the South American mainland failed.

Castro was stunned by Allende's death, but neither he nor the Soviet Union considered it a signal to end promoting revolution. In Cuba itself, Castro faced little serious opposition since most of his regime's likely opponents had fled to Florida in the 1960s.[2] Because he faced no danger at home, Castro was free to launch overseas ventures in the name of world communism, something he appeared more eager to do than other Communist leaders.

The next opportunity for Soviet-Cuban collaboration came on the African continent. The Soviet Union considered it impolitic to intervene directly in the affairs of emerging nations, and in any case such intervention was fraught with international consequences that the Soviet Union wished to avoid. The immediate target in the mid-1970s were African territories of the former Portugese Empire. As the Portugese government underwent several upheavals at home, it suddenly began to divest itself of its large African holdings;

---

[2] There was another exodus of over 100,000 people to the United States in 1980, but this emigration seemed to contain few politically active people.

new nations were abruptly born with hardly any preparation for an orderly transition to a native government.

In the large West African country of Angola, with its Portugese rulers now withdrawing, several native groups began to contend with each other for the right to replace the colonial government. The Soviet Union decided to back the group most advantageous to its interests, and in 1976 it provided a proxy Cuban military force with the transportation, arms, and supplies needed to ensure the victory of its clients in Angola. The strategy worked, but Cuban forces did not withdraw from the continent after the success in Angola. Instead they became a sort of Communist "Foreign Legion" fighting wherever the interests of the Soviet-Cuban bloc seemed to indicate was a suitable area. The Cuban forces were called upon to assist a new Soviet-oriented regime in Ethiopia and were said to have backed a rebel invasion of Zaire in 1978. Their presence has given many African leaders pause for thought, while others have made haste to use them where their own military prowess seemed insufficient to achieve immediate goals.

In most African and Asian countries, the meanings of the words *socialism* and *capitalism* have altered significantly from the original conceptualizations of Marx and Engels. *Capitalism* in particular has served as a virtual synonym for colonialism and suggests to these countries the years of Western European dominance over their economies and in most cases over their territories as well. *Socialism*, considered the opposite of "capitalism/colonialism," is often accepted without further definition or exposition as signifying something that must be good in and of itself. There are numerous African and Asian leaders who describe themselves as socialists, but their perception of socialism is often very topical and skewed toward the needs of their own countries and causes. By way of example, one might glance briefly at two of the better-known champions of socialist change in Africa, Julius Nyerere (1922–) and Franz Fanon.

Nyerere, the president of the East African country of Tanzania, is sometimes known as the "father of African socialism" and is well versed in classical Marxism, discoursing at times on such venerated subjects as historical materialism and determinism. However, he rejects the premise of classical Marxism that a mature capitalist society is a prerequisite to the development of a later socialist society. As the leader of one of the most-impoverished nations in the world, he has committed his nation to by-passing any indigenous development of capitalism, feeling that the experience of colonial exploitation is a sufficient capitalist phase. Instead he has concentrated on developing an egalitarian society. The history of independent Tanzania has had some parallels with Soviet history, for instance, nationalization of major industries and corporations and the forced resettlement of peasants into collective villages. Nyerere is hardly a Stalin, however, and although Tanzanian life is very austere there is no wanton terror. Even in its continued poverty, Nyerere's Tanzania enjoys better life expectancy, education, and other advantages than it did under colonial domination.

There has been little Soviet commitment to Tanzania despite the latter's espousal of a committed socialist society. On the contrary, until 1979, the Soviet Union sent substantial aid to Nyerere's neighbor, the volatile and hardly socialist regime of Idi Amin in Uganda. In 1979 Nyerere sponsored the overthrow of Amin—with the Soviet Union sufficiently prudent not to intervene—and Nyerere continued to show his unhappiness over the ongoing presence of Soviet-supported Cuban troops in Africa.

Others in the new Africa who have aspired to the defeat of capitalism have found a voice in the black psychiatrist Franz Fanon (1925–1961), whose brief revolutionary career was launched during Algeria's war for independence in the 1950s. Although heavily influenced by French Marxists, Fanon rejected the assumption that the proletariat was the most promising instrument for building socialism, noting that French workers were quite willing to accept the fruits of imperialism with little or no thought for its impact on the colonial peoples. The real revolutionary potential, he claimed, lay with the poor peasantry of colonial lands, living on the brink of survival, and with the urban unemployed and homeless. His best-known work, *The Wretched of the Earth,* is virtually a new Communist manifesto, calling upon the impoverished people of colonial lands to rise up against the economic, racial, and cultural exploitation of imperialism. It is literally a call to arms, and one that has frightened Europeans more than it has stirred the impoverished masses to whom it is addressed. It is, however, a credo that cannot be ignored: that poverty, racial oppression, imperialism, and the other indignities inflicted on the peoples of

Africa may well spawn a violent revolution as the only path to a social-ist society in which the African will receive justice. Fanon died young, the same year as his book, *Wretched of the Earth* appeared. A more mature Fanon might have developed alternative approaches toward the same goal or delivered his message in a way that would be better received by African leaders themselves. Nevertheless, what many understood was the anger in his words and his claim that Africa had little to gain by imitating Europe. The new Africa he envisioned would tear itself away from all European values, violently if neces-sary, and build its own society of revolutionary socialism.

## THE DISCONTENT WITH ESTABLISHED COMMUNISM

It has now been more than a century since the founding of the first Marxist party in Germany. In that time the world has undergone tre-mendous upheavals highlighted by two destructive wars in this cen-tury. In addition there has been, in the past thirty years, an accelerated abandonment of colonial possessions by Western powers, sometimes gracefully and sometimes by prolonged conflicts; it has been a relent-less process that has revoked the Western domination of the earth's surface. As a result of these upheavals, be they war or the end of em-pire, the Marxist condemnation of capitalist society has reached a vast audience of willing respondents. Marxism in all its varieties, and socialism in some distinctly non-Marxist forms, have captured the loyalties of much of the world.

Some Marxists have been unhappy with this success because in many instances it has originated from terror or coercion. Studying the history of socialism, they have recalled the words of the young Karl Marx whose unpublished manuscripts of 1844 enjoined:

Communism is the necessary form and dynamic principle of the immediate future, but communism is not itself the goal of human development—the form of human society.

To these Marxists, Stalinism and other forms of coercive activity in the name of communism are an abomination and a contradiction of true Marxist ideals. A number of East European philosophers, most notably Leszek Kolakowski of Poland, Ivan Svitak of Czechoslovakia, and Georg Lukacs of Hungary, have promoted a doctrine of socialist humanism as an antidote to what many perceive as the brutality of Communist regimes in power.[3] For a while some Yugoslav Marxists who rallied around the journal *Praxis*, also identified with socialist humanism, criticizing not only the Soviet practice but Yugoslav short-comings as well. For most socialist humanists, who consider the terms socialism and humanism to be complementary and interdependent, the Soviet Union's greatest failing has been its abandonment of humanism and its concurrent failure to develop a genuinely socialist society.

The socialist humanists have been notoriously unsuccessful in their attempts to persuade Communist governments to embrace their definition of Marxism. Their great hope was the regeneration of Czech communism under the leadership of Alexander Dubček; in the brief euphoric months of 1968 the Czechoslovak regime spoke openly of creating "communism with a human face." The Soviet march into Prague abruptly terminated those hopes, and the Czechoslovak regime of the 1980s gives no quarter to such heresies. Even in relatively tolerant Yugoslavia the *Praxis* group was disbanded in 1975 for its "abuse of freedom," and ever since the voices of socialist humanism there have had a much more difficult time finding an audience.

Dissatisfaction with established Communist parties has come from another quarter: those who consider them too soft, devoid of revolutionary spirit, and hopelessly coopted into bourgeois society. In May 1968 when student demonstrations in France triggered massive strikes by discontented workers, the Communist Party was caught off guard and only reluctantly and half-heartedly supported the uprising. When student violence in Paris led to apparently mindless vandalism and destruction, the Communists appeared as concerned as anyone else that order be restored. One of the student leaders, Daniel Cohn-Bendit, bitterly summed up the wrath of his fellow revolu-

---

[3] Lukacs, who was an adviser to Nagy in the ill-fated Hungarian uprising of 1956, is now deceased; Kolakowski and Svitak have been forced into emigration.

tionaries in his book *Obsolete Communism,* a title which aptly summed up the sense of betrayal that Cohn-Bendit and his fellow radicals felt about French communism. The espousal of Eurocommunism by several Western Communist parties since that time has understandably exacerbated this feeling, representing as it does an accommodation with democratic (capitalist) society.

The discontent of revolutionaries in the West, particularly younger revolutionaries, with what they perceive as the deradicalization of established Communist movements has manifested itself in a number of ways. In the late 1960s there was a groundswell of groups, such as the Progressive Labor Party in the United States, that identified with China instead of with the Soviet Union. Even though these groups enjoyed a high visibility in the Western media, they never achieved much importance, and they lost some of their attractiveness for radicals when China began to develop closer ties with the United States in the 1970s. A more-striking phenomenon has been the reappearance, or perhaps more correctly the survival, of Trotskyite groups on the Left fifty years after what was presumed to be Trotsky's total political defeat. From a dwindling but persistent political force in the political life of Sri Lanka, to a thriving publishing house in the United States, to a viable American youth group known as the Socialist Alliance, Trotskyism has survived as a world-wide presence in many wide-ranging forms. The persistence of anti-Trotsky literature in the Soviet Union is in itself remarkable; Soviet writers, not content with denunciations of the Chinese leadership as "Trotskyite," have continued to produce "historical" studies on the infamy of Trotskyism in the Soviet Union.

In the 1980s Communist regimes have developed new relationships with the non-Communist world. In 1970, most observers would have considered Communist China the most difficult Communist power to contain, and therefore the most worrisome for the West. A decade later China has repaired its relations with the West, even to the extent of urging the United States to maintain and increase its vigilance against the Soviet Union. On the other hand, the once highly publicized "détente" between the Soviet Union and the United States collapsed in December 1979 when the Soviet Union invaded the Asian country of Afghanistan and installed a Soviet-named government there. Whether the Soviet action in Afghanistan was motivated by expansionism, fear of Islamic revivalism spreading into Soviet Central Asia, or simple strategic considerations remained unclear. The action in any case was disheartening to those who believed that the Soviet Union had forsworn aggression to extend Communist control. Once again serious questions were raised as to how the Soviet Union perceived its avowed role as the leader of world communism.

The mistakes, conflicts, and problems of socialist societies are evident to any observer, but they do not belie the fact that in the modern world some form of socialist or socialist-oriented approach to organizing society has been preferred in disparate countries throughout the world. Stalin and Mao Zedong have been at least partially repudiated posthumously by their respective societies, but the variety of communism that each developed continues, albeit with less trauma. To date, the differences between modes of socialism seem greater than the common bonds, but the persistence of socialism as an ideological principle for organizing societies seems to be a permanent feature of the modern-day world.

# SELECTED READINGS

ETIENNE BALIBAR, *On the Dictatorship of the Proletariat* (New York: Schocken Books, 1978).
Balibar seeks to analyze Eurocommunism's rejection of the traditional Marxist idea of the dictatorship of the proletariat.

PETER CALVOCAROSSI, *The British Experience, 1945–1975* (New York: Pantheon, 1978).
Calvocarossi offers a "generation" study of postwar Britain, including an analysis of how the "socialist experiment" has changed British life.

SANTIAGO CARILLO, *Eurocommunism and the State* (New York: Lawrence Hill, 1978).
Carillo, the Spanish Communist, is perhaps the most-outspoken supporter of Eurocommunism, espousing the view to Moscow as well as to the West. The book summarizes his case for Eurocommunism.

ERICH FROMM, ed., *Socialist Humanism: A Symposium* (Garden City: Doubleday, 1965).
This book is a collection of essays centering on the theme that Marxism and humanism are complementary and that neither has any true meaning without the other.

JOHN G. GURLEY, *Challengers to Capitalism: Marx, Lenin, Stalin and Mao*, 2nd ed. (New York: W. W. Norton & Co., Inc., 1980).
The author combines an historical overview of the challenges posed by his protagonists and carries those challenges to the present day, examining their *results.*

JERRY F. HOUGH, and MERLE FAINSOD, *How the Soviet Union is Governed* (Cambridge: Harvard University Press, 1979).
This substantial work not only explores the Soviet society's institutions but its rationale and objectives as well.

RICHARD LOWENTHAL, *World Communism* (New York: Oxford University Press, 1964).
The author, once a prominent German Socialist, sees communism as losing its unity and faith. His description of communism as a secular faith leads into his highly negative analysis.

PAUL A. ROBINSON, *The Freudian Left* (New York: Harper & Row, Pub., 1969).
This book seeks to blend the presumed revolutionary impact of Freud's work in psychiatry with modern critics of society, notably Wilhelm Reich, Geza Roheim, and Herbert Marcuse.

# Index

# 7573224